# Privatising Electricity

# PRIVATISING ELECTRICITY

## The Politics of Power

*Jane Roberts, David Elliott* and
*Trevor Houghton*

**Belhaven Press**
London and New York

First published in Great Britain in 1991 by
Belhaven Press (a division of Pinter Publishers)
25 Floral Street, London WC2E 9DS

**British Library Cataloguing in Publication Data**

A CIP catalogue record for this book is available from the
British Library

ISBN 1 85293 180 9 (hb)
    1 85293 181 7 (pb)


For enquiries in North America please contact
PO Box 197, Irvington, NY 10553

**Library of Congress Cataloging in Publication Data**

A CIP catalog record for this book is available from the Library of Congress

Typeset by Florencetype Ltd, Kewstoke, Avon
Printed and bound in Great Britain by Biddles Ltd,
Guildford and Kings Lynn

# Contents

# List of figures

# List of acronyms

| | |
|---|---|
| ACE | Association for the Conservation of Energy |
| ACORD | Advisory Committee on Research and Development |
| AEA | see UKAEA |
| AEU | Amalgamated Engineering Union |
| AGR | Advanced Gas Cooled Reactor |
| BA | British Airways |
| BC | British Coal |
| BG | British Gas |
| BNF | British Nuclear Fuels |
| BP | British Petroleum |
| BST | Bulk Supply Tariff |
| BT | British Telecom |
| BWEA | British Wind Energy Association |
| CCGT | combined cycle gas turbine |
| CEGB | Central Electricity Generating Board |
| CFC | chloro-fluoro-carbons |
| CHP | combined heat and power |
| $CO_2$ | carbon dioxide |
| CPRE | Council for the Protection of Rural England |
| DGES | Director General of Electricity Supply |
| EC | European Community |
| ECC | Electricity Consumers Council |
| EDF | Eléctricité de France |
| EEO | Energy Efficiency Office |
| EETPU | Electrical, Electronic, Telecommunications and Plumbing Union |
| EFL | external finance limit |
| EMA | Engineers and Managers Association |
| ESI | electricity supply industry |
| ETSU | Energy Technology Support Unit |
| FBR | Fast Breeder Reactor |
| FGD | flue gas desulphurisation |
| FOE | Friends of the Earth |
| GDP | gross domestic product |

| | |
|---|---|
| GEC | General Electric Company |
| GMBATU | General Municipal Boilermakers and Allied Trades Union |
| GNP | gross national product |
| GW | gigawatt |
| HDR | hot dry rock geothermal energy |
| HMIP | Her Majesty's Inspectorate of Pollution |
| IEM | Internal Energy Market |
| IMF | International Monetary Fund |
| IPCC | Intergovernmental Panel on Climate Change |
| kW | kilowatt |
| kWh | kilowatt hour |
| LRMC | long run marginal cost |
| MANWEB | Manchester and North Wales Electricity Board |
| MMC | Monopolies and Mergers Commission |
| Mtce | million tonnes coal equivalent |
| MW | Megawatt |
| NCB | National Coal Board |
| NEDO | National Economic Development Office |
| NEW | Northumberland Energy Workshop |
| NFFO | non-fossil fuel obligation |
| NGC | National Grid Company |
| NHS | National Health Service |
| NIREX | Nuclear Industry Radioactive Waste Executive |
| NMO | non-market objective |
| NNC | National Nuclear Corporation |
| NORWEB | North West Electricity Board |
| $NO_x$ | oxides of nitrogen |
| NSHEB | North of Scotland Hydro-Electric Board |
| NUM | National Union of Mineworkers |
| OFFER | Office of Electricity Regulation |
| OFGAS | Office of Gas Supply |
| OFTEL | Office of Telecommunications |
| PEP | Personal Equity Plan |
| PES | Public Electricity Supplier |
| PPS | Parliamentary Private Secretary |
| PSBR | Public Sector Borrowing Requirement |
| PUC | Public Utility Commission |
| PWR | pressurised water reactor |
| R & D | research and development |
| R, D & D | research, development and demonstration |
| REC | Regional Electricity Companies |
| RPI | retail price index |
| SGHWR | steam generating heavy water reactor |
| SMP | system marginal price |
| $SO_2$ | sulphur dioxide |
| SSEB | South of Scotland Electricity Board |

| SWEB | South West Electricity Board |
| THORP | Thermal Oxide Reprocessing Plant |
| TUC | Trades Union Congress |
| TWh | terawatt hour |
| UKAEA | United Kingdom Atomic Energy Authority |
| VAT | value added tax |
| VAWT | vertical axis wind turbine |
| WEG | Wind Energy Group |

# Explanatory note on units

## Generation capacity

1 kilowatt (kW)   =   1000 watts
1 Megawatt (MW)  =   1000 kW
1 Gigawatt (GW)   =   1000 MW
1 Terawatt (TW)   =   1000 GW

A typical large, modern nuclear power plant has around 1.3 GW of installed capacity. Generating sets at modern coal stations are rated at 600 MW each. This is an output figure: input energy will be about three times this figure, depending on the efficiency with which the plant converts primary energy into electricity. Overall the UK has around 70 GW of installed electricity generating capacity.

## Consumption

A 1 kW one bar electric fire run for one hour consumes 1 kilowatt hour (kWh). The UK currently consumes approximately 250 Terawatt hours (TWh) per annum.

# Chronology of events

| | |
|---|---|
| March 1987 | Permission granted for Sizewell 'B' |
| June 1987 | Conservatives win third General Election |
| August 1987 | CEGB application for permission to build Hinkley 'C' |
| February 1988 | White Paper 'Privatising Electricity' published |
| July 1988 | Energy Committee Report on privatisation of ESI |
| October 1988 | Hinkley 'C' Inquiry opened |
| December 1988 | Electricity Bill published: second reading debate |
| January 1989 | Commons Committee stage of Bill commences |
| April 1989 | Second reading in Lords |
| May 1989 | Government defeat in Lords on energy efficiency amendment |
| July 1989 | Bill enacted<br>Magnox stations withdrawn from privatisation<br>Energy Committee Greenhouse Report<br>John Wakeham replaces Cecil Parkinson as Secretary of State for Energy |
| November 1989 | AGRs and PWRs withdrawn from ESI sale |
| December 1989 | Lord Marshall resigns as Chairman-designate of National Power<br>Flotation of the ten Water Companies |
| March 1990 | Vesting of new plcs |
| August 1990 | Iraqi invasion of Kuwait |
| September 1990 | Consent granted for Hinkley 'C' |
| November 1990 | Margaret Thatcher replaced as Prime Minister by John Major |
| November 1990 | Resignation of Robert Malpas as Chairman of PowerGen |

| December 1990 | Flotation of the twelve RECs |
| March 1991 | Flotation of National Power and PowerGen |
| Summer 1991 | Scheduled flotation of the Scottish electricity companies |

# Introduction

The title of this book is not original; *Privatising Electricity* was also the name of the White Paper (Department of Energy 1988a) issued eight months after Margaret Thatcher won her third term as Prime Minister. The White Paper expounded the theory of electricity privatisation; the present account charts the practice, while pointing out the shortcomings and defects in the Government's original proposals.

The manifesto on which the Conservatives fought the 1987 Election had pledged to continue the privatisation programme by selling the water and electricity industries. A further promise had been the development of 'abundant, low cost supplies of nuclear electricity'. At the time of writing, four years on, this second commitment seems surreal. It will not be in the next Tory manifesto; as a direct result of the privatisation of the Electricity Supply Industry (ESI) the economics of nuclear power have been so thoroughly discredited that the Pressurised Water Reactor (PWR) programme has been shelved. The civil nuclear programme will not be reviewed until 1994, well into the next Parliament.

The genesis of this study was the question 'How did such a series of fundamental misjudgements arise?' What were the philosophies, prejudices, ideologies, competences of the various actors in the Government, civil service and ESI that led to a systematic bias towards, and protection of, the nuclear industry through thirty years of tortuously difficult development? Secondly, what led to a belief that it would be possible to privatise nuclear power, and then to the dramatic abandonment, not just of nuclear privatisation, but of the residual PWR programme, once the going got tough?

The question of nuclear power cannot, however, be tackled in isolation. Nuclear power dominated the early stages of electricity privatisation to the detriment of other very pertinent issues and so it dominates large parts of this book, but the question 'Why a bias towards nuclear power?' implies another set of questions: 'Why is there not a bias towards energy efficiency/renewables/coal?' Politics is the study of power; the power to make choices. We hope to have revealed how and why choices have been made in and about the ESI, both under nationalisation and during the privatisation process.

This book explores the contradictions inherent in many of the choices that have forged recent UK energy policy. These have been ostensibly based

1

on the Lawson doctrine of 1982, that Government's role in energy policy should not extend beyond facilitating the operation of free market forces. We argue that, while market forces undoubtedly have their place in the electricity sector, social and environmental imperatives mean that targeted intervention must also play its part. The poor cannot be induced to reduce their electricity bills by insulating their homes if they do not have the capital to do this. The growing international pressure for reductions in carbon dioxide emissions will not be accommodated by market forces alone.

The material in this book falls into three parts. Part I reviews some relevant economic theory, and looks at the history of both privatisation and nationalisation in order to set the scene for the ESI sale. The economic basis of the case for liberalisation is often poorly understood. We therefore critically examine what market forces can achieve in Chapter 1. This provides a basis, not only for analysis of the economic policies associated with Margaret Thatcher's Governments, but also for discussion of the environmental economics contained in the 'Pearce Report' (Pearce 1989). Those seeking less theoretical analysis could skip this chapter, although the arguments it contains are referred to throughout the book.

Chapter 2 briefly reviews the course of privatisation policy since 1979, drawing particularly on the Telecom and Gas sales to illustrate the conflict between liberalisation and strategic objectives inherent in the privatisation of monopoly providers of essential services. A conceptual model of this conflict is described, on which much of Part 2 is based.

The pre-privatisation structure of the industry is described in Chapter 3. The corporatist nature of the nationalised ESI, and of its relationship to other sectors of the energy supply economy, especially coal, will be noted. This centralised structure presented formidable barriers to new technologies, such as renewable generation and CHP, as well as inhibiting the development of end-use efficiency.

Part II is concerned with the process of the ESI privatisation. The structure is a balance between a chronological and a subject based approach, as befits such a complicated story. The liberalising provisions of the English and Welsh White Paper were intended to fragment the monolithic ESI caucus. Chapter 4 describes what the Government's objectives were at the outset of privatisation (both hidden and open), using the conceptual model developed in Chapter 2. Competition, efficiency (both in its general sense, and in the sense of energy efficiency), security of supply and the mix of fuels, and social and environmental objectives are defined and critically analysed. An agenda containing a third set of objectives – those the Government deemed irrelevant to the privatisation process – is also described.

How the Government's objectives fared as they were translated into reality is next assessed. Three topics are dealt with separately – nuclear power (Chapter 6), energy efficiency (Chapter 7) and renewable energy (Chapter 8). Chapter 5 lays the foundation for these subjects by giving an

2

# Acknowledgements

Any perusal of the text will quickly demonstrate the debt we owe to the Energy Select Committee of the House of Commons, whose wide-ranging investigations of relevant policy areas have made our research so much easier. In particular, the authoritative memoranda of evidence commissioned by the Committee, and the minutes of examination of witnesses have been invaluable as snapshots of official and unofficial thinking as the privatisation process progressed. Jane Roberts' SERC supported PhD studies into the interactions between electricity privatisation and the Hinkley 'C' Inquiry provided another important source, as did the research of the Technology Policy Group of the Open University, which pursues a general research interest into the effects of restructuring on the technological infrastructure, both in the UK and abroad. Earlier versions of parts of the analysis in this book were published in the Journal *Technology Analysis and Strategic Management* Vol. 1 No. 2 (1989) and Vol. 2 No. 3 (1990). A grant from the Rowntree Memorial Foundation to Bristol Energy Centre, to pursue their Hinkley 'C' Inquiry research into electricity use by low income families, made possible much of Chapter 7. Thanks are also due to Martin Ince, who commented on an early draft, to Simon Roberts for useful discussions, to Sally Boyle who drew many of the figures and to Angela Perrett for preparing the index.

Jane Roberts
Dave Elliott
*Technology Policy Group*
*Open University*
Trevor Houghton
*Bristol Energy Centre*

March 1991

5

# PART I

# 1 Markets – theory, practice and pragmatism

'A market is like a tool: designed to do certain jobs but unsuited for others. Not wholly familiar with what it can do, people often leave it lying in the drawer when they could use it. But then they also use it when they should not, like an amateur craftsman who carelessly uses his chisel as a screwdriver.' (Lindblom 1977: 76)

Throughout the 1980s markets came out of drawers and were set to work, both in the UK and abroad. First World governments spent the decade seeking ways to introduce liberalisation and privatisation to both production and welfare. Market solutions were proclaimed as ways out of the impasse of the stagflationary seventies. Planning and demand management stood condemned (along with socialism) as out of date, inflationary and inherently flawed. The momentous events of 1989, the year of revolutions, saw the abrogation of the command economy as an instrument of production throughout much of the second world.

Yet pendulums swing, and it may be that in the 1990s enthusiasm about the efficacy of market forces will again be moderated by a more sober assessment of what they can, and what they cannot, achieve. Theory will be essential to this assessment, but the limits of its application to the real world must be recognised.

'Good economics is a balance of theory and abstraction on the one hand against hard reality on the other'. (Huhne 1990: 14)

Economics lays claim to being a science, but economies are open systems. They cannot be subjected to controlled experiments to determine their fundamental laws, as is possible in the closed systems available to the laboratory sciences. This limits the role of economic theory as a predictive device; it can be used to conceptualise relationships between observed data, but in open systems there are limits to the extent that theory is practically adequate to do this (Sayer 1984). A pragmatic, not an ideological, approach is needed. Pragmatism depends on theoretical insights, but the neglect of empirical evidence transforms theory into ideology (Huhne 1990).

## What markets can do

As an instrument of coordination, the market is a remarkable device, harnessing together the producers and consumers of the global economy in a matrix of demand and supply, mediated by the price mechanism. Such is the complexity of this matrix that its management by even the most sophisticated computerised command system would be an impossibility. Although theoretical models of unfettered free market systems can be compared with similar models of comprehensive command economies (in which market mechanisms play no part), all industrialised societies use a combination of the market and intervention. The choice is not between two ideal–typical models. For a society as a whole a balance must be struck between the free play of market forces and Government intervention in pursuit of non-market goals.

The 'invisible hand' of Adam Smith is often cited at this point in any discussion of how the market achieves such coordination. A less usual account draws an analogy from the engineering theory of weak and strong power controls. A hydraulic brake is a strong power control, but the relay circuit that activates it is weak – it uses small amounts of power to control much larger amounts.

> 'The ideal market could be seen as a weak power structure instantly responding to the changing needs of consumers, by contrast with the simplifying, standardising and remote state.' (Mulgen 1988)

Lindblom (1977) makes the same point about the comparative clumsiness of command (authority based) systems when he characterises them as having 'strong thumbs, no fingers'.

The price mechanism lies at the heart of the market's ability to coordinate supply and demand. Prices concisely, cheaply and efficiently summarise large amounts of information about the production costs of a good. However, prices can only convey information about the money costs of production. Social and environmental costs will only be signalled to consumers if mechanisms exist to incorporate these into the cost structure of the producer. Similarly, markets may leave some benefits unaccounted for. Consumers may decline to pay, as individuals, for the collective social and environmental benefits of products.

Maximum benefits are claimed to flow from the operation of market forces when production is competitively organised (e.g. Veljanovski 1987). The introduction of competition to some parts of the UK Electricity Supply Industry (ESI) was the cornerstone of that industry's privatisation. It is important then that, at the outset, the theory and practice of competitive markets is analysed. Note that in the following discussion, for the sake of simplicity, 'cost' includes items that might usually be thought of as profit, such as the cost of capital (both debt and equity) and the takings of the entrepreneur.

## Perfect and imperfect competition

Perfect competition, based on textbook supply and demand curves, does not exist in the real-life markets of industrialised societies. Its use is as an ideal–typical concept to produce theoretical models. The theory depends on the assumption of a competitive market of multiple producers, each making identical products, none of whom have sufficient market share to be able to affect prices, and who do not collude to restrict supply, and thereby raise prices. In such markets price will be set in response to consumer demand for the product. High demand will give a high price and vice versa. Under conditions approaching perfect competition producers are price takers; they have no choice but to accept the current market price of their produce.

Imperfect competition occurs when one or more producers of a good are so large that they can affect the market price by expanding or contracting production, that is, they have market power. Product differentiation (into different models or brands) will divide markets into smaller sub-markets (albeit competing), thereby increasing the relative size and the market power of producers. Producers with market power can act as price makers (Holland 1987). At any given level of consumer demand, the greater the market power of a producer, the greater the ability to set, rather than passively accept, prices.

When a few producers exercise significant market power within a market sector it is termed oligopoly. Here the possibility emerges that, in addition to using their individual market powers to affect prices, firms might collude, either overtly or tacitly, in order to drive prices higher or even, in some cases, lower. High prices obviously benefit firms by increasing profits, provided they are not set so high as to depress demand to such an extent that overall revenue falls. Low (predatory) prices can be maintained by oligopolies to discourage emerging competitors from entering the market.

The extreme case is that of a single supplier in a market: a monopolist. Pure monopoly is as rare as perfect competition, as most market sectors face competition from substitute products. The ability to make, rather than to take, prices is never absolute.

## Allocative efficiency

A text book model of a perfectly competitive market can be used to show that, in the long term, the price taken by producers will equal the cost of producing the last unit of production. This price is called the long run marginal cost. It is not the same as the average cost of production, which is

11

the total cost of producing a quantity of units divided by that quantity. The interaction between marginal and average cost is shown in Figure 1.1. That this is a perfectly competitive market is shown by the gap between the cost/production curves of this hypothetical individual producer and the demand curve. Multiple producers will be necessary to produce a quantity sufficient to meet consumer demand.

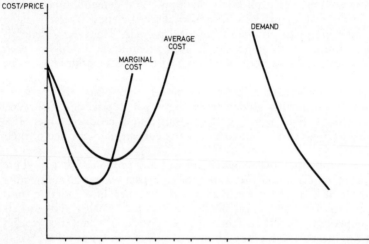

**Figure 1.1** Marginal cost, average cost and demand in a competitive market

Marginal costs fall until economies of scale are exhausted, then steadily rise. Average costs also fall and rise, but less steeply. The quantity demanded is far in excess of that which this single producer can make before marginal costs rise. There is therefore room in the market for multiple producers, each with similar cost curves.

For a small producer in a competitive market the average cost of units of production will initially fall with greater quantity produced, as fixed and past costs are spread over larger numbers of units. Benefits of scale are, however, limited, and average cost begins to rise with quantity once, for example, more expensive labour is necessary further to increase production through overtime working. Marginal cost falls and rises at a faster rate than average cost because it represents the cost of the last unit of production only. Both the fall in cost due to economies of scale and the subsequent rise in cost are fully borne by this last unit, not averaged over total production.

Once marginal costs rise above prices, it will no longer pay the producer to increase output. If price significantly exceeds long run marginal cost (LRMC), competitors will move into the market, thereby increasing supply and reducing the price. Competition therefore squeezes prices towards, but not below, LRMC. The model assumes that the entire production output will be sold at the price equivalent to LRMC.

The model can be used to show that such a solution is 'allocatively efficient' in the sense that when price equals LRMC the combined benefits to consumers and producers will be maximised. Perfect competition will give maximum allocative efficiency; but real markets are never perfectly competitive. In oligopolistic or monopolistic markets price will usually exceed LRMC. Unlike perfect competitors, oligopolistic producers see prices fall in response to increased production. Production will therefore be limited to a quantity which maximises total revenue, and the cost of the last unit of production will be below its artificially high price. This solution is inefficient. The national economy loses the foregone output – this is called the social cost of monopoly. Also, higher than necessary prices lead to higher than necessary profits, resulting in a transfer of wealth from consumers to the monopolist. Governments may therefore intervene in order to attempt to correct these inefficiencies.

As with price, the concept of allocative efficiency only takes account of money costs and benefits. In a hypothetical competitive market for cigarettes, free from Government intervention via taxation and advertising restrictions, if price equals LRMC, the sum of benefits to consumers and producers (and therefore to society as a whole) is maximised. In fact, the drain on society via increased health spending in this situation would be extremely inefficient. Most governments tax tobacco and thereby reduce consumption of cigarettes, partly to raise tax revenue, but also to discourage smoking. Allocative efficiency as a theoretical concept is blind to external costs and benefits.

## Productive efficiency

When goods are produced at least cost to the manufacturer this demonstrates maximum productive efficiency. Although this is a different concept from allocative efficiency, in models of perfect competition the two coincide. Perfect competition will give perfect productive efficiency because, unable to influence the price of their products, producers can only maximise profits by keeping costs as low as possible. In contrast to allocative efficiency, a degree of imperfection in the market will not affect this – provided there is some competition between producers, pressure on costs will remain. Once imperfect competition merges into out and out oligopoly, these pressures have eased. The greater the ability to set prices, the more likely it is that management will tolerate inefficiency, knowing that some of the cost of this will be passed on to consumers. However, productive inefficiency will always eat into profits to some extent, even in a monopoly.

## Beyond imperfect competition

After mastering the intellectual elegance of textbook economics it comes as a disappointment to realise that empirical evidence suggests that marginal

13

pricing is rarely used by producers, who rely instead on long run average costs plus a mark-up to set prices.

The concept of marginal cost can be illustrated by the traders, most often encountered in home counties suburbia, who will knock on doors of houses with driveways offering to resurface them. The patter goes: 'I've just finished a job up the road and have just enough hot tarmac left to patch up your potholes, so I can offer to do the job for half the usual rate'. In these circumstances marginal pricing is a simple and rational option. However, looking at the decisions facing the management of even a small production line based factory, it will be found that, once simplifying assumptions are removed, the sums become problematic. Marginal costs will vary daily, with inputs (raw materials, absenteeism). They will vary with shift length (a six hour shift with one break will give a different marginal cost per item than an eight hour shift with two breaks). Sums which are difficult for a single production line become impossible for a large factory, let alone a multinational company. Holland (1987) has claimed that marginal analysis is 'as relevant to the pricing and profits of the modern capitalist corporation as is astrology to astrophysics' (1987: 339).

In addition, marginal costs may not necessarily rise as shown in Figure 1.1. Natural monopolies are defined by their cost structure – by marginal costs that are always lower than average costs (Figure 1.2). Thus network industries, such as gas, electricity and water, which have large sunk costs, will have marginal costs still falling, and therefore below average costs, when the demand and cost curves meet. In these cases prices will be set in excess of marginal costs, as average costs have to be covered if the firm is not to make a loss. Cost-plus pricing becomes a necessity.

This is not to say that prices are set completely independently of demand, as firms will vary the percentage mark-up in response to demand in an attempt to maximise profits. If a lower mark-up results in proportionately more sales, and therefore greater overall profits, the lower figure will be used. However, the idea that prices equal long run marginal costs and therefore bring perfect allocative efficiency is a theoretical insight into, and not a complete explanation of, the behaviour of firms in the real life economy.

## Prices

Prices convey information. They give information to consumers about the money costs of production of goods. They give information to producers about the willingness of consumers to pay. The combination of these can then to some extent adjust quantity of production to consumer demand, leading to a degree of allocative efficiency. However, because of market imperfections, this allocative efficiency is often far from perfect.

What prices often do not take into account are the non-money costs and benefits of production and consumption – the externalities. Without Government intervention, the ability of markets to take external costs and

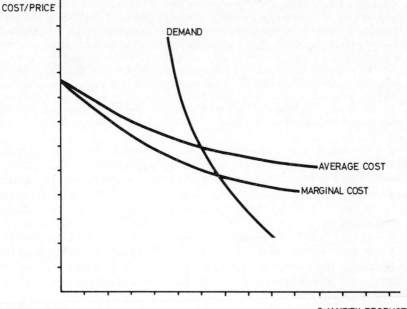

**Figure 1.2** Marginal cost, average cost and demand in a monopolistic market

Large fixed costs mean that the producer benefits from economies of scale up to the point when total consumer demand is met. One producer can economically supply total demand. Note that marginal costs do not rise above average costs in this example. Pricing based on marginal costs will therefore lead to the producer failing to cover costs.

benefits into account is limited to the extent to which producers and consumers will voluntarily act in accordance with social and environmental imperatives. Governments, therefore, intervene in markets in order to correct for externalities. There are two basic ways of doing this: by command, or by using the market mechanism itself. The next two sections examine the ways in which non-money costs and benefits can be incorporated into prices.

## Signalling non-money costs

The 'tragedy of the commons' conundrum demonstrates the inevitability with which communally owned resources will become over-exploited if production is for private gain.

'The "commons" theme is exemplified by the dilemma facing a medieval cattle herder who, along with all his neighbours, has free access and equal rights to graze his cattle on commonly owned pasture. If we assume that a certain number of cattle at a given point in time eat the grass at the same rate as it grows (that is,

15

there is a steady state in the production and consumption of grass), then the addition of *just one* extra cow will inevitably produce diminishing marginal returns. The herder reasons that if he adds his cow most of the benefits will accrue to him personally while most of the costs will be spread over all the other herders (but in such a manner that no individual is noticeably or unfairly injured). He also knows that if he does not add his cow (and there is no law to stop him) other herders might still add theirs. So the only rational solution is to add the cow. Of course every other herder comes to precisely the same conclusion through a process of similar logic, so the commons becomes hopelessly overgrazed.' (O'Riordan 1981: 28)

The environment is a 'commons'. When sulphur dioxide emissions from British power stations poison Scandinavian lakes, the price of UK electricity is not affected as no mechanism exists to enforce compensation payments. Motorists do not bear the full costs of their journeys. They pay for their cars and their fuel, but not for the pollution they emit into the atmosphere, nor for the noise and danger they inflict on the streets that they pass through. Such costs are called 'externalities' because they are external to producers' cost structures and to prices. Market mechanisms can account for them by 'internalising' them – that is, making the polluter pay. Methods which value some aspects of environmental quality have been developed, and market mechanisms exist that would force producers to take these costs on board.

It has already been noted that changes in the market model lead to changes in the quality of the information conveyed by price. If governments intervene to enforce a pollution charge the information content of price is thereby enhanced, provided the charge is appropriately set. The Pearce Report (Pearce *et al* 1989) suggests that such methods, properly structured, can be a more efficient way to impose standards than simple emission control by command, because each plant can choose the most cost-effective option. Plants where pollution reduction is cheap will choose to clean up rather than pay for the permit or charge. Under a command system such firms might emit up to the permitted maximum. Firms where clean-up costs are high will pay the full price of their pollution, and pass some of this on to their consumers. Thus the externalities of production, to some extent, can be accounted for.

For pollution caused by consumption the situation is more complicated. A permit system is only administratively possible if outputs can be independently monitored by the issuing agency: this applies to factories, but not to individual consumers. However, the alternative of pollution charges has some applicability to pollution caused by end-use. In the case of carbon dioxide emissions, rather than trading in permits, a tax on fuels proportional to their carbon content can be imposed, so that motorists, central heating owners and industry alike bear their share of the costs they impose on the atmosphere by burning fossil fuels. However, other end-uses are too diverse and context dependent to be taxed in this way. Cigarette smokers can be taxed on the social cost of their habit with regard to primary health effects, but nuisance from passive smoking cannot be accounted for. There is no

16

equivalence in the nuisance caused by a smoker who illegally lights up on the London Underground, one who smokes in a crowded office, and one who smokes while out on a solitary stroll. Sanctions – either legal or social – not taxes, are the appropriate mechanism of control.

Other examples of potential market-based regulatory mechanisms are mandatory deposit schemes on bottles, subsidies to polluters to cease or reduce pollution, and compensation schemes to redress the grievances of those affected by pollution. The potential to use market mechanisms to control and, if consumption is sensitive to price, reduce the wear and tear on the commons is real. Valuation remains problematic, but Pearce *et al* believe that:

> 'By at least trying to put money values on some aspects of environmental quality we are underlining the fact that environmental services are *not* free. They do have values in the same sense as marketed goods and services have values. The absence of markets must not be allowed to disguise this important fact.' (Pearce *et al* 1989: 80–1)

It is important to recognise that:

1   Bringing environmental and social costs into account in this way is a form of (not a replacement for) intervention, either directly by Government or by an autonomous agency sanctioned by Government. It is not allowing market forces to have free rein but precisely the opposite (Jacobs 1990).
2   Markets can be elegant mechanisms to transmit information by price. Like all systems, however, output is only as good as input. Some social and environmental costs of production cannot be, even approximately, valued. End-use costs tend to be even more intangible. Other means of intervention, complementary to market mechanisms, are at the disposal of Government in these cases.
3   A reading of the Pearce Report gives the impression that the primary difficulty with making the polluter pay is the methodological one of valuing the environment. Thorny as this problem may be, it is as nothing compared with the political difficulties that would be encountered in implementing, say a carbon tax, against the wishes of big business.
4   The question of 'who controls the valuation process?' is also crucial. Different groups will hold different ideas of the value of environmental goods (Cotgrove and Duff 1981). Such divergences will be accentuated where vested interest is involved. An extreme example concerns the aboriginal people of Australia, whose sacred sites contain valuable mineral resources. The aboriginals hold the integrity of their land to be many times more valuable than the ore it contains: the mining companies hold precisely the opposite view. Whose valuation is to be used, and, if a model is constructed which can accommodate both views of the value of the land, who decides what weighting will be put on the respective valuations?

## Paying for external benefits

The emergence of the green consumer has shown that at least some are prepared to put their money where their consciences are. Green consumerism has unarguably had an impact on some producers and retailers, and successes in areas such as additives and aerosols mitigate the inevitable criticisms of the movement. These stem, fairly, from its excesses and, perhaps unfairly, from its limitations. Green consumerism is only one rung of a very tall ladder; the next stage will be reached when a significant body of consumers question the need for certain kinds of consumption in the first place. This stage will of course attract much less industrial support.

Whatever willingness there may be in a society to pay more for products which are less damaging to the environment, there is a class of goods for which individual consumers cannot usually pay. These are public goods, and just as the costs of pollution may be borne by all, so the benefits of public goods are enjoyed by all. But the obverse does not apply. The benefit of pollution accrues to the polluter, but no individual pays for public goods.

Street lighting and cleaning, traffic control, law enforcement and defence are all examples where collective provision, funded by taxation, is inevitable. Beyond such basic services, societies choose which activities will be provided collectively and which on an individual basis. The less willing, or able, individuals are to pay for a service, the more likely it is to be collectivised.

## Liberty and democracy

Liberalism shares its etymological root with liberty, and proponents of the free market claim it is a necessary, but not sufficient, basis for political freedom. The best known modern exponent of this view is Friedman.

> 'Economic arrangements play a dual role in the promotion of a free society. On the one hand, freedom in economic arrangements is itself a component of freedom broadly understood, so economic freedom is an end in itself. In the second place, economic freedom is also an indispensable means toward the achievement of political freedom.' (1962: 8)

The latter point follows because the ability to promulgate political dissent can only be guaranteed in a market economy. If the state controls access to the media, protest is at the discretion of the state. In a market economy, although dissent can be discouraged by the state, money can buy paper and printing at least, and television time at best. Suppression is more difficult, although not impossible (Miller 1989). Friedman points to the evasion of the McCarthyite blacklist by Hollywood scriptwriters in the 1950s to show that markets can ameliorate censorship. Of course, if money is the means by which public opinion can be influenced, then powerful vested interests have a greater opportunity to do this than other groups. Veljanovski (1987) notes the link between political and economic power, claiming that the absence of market power in competitive markets precludes tyranny. Even potential competition can act to erode power bases. Additionally, markets

18

can be seen as democratic mechanisms where consumers use money to 'vote', although market votes are not distributed equitably (Miller 1989).

Some arguments linking markets and political freedom are not well founded, for example Friedman's claim that free markets can organise production of goods and services without coercion:

> 'So long as effective freedom of exchange is maintained, the central feature of the market organisation of economic activity is that it prevents one person from interfering with another in respect of most of his activities. The consumer is protected from coercion by the seller because of the presence of other sellers with whom he can deal. The seller is protected from coercion by the consumer because of other consumers to whom he can sell. The employee is protected from coercion by the employer because of other employers for whom he can work, and so on. And the market does this impersonally and without centralised authority.' (1962: 14)

In practice, of course, markets are a mixture of voluntary and coerced exchanges. Want has forced all but the rich to do work they find uncongenial from time immemorial. Therefore to characterise the relationship between wage earner and employer as voluntary tells only half the story. The freedom to starve (which is what unemployment would mean without Government intervention) is no freedom at all.

In the real world, collusion is impossible to eradicate and, as noted earlier, the incidence of market power is widespread.

> 'Maybe if the choice was between a concentration of power in public hands or tens of thousands of small, intimately competing small businesses, the voter would think there was safety in numbers. But that is not the choice. The choice is between a growing concentration of private power held in a few – closely linked – hands, not accountable to the community. Or greater accountability to workers, consumers and to the people – from within the public sector.' (Benn 1979: 54)

Holland (1987) notes the difference between 'freedom from' and 'freedom to', pointing out circumstances where Government action (say demand management to boost employment) increases choices available, and therefore the freedom of citizens.

Just as perfect competition promises perfect allocative efficiency, so proponents of free market capitalism promise freedom. In both cases the truth of the theory provides insights into the praxis, but cannot comprehend entirely the complexities of the real situation. Absolute individual freedom in an industrial society is anyway a nonsensical proposition. Balance must be struck between individual and collective freedoms – and individual and collective responsibilities.

## What markets cannot do

The most fundamental objection usually raised against unfettered free markets is that they cannot guarantee minimum living standards, and indeed are likely, through their operation, to produce the inequities that they are unable to mitigate.

The other major defect of markets is their inability to plan for the long term. This applies as much to the individual firm as to the macroeconomy. Producers (whether individuals or large firms) will be reluctant to prejudice today's profits for the the sake of jam tomorrow. Long sighted investment decisions, for example in research programmes, are not favoured by competitive conditions. Indeed, the higher the degree of monopoly in an industry, the more likely it is to invest in innovation. Nationally important macroeconomic aims, for example full employment or self sufficiency in strategically important commodities, may not be automatically achieved by the use of market forces alone.

Markets also fail at times of national emergency, when the collective interest must override the individual. In time of war collectivism is widely used in order that the productive resources of the nation can be more effectively harnessed to its defence. It is too early to judge whether the threat posed by the greenhouse effect is of an order of magnitude greater than that posed in 1940 by Hitler. But it may be that, while Hitler threatened liberty, democracy, and the right to life of some minority groups in Europe, the greenhouse effect has the potential to end all human life on this planet. Should it turn out that the stakes are so high, the actual effectiveness of ameliorative action will be more important than its theoretical basis. This study of the privatisation of the UK ESI hopes to demonstrate the superiority of pragmatism over dogmatism.

# 2 The limits of liberalisation

'Although the size and extent of natural monopolies have clearly to be constrained to what is truly "natural", I firmly believe that where competition is impractical privatisation policies have now been developed to such an extent that regulated private ownership of natural monopolies is preferable to nationalisation.' (John Moore, Financial Secretary to the Treasury 1985: 95)

## The origins of the UK privatisation programme

### The 1970s

The policy of privatisation has its roots in the problems of governance and economic management experienced by UK Governments in the decade before 1979. These years saw a decline in the political authority of Government, and 'unremitting economic crisis' (Budge *et al* 1988). Since World War I British Governments had displayed a tendency towards quasi-corporatist solutions (Middlemas 1979), and this trend accelerated in the 1970s in response to the crisis. When the Heath administration fell in 1974 as a direct result of trade union hostility it seemed to confirm that Government could rule only with the consent of economic interests.

By 1974 some were predicting full state control of privately owned industry within ten years (Pahl and Winkler 1974). The State's role as a major industrial producer increased as failing private enterprises (Rolls Royce, British Leyland) joined the existing nationalised industries. The culmination of this process was when the 1974–9 Labour Government sought, found, and then lost, the cooperation of industry and unions in the Social Contract. The barriers between Government, union and industry became increasingly blurred. Yet, paradoxically, as the sphere of influence

21

of the State grew, its power diminished. Governments needed to bargain to survive.

During the mid seventies public expenditure as a proportion of Gross National Product (GNP) was rising at a time when economic growth was sluggish due to the recession caused by the oil price shock of 1973. Inflation and unemployment rose in tandem, and Keynesian demand management was powerless to cope with one without exacerbating the other. After the IMF loan negotiations of 1976 the Government was unable to deliver its side of the Social Contract bargain. There was subsequent widespread industrial unrest and Labour lost the 1979 General Election.

The tendency of a social democratic state to over-extend itself to the point where it finds itself unable to survive without bargaining, and simultaneously weakened in its bargaining power, has been characterised from the left as 'legitimation crisis' (Habermas 1976) and by neo-conservative and liberal economists as 'overload' (Birch 1984). The process was sharply reversed by the Conservative Government that took power in 1979 (Middlemas 1983). The years in opposition in the mid-70s had led to a shift in the mainstream of Conservative Party thinking towards monetarism and support for free markets. The post-war bipartisan consensus, based on adherence to Keynesian interventionist economic management, had ended (Heald and Steel 1986). Rejecting both corporatism and state control of industry the Thatcher Governments sought to 'roll back the state', thereby restoring the authority of Government (Gamble 1988). Two distinct strategies were adopted, sometimes in tandem:

Privatisation: the transfer of ownership of assets from the public to the private sector.

Liberalisation: the introduction of deregulation and competition to regulated and monopolistic industries.

Note that the term 'privatisation' is often used to describe acts of liberalisation – for example the franchising of local authority or NHS services. To avoid confusion, throughout this book the narrower definition given here will apply.

### The first Thatcher term – Liberalisation

With hindsight, privatisation of nationalised industries seems an obvious tactic for a Government holding the general policy objective of disengagement from the economy. In fact, the perceived difficulties of selling the nationalised monopolies meant the programme gained little momentum in the first term of office, when priority was instead given to liberalisation. Thus the first phase of privatisation was of industries typically already found in the private sector, with few special characteristics that would predispose them to state ownership, for example Amersham International, Britoil, BP and ICL. These early sales raised comparatively small sums for the Treasury at a time when monetary policy was very tight, and tax revenue under pressure due to recession. The income generated would therefore have been particularly welcome, and the transfer of ownership was politically expedient and administratively simple.

The sale of 51 per cent of British Telecom (BT) in 1984 marked the beginning of the second phase – the sale of the public monopolies, including the so-called 'network' industries. The telephone, gas, water and electricity sectors are all natural monopolies (see Figure 1.2). These industries are characterised by supply networks which it would be expensive to duplicate, although fibre optics has brought down the cost of duplication in telecommunications. Lack of competition means that regulation is necessary to safeguard consumers' interests against monopoly power; however, even in network industries some degree of liberalisation is often possible by introducing competition into non-network activities. The possible extent and nature of this competition is dependent on the technological characteristics of the industry.

During the first years of Conservative Government several legislative measures to liberalise the public sector were passed, and these had mixed success. The British Telecommunications Act 1981, Oil and Gas (Enterprise) Act 1982 and Energy Act 1983 aimed to liberalise the telephone, gas and electricity sectors respectively. Thus, well before its privatisation, BT was exposed to competition in peripheral activities, through the ending of the statutory monopoly on telephone terminal equipment, and value added network services (such as weather information and the talking clock), and the supply of terminal equipment. Development of fibre optics meant Mercury could be established as a trunk competitor to BT, provided it could gain access to BT's local networks at a non-prohibitive cost. Competitors did enter the deregulated telecommunications markets, although these represented a very small portion of BT's activities. The heart of its business, voice telephony, remained regulated and protected from competition from all but Mercury, from 1983 until 1990, when it was announced that regulation was to be further relaxed. The UK telecommunications regime was often cited as the most liberal in the world. However, most of the benefits of liberalisation accrue to business, rather than domestic, users (Braun 1990).

Liberalisation of the gas industry had little success. British Gas (BG) was divested of its oil assets, but retained its *de facto* monopoly on mains gas supply despite loss of the statutory monopoly. Although access to British Gas pipelines is theoretically available to alternative suppliers wishing to reach industrial customers, barriers exist to prevent this. British Gas owns all existing gas supplies, the average cost of which is below newly discovered fields, and can use predatory pricing to protect its industrial markets (National Consumer Council 1989). By 1989 it was necessary for the Department of Trade and Industry to insist that BG ensure that at least ten per cent of gas supplies from new fields be delivered by competitors – an example of liberalisation by regulation.

The 1983 Energy Act is considered in detail in the next chapter, but is generally reckoned to have failed in its attempt to introduce competition into the generation of electricity (Hammond, Helm and Thompson 1989). Despite the removal of the statutory monopoly previously enjoyed by the CEGB in England and Wales new entrants did not enter the market to any significant extent.

## Objectives of privatisation

The liberalisation of BT did not address the telecommunications industry's main problem in the early eighties: that of finding the money for investment in new systems and equipment at a time of rapid technological change. BT needed large capital sums, but monetary policy was tight, so these had to be sought from the private, not the public, sector (Veljanovski 1987). Attempts were made to devise a 'Buzby Bond' whereby the still nationalised BT could raise money from the capital markets in the same way as a private company, but the project foundered. While BT remained wholly in the public sector, the Government stood as guarantor for its debts. Therefore its borrowings were deemed to increase the Public Sector Borrowing Requirement (PSBR), whether they were raised from public or from private sources. As such they prejudiced one of the Government's fundamental economic objectives, that of reducing the PSBR. Privatisation of BT was thus forced upon the Government, who were then surprised at the ease with which it was accomplished. Although the primary motivation was to free the industry from the financial constraints of the public sector, other advantages to the Government followed, and these have relevance to subsequent privatisations. The specific objectives of each privatisation are different, complex and often contradictory.

The programme is often criticised as being a crude money raising device – 'selling off the family silver'. In fact the PSBR effects of the various sales have been mostly cosmetic. When a limited company sells a subsidiary its balance sheet bottom line is unaffected, provided the cash received equals the book value of the asset. Foregone profits from the subsidiary company are replaced by interest on the cash. Although the Government does not produce an annual balance sheet the effect of asset sales is no different than it would be for a company. So it can be argued that privatisation has been a way of financing the PSBR, not reducing it (Brittan 1984). However, the nationalised monopolies were not sold at their book value, but at a considerable discount in most cases, and with the aid of expensive publicity campaigns and incentive schemes. If a plc sold assets for less than they were worth it could reduce its borrowings, but its balance sheet worth would be reduced by the amount of the loss it had sustained on the deal. If the cash received generated or saved a sum of interest smaller than the profits of the sold asset the company's long term profitability would be affected. This is the situation with the privatisation programme. Although sale proceeds have, in some cases, reduced the PSBR in the year of the sale, the long term revenue loss may force increased borrowing in years to come. Although this will be offset by the investment programmes of the privatised industries being transferred from the public to the private sector, the net effect has been a balance sheet loss to the Government.

Whatever the financial complexities, political PSBR factors weighed heavily in the privatisation programme. The 1979 Government took office pledged to reduce the PSBR by decreasing public expenditure. The strict monetarism of the first term had led to recession and high unemployment (three million in 1983) and public expenditure as a proportion of GNP had in fact increased. Once convinced by the BT sale of the viability of utility privatisation, the Government seized upon the policy as an *ad hoc* response to this failure (Brittan 1986). Any success story on the economic policy front was welcome.

'Popular capitalism' then emerged as an objective. Issues sold well below the first day trading price ensured that buyers were well satisfied with their bargains, and the promotion of wider share ownership became an end in itself, developed beyond the privatised sector with fiscal incentives such as PEPs. This objective served the Government's ambition to promote an enterprise culture, as did the shareholdings reserved for workers in the privatised industries. John Moore, when Financial Secretary to the Treasury, claimed that the existence of large numbers of shareholder/customers in the former nationalised industries would give simultaneous pressure for both efficiency and price restraint, thereby bringing benefits to the economy as a whole. The nationalised industries were widely perceived as inefficient and out of touch with consumers. Regulated private ownership was to be preferred to public ownership, because, as well as pressure from shareholder/customers, scrutiny by lending institutions would ensure productive efficiency (Moore 1986). This approach has been criticised on the grounds that ownership is less important than effective competition in producing efficiency (Kay and Thompson 1986).

The transfer to private ownership of a public monopoly may improve its productive efficiency, but this will be as a result of reduced Government interference and the introduction of capital market pressures, not because of public ownership *per se*. Shareholders do not usually impinge on the day-to-day activities of a company's management, but if inefficiency leads to declining profits, the share price will fall, leaving the company vulnerable to takeover and its management vulnerable to the sack by the new owners. This threat keeps managers on their toes. However, the market for corporate control is most effective on small and medium size quoted companies; despite the trend to larger takeovers in recent years, very large companies remain fairly safe from hostile takeover bids. Breaking a national monopoly into smaller regional monopolies may increase productive efficiency by making the threat of takeover more real.

Where there is natural monopoly, competition can bring allocative efficiency only to peripheral activities. However, allocative efficiency can be improved, to some extent, by splitting a national monopoly into regional companies. Comparisons between the regions will give the regulator information on which to assess the relative efficiencies of the regional companies, and devise incentives for the most efficient. Real (albeit duopolistic) competition across regional boundaries may also be possible.

The objectives of the privatisation programme were thus: to free the industries from Government interference, especially by way of investment constraints; financial and political PSBR considerations; the promotion of 'popular capitalism'; and hopes of increasing productive and allocative efficiency. It is wrong to claim, as some have (Lyons 1989), that the privatisation programme was entirely doctrinally led. Pragmatism, not to say expedience, pervaded the programme from the sale of BT to the sale of the water authorities. The overriding objective was to accomplish the sales quickly in order to reap the perceived political benefits.

The most obvious casualty of this approach was liberalisation. Whereas the first Thatcher term was characterised by attempted liberalisation with only token privatisation, in the second term the reverse priorities applied. Liberalisation may be the ideological companion of privatisation, but in practice liberalisation impedes the pragmatic goals of privatisation. This conflict between the Government's dual goals is often complicated, in the case of nationalised monopolies, by the presence of externalities which necessitate the imposition of non-market objectives on prospective privatised companies.

## Objectives in conflict

### Non-market objectives

Non-market objectives (NMOs) are social, environmental or strategic objectives which a private company might choose not to pursue if only commercial criteria applied. In the public sector responsibility for non-market objectives is assumed by management, in consultation with Government, and the cost is cross-subsidised from commercial activities. If the Government wishes to ensure that non-market objectives are met subsequent to privatisation, it must regulate, either by command or by using market mechanisms to provide incentives. Examples of social non-market objectives are the rural pay phones and emergency service which BT must provide under the terms of its licence. The environmental non-market objective of improving water quality has been imposed, by regulation, upon the private water companies. The strategic non-market objective of reducing national dependence on fossil fuels for electricity generation has, after much difficulty, been met by the imposition of a non-fossil fuel obligation (NFFO) on the privatised regional electricity companies.

## Triangular conflict

Just as the objectives of privatisation and liberalisation themselves are in conflict, so the imposition of non-market objectives on an industry in the throes of privatisation adversely affects the prospects for these former goals. The triangular nature of the resulting conflict is based on three pairs of oppositions: privatisation versus liberalisation; privatisation versus non-market objectives; and liberalisation versus non-market objectives. The bases of these are now examined in turn.

### Privatisation versus liberalisation

Kay and Thompson (1986) have identified the 'paradox of privatisation' whereby the management of industries faced with privatisation, conscious that in the private sector they could be subject to more rigorous incentives and disciplines, resist attempts by the Government to introduce liberalisation or deconcentration. Concessions are therefore made by the Government to ensure the management support essential for a smooth transfer of ownership and thus liberalisation is diminished. In addition, a monopoly commands a higher market price than an industry subject to competition and this will prove a disincentive to liberalisation for a Government keen to reduce the PSBR.

Any privatisation, once decided upon, is best accomplished expeditiously. Delay, particularly in the sale of large industries, could impinge on macro-economic policy by forcing a rise in the PSBR. Fundamental liberalisation will involve time-consuming restructuring of the affected industry. If opposed by management, delay could become interminable.

Electoral considerations also apply. It would not be sensible to plan a privatisation to span two terms of office. A Government always prefers to face the electorate with as little unfinished business as possible. This is especially true of privatisation, which is often politically difficult to accomplish. For a major industry, from White paper to flotation can easily take two years without any restructuring at all. Although industries may be prepared for privatisation (by way of rationalisation, feasibility studies, price rises, balance sheet strengthening and changes in management), in the term of office prior to that in which they are actually sold, such preparations rarely involve liberalisation.

### Privatisation versus non-market objectives

Similar considerations apply when the regulatory regime of a privatised industry is being developed. The greater the regulatory burdens imposed, the smaller will be the market value of the company. The Treasury is reluctant to bear the cost of the various strategic and public service functions that the nationalised monopolies have traditionally financed by cross-subsidisation from their other activities. Lack of direct subsidy means cross-subsidisation must continue in the private sector and prices to customers will be higher than they would otherwise have been.

27

Profit seeking plcs would obviously rather not have the bother of meeting non-market objectives, but where their remit is limited to a small proportion of total turnover and the long term cost of the obligation is known with reasonable certainty, the NMOs will not be difficult to impose. The situation becomes more complicated where the future cost of obligations is unpredictable. If, in addition, NMOs represent a significant proportion of turnover, the offer price of the company will be significantly depressed as a result.

*Liberalisation versus non-market objectives*
Liberalisation is often used as a synonym for deregulation, so it is almost a truism to observe that liberalisation and regulation are in conflict. The specific form this conflict takes in the privatisation process follows from the prevalence (noted above) in nationalised industries, of cross, rather than direct, subsidisation. The distinction between direct subsidy and cross-subsidy has important implications for competition and regulation.

With a direct subsidy, the cost of maintaining an unprofitable service is borne by the taxpayer. Prices charged for normal, commercial services are theoretically unaffected, although there is always the danger that the service provider might overcharge the subsidy-payer, using the excess either to lower commercial prices or raise profits. Cross-subsidy means the service provider has to finance non-commercial services by raising prices on commercial operations. Therefore other consumers, not taxpayers, pay. The provider in this case will be in danger of losing market share to competitors who do not have the responsibility to provide non-commercial services. Regulation will therefore be necessary to enforce the provision of the non-commercial service and to protect the provider from 'cream-skimming' competition.

PSBR pressures have ensured that, in every privatisation, the Government's preference has been for continued cross-subsidy, rather than direct subsidy from public funds. As cross subsidy implies protectionist regulation, non-market objectives conflict with liberalisation.

# A conceptual model of triangular conflict

It is possible to conceptualise this triple conflict in diagrammatic form. The model, which is qualitative, is extensively used in Part II of this book, in order to analyse the ESI privatisation. Its use is as a concise and visual expression of the triangular conflict.

Privatisation, liberalisation and non-market objectives can be thought of as vectors, at 120° to each other, pushing against a flexible but inelastic boundary (Figure 2.1). The boundary defines the limit to which these three groups of objectives can be realised for any particular privatisation.

N is the nationalised utility. Progress along the direction P represents a lucrative (to the Treasury) transfer to the private sector. It is probably

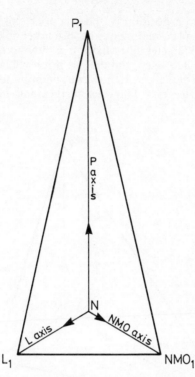

**Figure 2.1** The interaction of privatisation (P axis), liberalisation (L axis) and imposed non-market objectives (NMO axis) with the boundary of possibility

N represents the nationalised industry: the axes represent the extent of changes wrought in the three directions concomitant with transfer to the private sector.

simplest to think of the length $NP_X$ as the difference, in cash in the Treasury coffers, between the nationalised and private industry. Balance sheet adjustment through debt loading or write off must be taken into account, as well as share receipts. The timeliness of the privatisation is also a factor here. A quick and easy sale this year will be regarded as more valuable to the Treasury than a difficult and politically uncertain sale three years hence. Progress along the L axis represents liberalisation – restructuring of the industry to improve competition. The NMO axis measures the extent to which non-market objectives are imposed on the privatised industry. These may be objectives which were previously cross-subsidised under nationalisation of the industry, or completely new obligations.

Because the boundary is inelastic, once the vectors reach it, further progress along one axis is only possible at the expense of retraction along another. The length of the lines ($NP_X$; $NL_X$; $NNMO_X$) represent the given sets of maxima in any particular privatisation attempt. Thus, if privatisation is to be accomplished expeditiously and at a price close to the value of the asset, liberalisation and commitment to non-market objectives must be kept low (Figure 2.1). If greater liberalisation is attempted, time consuming restructuring will be necessary, and the sale price will fall (Figure 2.2). $P_2$ is accordingly closer to N than $P_1$. If, however, onerous non-market objectives are imposed, the price may fall even further and liberalisation will be impeded (Figure 2.3).

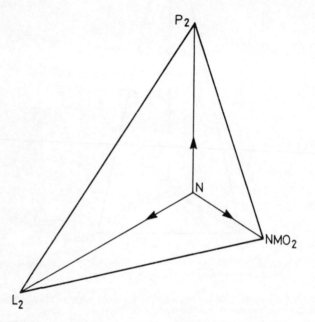

**Figure 2.2** The interaction of privatisation, liberalisation and imposed non-market objectives with the boundary of possibility in a hypothetical example

As the L and NMO axes are extended, $P_X$ approaches N (Figure 2.4). In this case the privatisation will be difficult, but not impossible, to accomplish and proceeds will be small. $NP_X$ may even acquire a negative value (Figure 2.5) in which case the Treasury will be left with a net loss on the sale after the debt write-offs necessary to bolster the balance sheet and, therefore, the share price.

For the Government department in charge of a privatisation the skill is to judge where the boundary lies and then to plan to find a balance between the three vectors which is such that the boundary is reached, but not exceeded. In such cases (e.g. Figures 2.1, 2.2, 2.3. 2.4 and 2.5) the joint gains from the sale will be maximised. An unambitious department might pitch its sights too low; Figure 2.6 shows that the boundary is slack in such a situation. Either greater sale proceeds, or more liberalisation, or more non-

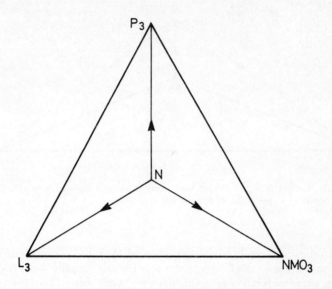

**Figure 2.3** The interaction of privatisation, liberalisation and imposed non-market objectives with the boundary of possibility in a hypothetical example

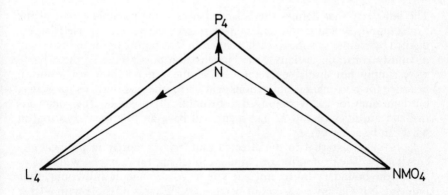

**Figure 2.4** The interaction of privatisation, liberalisation and imposed non-market objectives with the boundary of possibility in a hypothetical example

31

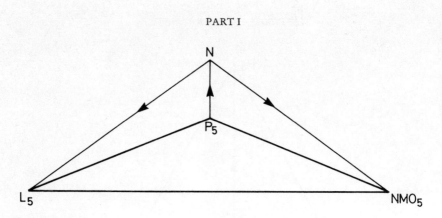

**Figure 2.5** The interaction of privatisation, liberalisation and imposed non-market objectives with the boundary of possibility in a hypothetical example

market obligations could have been achieved. At least, in this scenario, there is the consolation to the Government that the sale actually went through. If the new shareholders are grateful that they were able to buy the company cheaply this may provide some political reward to offset the damage caused by the inevitable criticisms of give away privatisations.

Figure 2.7 shows the opposite case, of a privatisation where the sponsoring department has been too ambitious. The boundary is broken, and the sale is impossible. The market will not pay the price demanded for a fragmented, competitive industry loaded with regulatory burdens.

## The art of the possible

The boundary that defines the balance between the possible extent of the privatisation, liberalisation and non-market objective axes is itself largely defined by factors specific to each utility sale. The nature of the industry will obviously constrain options – the liberalisation possibilities of the BT sale were simply not available in the case of the water authorities. Political pressure for non-market obligations will vary: onerous burdens for water, but light ones for gas were judged to be politically possible. The personalities and attitudes of top management will have an important bearing on what can be achieved.

Constraints external to the affected industry lie mostly in political circumstances. The promotion of popular capitalism, for example, will tend to shrink the boundary by forcing the sale to go through at a discount, thus reducing $NP_X$ in any given set of parameters. What is possible with a large Parliamentary majority might not be with a smaller one. What is possible early or in the mid-term of office may not be possible in the year prior to a General Election.

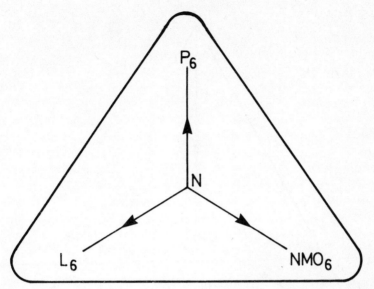

**Figure 2.6** The interaction of privatisation, liberalisation and imposed non-market objectives with the boundary of possibility in a hypothetical example

## The privatisation of the network industries

### The BT sale

Although the 1981 Act introduced significant liberalisation of telephony this was not pursued to its technological limits. For example, BT could have been split into regional companies, but to restructure in this way might have taken between two and five years and the Government was not prepared to wait. Further competition was technically possible from cable, but if British Telecom in the private sector was to continue to cross-subsidise the emergency service and public call boxes, it was necessary to shield it from competitors who had no such obligations. In addition, the market power of BT was so great that establishing even one competitor was a difficult task – to succeed the challenger had also to be protected.

BT and Mercury were therefore given a duopoly (until 1991) over the provision of voice telephony. Despite the establishment of the regulatory body, the Office of Telecommunications (OFTEL), this has been character- ised as an incentive to collude (Thompson 1986), although the price of trunk telephone calls has subsequently fallen. The opening of the market to further competition, announced in 1990, may similarly force down other call prices. How non-market objectives will fare in the new regime remains to be seen.

Moderate liberalisation, coupled with moderate non-market obligations, gave a situation similar to that in Figure 2.1. The 130p share price (49 per

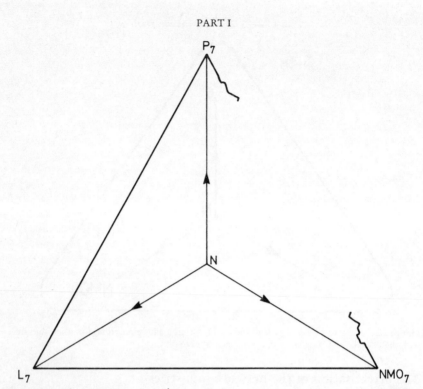

**Figure 2.7** The interaction of privatisation, liberalisation and imposed non-market objectives with the boundary of possibility in a hypothetical example

cent of the shares were retained by the Government) soared in the wake of the flotation in November 1984, but if, as is likely, the under-pricing was deliberate to ensure over-subscription, a full take up of shares and electoral popularity, $P_{BT}$ was on the boundary. The sale of the remaining Government stake in BT is expected in the autumn of 1991, partly to raise money, partly to pre-empt 'back-door' renationalisation by a post-election Labour Government for the price of a 2 per cent stake.

### The British Gas sale

After the comparative failure of the 1982 liberalisation attempt, British Gas was sold as a single entity, with no further opening to competition being attempted. Even peripheral activities such as gas showrooms were retained in the monopoly. British Gas management, especially its Chairman, Sir Denis Rooke, had fiercely opposed previous dismemberments, such as the forced sale of the stake in Wytch Farm oilfield. Separation of potentially competitive from monopoly activities, with the additional break down of the monopoly into 12 regional companies and one national transmitter would have introduced realistic capital market pressures and yardstick comparisons (Hammond, Helm and Thompson 1986), but expedience demanded a quick, easy sale rather than a protracted restructuring struggle with management. As a result the industry was sold with no further liberalisation and no significant non-market obligations.

The share issue followed the (by 1986) well-established pattern: the issue was 210 per cent over-subscribed, although the issue price was higher than expected, at 135p. Vouchers and extra shares were offered to long term shareholders in order to discourage short term profit taking.

## The Water sale

The privatisation programme took a setback when the October 1987 stock market crash coincided with the sale of the Government's remaining stake in BP. Although few individual shareholders lost money, had the crash come later in the offer period, or immediately after the sale, thousands of individual investors would have lost large sums of savings – a nightmare prospect for a Government committed to popular capitalism. As it was, most of the shares were left with the underwriters, and the Government felt obliged to offer an artificially high buy-back price.

Pressing on regardless with the manifesto commitment to privatise the ten English and Welsh water authorities the programme ran into further problems. Defeated in the House of Lords and threatened with prosecution by Brussels on water quality standards; attacked by environmental groups on the same issue and on the fate of the water authorities' massive land holdings; Nicholas Ridley and Michael Howard, the ministers at the Department of Environment responsible for the sale, reached a nadir when attacked by their own Prime Minister in March 1989 for their supposed mishandling of the privatisation.

The flotation, in November 1989, was successful to the extent that the shares were 5.7 times over subscribed. However, the amount of the net proceeds to the Treasury of the sale was negative: £5.3 billion was raised by the share issue, at a cost of £5 billion debt write off, £1.6 billion cash injection to the authorities and £100 million flotation expenses, leaving the Government £1.4 billion out of pocket on the deal. Figure 2.8 shows the way the opposing forces balanced out in the water sale. The negative gain to the Treasury is represented by $P_W$ lying below N. $NL_W$ is not long: water is a poor candidate for liberalisation and no attempt was made. Minor restructuring only was necessary for regulatory reasons as the regulatory functions of the old authorities were reconstituted in the new National Rivers Authority. The water authorities were already regionally organised, so yardstick competition may help the regulator simulate a competitive regime. Capital market pressures will also apply to a greater extent than they can with BT or British Gas as the companies are smaller fry. The major factor pulling down the price of water shares was the massive investment needed to improve water quality and meet EC standards. This is reflected in the extended NMO axis, although, had environmentalist critics had their way, the axis would have stretched much further.

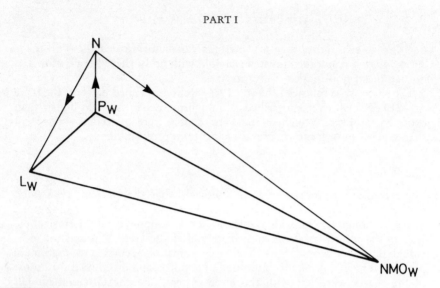

**Figure 2.8** The interaction of privatisation, liberalisation and imposed non-market objectives with the boundary of possibility in the sale of the ten Water Authorities

Despite the many difficulties on the way transfer to the private sector was accomplished. This was a considerable achievement: the price was the overall loss to the Treasury and the political capital expended in forcing the sale through.

## Lessons for the ESI sale

The water sale was far from complete when the White Paper on electricity privatisation was published in February 1988, but the BT and British Gas sales had left a legacy and much of this was positive. Experience had shown that privatisation was possible, and that political gains were there for the taking. But, increasingly, the conflicts noted in this chapter, particularly that between privatisation and liberalisation, were being noted. The consistent sacrifice of liberalisation objectives in successive privatisations was being criticised, some of this criticism coming from close to and within the Conservative Party. Shareholders were happy with their bargains, but the far greater number of telephone and gas consumers were dissatisfied. Criticism of the level of service, particularly of that provided by BT, was intense.

The water and electricity industries were the major privatisation commitments of the 1987 Conservative Manifesto. Privatisation, without significant liberalisation (where this was feasible), was looking increasingly problematic. This change in political mood did not affect the water sale. The industry, a thoroughgoing natural monopoly already fragmented into regions, was not a serious proposition for liberalisation. The electricity supply industry, however, was a different matter.

# 3 The nationalised ESI

'Virtually no one now bothers to pretend that if we were starting from scratch, we would choose to recreate the public sector monoliths that dominated key areas of the national economy in the post-war period. They are the tower blocks of the economy, the monuments to the public sector planning that lost sight of the customers' needs.' (Cecil Parkinson, opening the Second Reading debate on the Electricity Bill 12 December 1988)

## Nationalisation

### The structure of the ESI

Parts of the electricity industry were publicly owned (by municipalities) at their inception, in recognition of the social and strategic importance of a reasonably priced and secure electricity supply. In 1946 the incoming Labour Government found a plethora of over five hundred bodies, both public and private, involved in the generation and distribution of electricity in the UK, although there had been moves towards increased centralisation since 1927 (Curwen 1986). Although the Attlee administration was as ideologically committed to public ownership as the Thatcher Governments have been to privatisation, pragmatism underlay the nationalisation programme in the same way as it did the BT, British Gas and water authority sales. Inheriting a highly regulated, but fragmented, economy from the War years, rationalisation was as important an objective as the transfer of ownership that enabled it (Eckstein 1958).

The industry was taken into wholly public ownership by the Electricity Act (1947) which established twelve regional distribution corporations in England and Wales and two in Scotland (the area boards), and the British Electricity Authority, responsible for generation and transmission in England, Wales and Southern Scotland. A single corporation, the North of Scotland Hydro-Electric Board (NSHEB), was responsible for generation, transmission and distribution in the remainder of Scotland. Re-organisations in 1955 and 1957 resulted in a structure that was to endure for 32 years. The two Scottish Area Boards were merged with the BEA's Scottish interests to form the South of Scotland Electricity Board (SSEB), the remainder of the BEA being renamed the Central Electricity Generating Board (CEGB).

Thus the ESI in England and Wales was, on paper, organised horizontally (Figure 3.1). Organisations were functionally differentiated, so that generation and distribution were separated. Overall coordination was the role of the Electricity Council, established by the 1957 Act, and this led to a measure of informal vertical integration (Yarrow 1986). The members of the council were representatives of the CEGB and the English and Welsh area boards. In Scotland such a body was not necessary as the industry was vertically integrated, both Scottish boards bearing responsibility for generation and distribution within their respective areas.

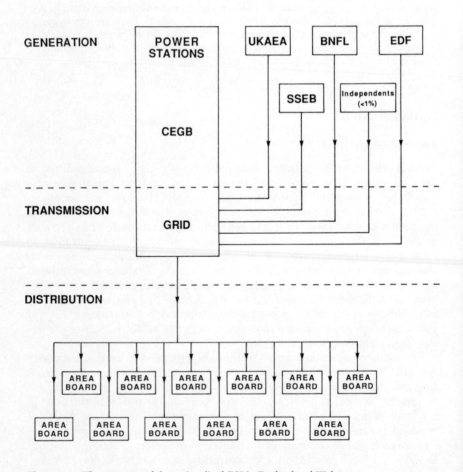

**Figure 3.1** The structure of the nationalised ESI in England and Wales

Although the bulk of electricity was generated by the CEGB, other bodies were responsible for some inputs into the National Grid. The UK Atomic Energy Authority (UKAEA) and British Nuclear Fuels both operated nuclear reactors, selling the power through the Grid. Following the construction of a cross-channel link, some electricity was imported into England and Wales from France, as well as from Scotland. But generation by commercially owned companies was negligible.

Transmission is the transfer of bulk supplies of electricity, at high voltage, from power stations to the area boards' networks. Distribution takes these supplies at lower voltages to consumers. Both of these activities are natural monopolies, based on capital intensive networks of cables, and character-ised by continuously falling marginal costs (see Figure 1.2).

Generation is not a natural monopoly. Once a resilient high voltage grid is available to transmit the power, it can accept inputs from plant of differing type, size and ownership, operating in a wide variety of locations. Because generation takes place in individual plants, each with a maximum capacity, it is characterised by rising marginal costs. Plants with the lowest cost per unit are operated at maximum capacity to provide the base load demand, supplemented, as demand rises through the daily and seasonal cycles, by more expensive capacity. This is not to say that it is potentially possible to organise generation into a perfectly competitive market. Features such as the non-storability of electricity, the high sunk costs of some types of power station, the under-utilisation of plant needed only to meet peak demand and the fact that the output is eventually sold in monopolistic retail markets, all limit the effectiveness of competition in generation to act in the consumer interest (National Consumer Council 1989).

## The implications of corporatism

The various actors in the nationalised ESI (the CEGB, area boards and also the Department of Energy) were organisations pursuing their corporate interests as vigorously as pressure groups such as Greenpeace or Friends of the Earth pursue theirs. This policy sector overlapped with others (for example the coal policy sector) and contained within itself sub-sectors (for example the civil nuclear power policy sector). All of these sectors can be strongly characterised as corporatist, in line with the classic definition of Schmitter (1979: 13):

'Corporatism can be defined as a system of interest representation in which the constituent units are organised into a limited number of singular, compulsory, non-competitive, hierarchically ordered and functionally differentiated cat-egories, recognised or licenced (if not created) by the state and granted a deliberate representational monopoly within their respective categories in exchange for observing certain controls on their selection of leaders and articula-tion of demands and supports.'

Pluralist political structures can accommodate interest groups in two ways: by allowing the less radical 'insider status' in a form of corporate pluralism (Jordan and Richardson 1987); and by allowing scope for Parliamentary and executive lobbying. Corporatism, however, operates as a closed system; outsider groups have little scope for influence. Policy is made within the very institutions responsible for its implementation (Jessop 1979).

While Schmitter's definition is not applicable to the UK political system as an entirety, it can be applied to some policy sectors (Marsh 1983), provided it is recognised that abstract models can never comprehensively describe complex, concrete political systems (Panitch 1980). Neither corporatist nor pluralist models describe the reality of interest group intermediation in the UK, but both provide insights into the workings of this reality. Policy sectors involving large economic interests will tend towards the corporatist model; civil nuclear power has been described as an 'outstanding example' of this (Marsh 1983). Schmitter's analysis is of corporatism as a political system, but corporatism also operates at an economic level. Economic corporatism implies monopoly, regulation, manipulation of markets, and producer (rather than consumer) led decisions. It was anathema to Thatcherism at both the political (interest group) level and the economic level.

Conflicts are resolved in corporatist systems by intermediation – by bargaining in search of consensus. By entering into a corporatist relationship with industry, government offers partnership in policy making in return for cooperation and influence in implementation. The state extends itself into the industrial sector and is thereby weakened in its authority. This was dissonant with the political style of Thatcherism ('conviction politics') and with the strategy of rolling back the state discussed in the previous chapter.

The conflict between the economic workings of corporatist systems, and the free market liberalism espoused by the Thatcher Governments is obvious. It is important to remember, however, that pragmatism, rather than ideology, guided the 'rolling back of the state' in the eighties. Where necessary, State involvement in the economic sphere continued (defence, agriculture) perhaps with limited attempts at liberalisation. In many areas the boundaries of the state rolled forward. Local authority finance and internal trade union organisation are pre-eminent examples of this. At the pragmatic level Thatcherism was forced to coexist with corporatism. Those who have traditionally used the term corporatism as synonymous with tripartism might disagree with this assessment. Trades unions were systematically excluded from consultation with Government during the Thatcher years and tripartite institutions, such as the National Economic Development Corporation, downgraded. But although tripartism is one manifestation of corporatism, corporatist relations can exist even though unions are excluded.

Corporatist relations within the ESI and overlapping policy sectors were the status quo. This had a pervasive effect on the operations of the industry.

Insider interests (coal and nuclear power) benefited greatly, while outsider interests (consumers, renewable energy sources, energy efficiency) made little headway.

## Supply or demand?

The structure of the nationalised ESI guaranteed a pre-eminent role for the generating board in England and Wales. With a statutory monopoly on generation, no regional fragmentation, and a lion's share of the capital assets of the industry, the CEGB dominated the ESI south of the border. The Scottish boards, though much smaller, were vertically integrated, and therefore all-powerful, within their respective areas. In any ESI the generator has more scope for initiative than the distributor. It is the generator that decides how much plant will be constructed and of what type, and which shall be retired, therefore determining the fuel mix.

The dominance of the generating boards in setting the policy for the industry contributed to the supply led approach that characterised the nationalised ESI. Since the emergence of the environmental movement, its most fundamental criticism of the ESI has been directed at its emphasis on increasing supply to whatever level was necessary in order to meet projected demand, rather than focusing on meeting demand in the most energy efficient way, or at the lowest cost. The least-cost option is often to decrease demand, by conservation or the substitution of other fuels for electricity, rather than to increase supply. Matching supply to end-use requires decisions to be taken at a devolved level and the centralisation of the ESI precluded this. The least cost planning concept will be more fully discussed in Chapter 7.

Emphasis on creating supply, rather than on managing demand, was anyway inevitable in the long years of the economic boom of the Fifties and Sixties. Technological optimism and steady economic growth, coupled with a blissful ignorance of the importance of the environmental impacts of electricity generation, led to a succession of investment decisions that were to lead to serious over-capacity of generating plant by 1980.

There were other reasons for this over-investment. The size of power stations, and therefore their lead times, increased steadily until the hiatus in construction in the 1970s. Planners in the Sixties were, of course, unaware of the coming oil-price shock of 1973–4, and of the economic slowdown that would partially result from this. Neither was there a realisation that economic growth did not necessarily lead to a one-for-one percentage increase in electricity demand, as had been the case historically. As the British economy diversified into service, rather than energy intensive manufacturing industry, electricity demand grew at a slower rate than the economy as a whole.

Finally, the relationship of the industry with Government encouraged over-capacity, enabling the investment polices of the ESI to be manipulated by successive Governments in pursuit of strategic and macro-economic goals (McGowan 1988). Successive decisions on the nuclear power pro-gramme, the enforced purchase of British coal, the enforced use of British construction companies – these are all examples of Government inter-vention in pursuit of strategic goals. Macro-economic considerations have disrupted the economic regulation of the ESI.

## Economic regulation

The problems inherent in the pursuit of non-market objectives are mani-fested in, not created by, the privatisation process, and have dogged the nationalised industries since their creation. That the most monopolistic part of the ESI, the CEGB, should (apart from transmission) display limited tendency to natural monopoly can be attributed to the post-war enthusiasm for centralisation, coupled with the 1945 Labour Government's belief in the efficacy of planning. Through the ownership of the fuel and power, trans-port, and iron and steel industries the Government hoped to end the inefficiencies and shortages that had pervaded the Twenties and Thirties. It was hoped that state ownership could be a substitute for comprehensive economic planning (Armstrong, Glyn and Harrison 1984).

The dramatic improvements in efficiency that followed nationalisation seemed to vindicate this approach (Herbert Committee 1956). However, just as privatisation carries inherent contradictions, so did the post-war nationalisation programme. The vehicle chosen for the nationalised ESI was the public corporation based on the Morrisonian model. Such a corporation theoretically operates at arm's length from the Government of the day, with a requirement to break even financially, while providing both commercial and public interest services economically and efficiently. It was hoped that autonomy from Government would give the industries business flexibility and clear lines of responsibility. Public corporations were intended to bear much more resemblance to private sector companies than to the civil service.

Two conflicts are inherent in the Morrisonian model. There is no clear dividing line between decisions to be taken at Ministerial level and those to be taken by management. This leads to a conflict between the perceived need for industry autonomy, and the need of the Government to use the industry for macro-economic, strategic or social purposes. Nationalised industries cannot simultaneously operate at arm's length, and be used as instruments of economic planning. The second conflict is the familiar micro-economic one between the pursuit of commercial and non-market objectives. The boards of the nationalised industries were charged with finding a balance between these objectives, but no effective system of accountability developed to monitor, for example, the extent of cross-subsidy and the cost-effectiveness of non-market provision. Despite a series of Reports and White Papers deploring Government interference and pro-posing mechanisms of control that limited Ministerial discretion (Herbert

Committee 1956; HM Treasury 1961, 1967, 1978; NEDO 1976), neither of these conflicts were resolved.

The ESI was formally regulated by a dual system of statutory and financial controls, and it was with regard to the latter that the problems were mostly manifested. In addition there was available a system of retrospective accountability through investigations and Reports by Parliamentary Select Committees and (latterly) by the Monopolies and Mergers Commission (MMC 1981). Statutes leave only small discretionary powers with the Minister (or Secretary of State), and these are subject to judicial review and must therefore be exercised reasonably. However, successive Ministers have had the utmost discretion when setting the financial regimes of nationalised industries and both Labour and Conservative administrations have used this to the full.

After the 1978 White Paper the main financial controls were the financial target (calculated as a percentage return on assets) and, supposedly subsidiary to this, the external financing limit (EFL), prescribing the annual maximum increase or minimum decrease in the industry's debt. For any given nationalised industry a positive or negative EFL will increase or decrease (respectively) the PSBR. In an effort to introduce commercial disciplines to investment appraisal, a discounted cash flow system was implemented using a discount rate of five per cent.

The rationale of the financial target was to encourage a move to a more allocatively efficient pricing policy based on long-run marginal costs. However, this was impeded by the conflict between the macro-economic goal of reducing the PSBR and the microeconomic goal of meeting the financial target. Just as in the Seventies electricity prices had been kept below long run marginal costs in order to counter inflation, so the squeeze that the Government put on the PSBR throughout the Eighties meant tight EFLs, and prices significantly in excess of long-run marginal costs. Latterly, the prospect of privatisation reinforced this policy, in the hope that high profits would make the industry easier to sell (Rodriguez 1987).

In addition to the formal mechanisms, informal ways existed for the Government to influence the ESI and vice versa. Board members were appointed by the Minister and there was extensive consultation between the boards on the one hand, and the Department of Energy (or its predecessors) on the other. In this corporatist sector policy was forged, and disagreements resolved, by bargaining behind closed doors.

## The insiders

The generating boards, distribution boards, the coal industry, and the power plant construction industry formed self-contained, yet overlapping, circles of influence within the overall ESI policy sector. The strong links between these groups created a powerful interest in favour of the status quo, while new technologies or ideas which threatened the interests of those within, such as renewable generating technologies, combined heat and power (CHP), and energy efficiency, remained out in the cold.

## Nuclear power

Tony Benn (Secretary of State for Energy between 1975 and 1979) has famously said that 'In my political life I have never known such a well-organised scientific, industrial and technical lobby as the nuclear power lobby' (Benn 1979: 81). This is no coincidence. The technological characteristics of nuclear power determine the institutional structures necessary to sustain a programme of reactors. If the structure is not sufficiently centralised, powerful, and well organised, the programme will falter. The history of the UK nuclear power programme is analysed in greater detail in Chapter 6: for now it is sufficient to note that, by the mid-seventies, the civil nuclear policy sector was probably the most extreme example of corporatism in action in the UK.

## The power plant constructors

The UK power plant industry had traditionally been regarded by governments as a candidate for strategic protectionism. A viable construction industry implies large investment in plant and in a skilled workforce. A steady procurement programme facilitates this investment – fluctuations between glut and famine in the order book result in cyclical over and under-investment. The nationalised ESI had invariably 'bought British', due to Government persuasion, manifested in the corporatist relations between the constructors and the CEGB. Major firms, such as GEC, became part of the ESI caucus (Sedgemore 1980). Pressure from the construction industry was an important factor in the genesis of overcapacity. A series of nuclear and conventional power station orders were made in advance of capacity need throughout the 1970s, to keep the power plant industry alive at a time of order famine. The bringing forward of capital expenditure that this necessitated resulted in substantial extra costs being borne by consumers (MMC 1981).

## Coal

The coal mines were nationalised in the same year as the ESI, 1947. The slump in world trade in the inter-war years had greatly depressed the industry, and nationalisation was the culmination of thirty years' trade union pressure for public ownership. Private ownership left a legacy of poor investment and atrocious labour relations, and the parlous state of the industry was demonstrated by the severe winter and fuel crisis of that year.

The first decade of public ownership saw a short-lived recovery in output before competition with other fuels, mainly oil, but also nuclear power, ate into coal's market share. Government policies in these years sought to manage, rather than arrest, the decline of the industry. The National Coal Board (NCB) was given a high degree of protection by means of a statutory monopoly, limits on open cast production, taxes on oil, and import restrictions. Latterly, the switch to natural gas further eroded coal's share of the market. As overall demand fell the proportion of total coal production sold to the ESI steadily rose (Robinson 1989). This mutual dependence in a bilateral monopoly raised important questions of pricing and regulation (Cook and Surrey 1977; Robinson 1989) and these were compounded, particularly in the 1970s and 80s, by the intervention of successive Governments, seeking variously to protect the coal industry or to rationalise it.

The oil price hike of 1973–4 led directly to the Labour Government's 1974 Plan for Coal. This was an agreement between the Government, NCB and union side, which envisaged a major capital expenditure programme in order to exploit new reserves and expand capacity. Although the plan was to be redrawn almost immediately (Department of Energy 1977) because of the underestimation of capital expenditures and problems with the planning system, the tripartite basis of decision taking within the coal sector was seemingly confirmed in 1978 when 'at the miners' union's annual conference at Torquay, a planning agreement, the first of its kind between a nationalised industry and the Government, was signed' (Benn 1979).

Not surprisingly, different priorities were asserted by the new Conservative Government following the 1979 election. The NCB was put under a statutory obligation to break even, and this, coupled with the fall in demand triggered by the economic recession of the early Eighties, meant an overall retraction in capacity, not the expansion envisaged in the 'Plan for Coal'. Pit closures accelerated following the defeat and schism of the National Union of Mineworkers in the 1984–5 strike. By 1990, 100 out of 169 pits had been closed and 140 000 jobs lost since the strike.

The attitude of the Thatcher Governments to the coal industry has been forged by hostility (a throwback to the fall of the Heath Government in 1974) and dependence. Industry in general, and the ESI in particular, needs supplies of British coal. Port facilities for importation are extremely limited and proposals to build new coal importation docks can have only a small impact in the context of total UK demand. The international steam coal market is anyway tiny, and demand from the UK would quickly push prices towards those offered by the (now re-christened) British Coal Corporation (BC), once the cost of transport to inland sites was taken into account (Prior 1989).

The generating boards, BC and Government were locked in a triangle of mutual dependence. Although after the change of Government in 1979 the relationship cannot be characterised as cosy, reluctant recognition of the nation's dependence on the coal industry ensured continued protection by the Thatcher Governments. There was a series of 'joint understandings' between the CEGB (and the SSEB) and BC over coal prices. Under these understandings, the generating boards agreed to purchase coal from BC in greater quantities and at a higher price than they would otherwise have done. The Government condoned these cross-subsidising arrangements, no doubt in order that the electricity consumer, rather than the Treasury, should, to some extent, bear the coal industry's losses.

Throughout its post-war tribulations the coal industry has had the consolation of being inside the policy fortress. Forced, during the Eighties, to pursue the short term objective of breaking even, rather than plan in the long term for expansion, BC could still depend on its position in the corporatist caucus to protect it somewhat from the chill winds of the free market. Other energy interest groups were not as well placed.

## The outsiders

Outsider groups were knocking on the door of the ESI sector during the Seventies and Eighties, but uniformly failed to be admitted beyond the front porch. Technologies offering environmental benefits over the supply-led coal/nuclear policy sought by the ESI lacked a powerful lobby. Voluntary environmental pressure groups found their considerable influence on public opinion largely failed to be translated into policy. Consumers, although represented by statutory Area Consultative Committees, lacked a powerful voice.

Even when business interests acted in an attempt to create a niche for alternative technologies they made little headway. The Association for the Conservation of Energy (ACE), the Wind Energy Group (WEG), the Combined Heat and Power Association and the Association of Independent Electricity Producers are all examples of pressure groups established by groups of industrial firms in order to campaign for the policy changes necessary for alternative technologies to flourish. This is not the usual way that firms operate as pressure groups. It is far more usual for business to be drawn into discreet insider consultation than to have to campaign alongside the voluntary groups, such as Friends of the Earth, using the media and Parliamentary Committees in the hope of advance. The existence of these groups on the periphery of the ESI policy sector is a telling indication of just how tightly closed to outside influence the main arena was.

### Renewables

With the exception of tidal barrages, renewable generating technologies tend to be small scale. Promotional material published by the nuclear industry often emphasises this as a disadvantage (e.g. BNF 1988), but proponents of renewables see their modular nature and short lead times as an advantage. Renewables offer flexibility in implementation, in contrast with the large plant programme favoured by the nationalised ESI throughout the Sixties, which led to the over-capacity of the Seventies and early Eighties.

46

The 'big is beautiful' philosophy of the ESI planners, and the centralised structure that underlay it, ensured that renewables were not deployed to any significant extent by the CEGB or SSEB. No sufficiently powerful lobby existed to promote the development of these technologies. Outside the policy making sector, groups such as Friends of the Earth and WEG were advocating Government support in order to develop the renewables to the point of commercial deployment. Inside the sector, the Department of Energy gave responsibility for overseeing and assessing the UK's various renewable projects to the Energy Technology Support Unit (ETSU), based at the Harwell laboratory and run by the United Kingdom Atomic Energy Authority (UKAEA). Although ETSU has repeatedly protested its independence, its location at Harwell, as a division of UKAEA with key staff members recruited by and returning to the UKAEA, has led to continued disquiet amongst outsiders concerned about the possibility of a pro-nuclear bias. Such fears were confirmed, for some observers, by the controversy over the funding of the wave energy research programme.

Wave energy had been seen as one of the most promising of the renewable technologies. In September 1980 John Moore, then Under Secretary of State for Energy, commentated: 'whatever other problems our wave energy researchers may face, lack of Government support will not be among them'. However in 1982, following a review carried out by ETSU for ACORD (the Government's advisory committee on research and development), it was decided, on the basis of the review's unit cost estimates, that further work on deep sea wave power should be wound down. ETSU's report concluded that there was only a low probability of any design achieving an energy cost below 8p a unit (ETSU 1982a). The research teams strenuously challenged this assessment. For example, Professor Stephen Salter, inventor of the 'nodding duck' wave device, estimated that it could produce electricity at around 5p/kWh and some of the researchers' estimates for other devices were even lower. But the ETSU/ACORD view prevailed and the UK deep sea wave research effort ground to a halt.

In 1988 an account of the whole episode – replete with allegations that a consultant's report on the Duck had, in part, had its conclusions reversed – was put before a House of Lords Select Committee which was reviewing the European renewable energy programme. While unwilling to make a judgement on the allegations, the Committee did conclude that off-shore devices 'should be further examined' (Select Committee on the European Communities 1988).

Pressure for a rethink was further fuelled by Norway's success with two shore based devices, which generated power at about 4p/kWh. Some funding for similar UK work was provided and then, in 1989, a new ETSU review of wave power, including deep sea wave power, was set in hand. Observers detected an implicit admission that the earlier assessment had been faulty, if not corrupt. This view was reinforced by the Department of Energy admission in April 1990 that ETSU had inadvertently passed on incorrect data on the Duck to the consultants contracted to prepare the original review.

This had had the effect of raising the estimated cost of wave electricity to 9.8p/kWh, when the true figure would have been 5.2p/kWh. The House of Commons Energy Committee examined this matter, and in August 1990 concluded that 'there is a case to answer' commentating that:

'If the review identifies significant errors in earlier assessments of wave energy such as Salter's Duck, we recommend that an independent body be established to examine how such errors came to be made (in particular whether there was any deliberate distortion of the evidence) and to publish its findings' (Energy Committee 1990a: para. 18).

Whatever the eventual outcome, it seems fairly clear that some form of institutional bias has been at work. While the bulk of ETSU's staff no doubt are fully committed to renewables, this is less likely to be the case in the higher levels of decision making and it is hard to disagree with Professor Salter's conclusion that 'in future we should not have nuclear people in charge of renewable energy' (Select Committee on the European Communities 1988).

## Combined heat and power

A modern coal fired power station produces electrical energy equivalent only to about 35 per cent of the total energy theoretically available from the fuel. CHP uses the waste heat from thermal power stations, which is usually vented into the atmosphere via cooling towers, to heat either industrial or domestic buildings. Refuse, oil and gas are alternative fuel sources to coal.

There are small scale applications of CHP in the UK, but implementation of the technology is far below what is technically and economically possible. The Marshall Report (1979) identified 35 cities and towns as suitable for the establishment of economic CHP, but very little has come of this beyond feasibility studies.

Structural reasons are again at the heart of this failure. No sufficiently powerful institution existed in whose interest lay the development of CHP. Although the CEGB was empowered to investigate CHP schemes, and to charge for heat generated, its centralised structure gave it no incentive to do this. The Board was set upon a policy of building big, and if possible, nuclear power stations. These, by their very nature, have to be located away from centres of population where the demand for heat is. The over-capacity of the Seventies and early Eighties resulted in the premature closure of smaller, older stations, situated in or on the borders of towns, and therefore potentially well suited for conversion to, or replacement by, CHP plant.

## Energy efficiency

The issue of energy efficiency is one which spans the breadth of the whole energy policy sector, going far beyond the ESI. An interest group perspective gives some insight into why energy efficiency has failed to gain priority from successive Governments, but only in the context of other, inter-linking, factors which are as important – especially when comparing Britain's performance with that of other developed countries. The weak position of the energy efficiency lobby has been dictated by the relative wealth of the UK's energy resources, which has placed efficiency well down the political priority list. In addition, lack of an overall Government energy policy, in the form of directive planning, has left the proponents of low energy strategies with no focus for their campaigns.

In recent times, the fortunes of natural gas have been most influential. The discovery of substantial reserves in the North Sea, and the far sighted decision by the then British Gas Corporation to invest in a huge programme of conversion from town gas to natural gas, were crucial to subsequent energy policy decisions. The conversion programme was carried out in the period between 1967 and 1973. In consequence the new natural gas grid was largely in place and supplying a cheap and convenient fuel at the time of the first oil crisis.

With gas and oil in the North Sea, and large coal reserves, there was little reason to panic in the UK, and therefore little reason to embark on large scale energy efficiency programmes – unlike our European and American counterparts. Natural gas rapidly took up the demand from central heating in homes and from many industrial processes. By 1988 45 per cent of non-transport final energy consumption was met by natural gas. The effect of energy wealth on efficiency was compounded by lack of Government planning. In the 1970s, energy planning and energy forecasts became the subject of fierce political debate centring on the future of coal and nuclear power. The 'alternative' lobby had some successes in championing energy efficiency through the production of a number of energy models setting out low energy scenarios for the UK (e.g. Leach *et al* 1979; Earth Resources Research 1983). Concentrating on end-use, these studies received an increasing amount of official recognition, and their production was encouraged by Tony Benn when Secretary of State for Energy. Even this small headway, however, was largely illusory. In 1979, in a chapter devoted to energy policy, Benn wrote only one short paragraph on efficiency:

> 'Nor should we assume that a lower level of energy consumption would necessarily be in the general interest. It could have implications for employment and for the standard of living. We have to be careful that we don't accidentally back into solving the energy crisis by a permanent slump.' (Benn 1979: 90-1)

In the same chapter Benn complains of the partial information available to him, as Secretary of State, when taking decisions on the nuclear industry. Benn's PPS, Brian Sedgemore's account of the 1978 AGR decision implicates the Department of Energy as an institution set in its pro-nuclear, and, by implication, supply-side, policies and determined to steer the Secretary of State to its course, rather than any he might have charted (Sedgemore 1980). Certainly the above quotation is an accurate summation of official thinking, both in the Seventies and Eighties.

49

Abroad, where energy supply security was in question, energy efficiency was seen as a matter for government intervention. In the USA, many state utility regulatory bodies have adopted least cost planning which gives a far greater emphasis to energy efficiency options. Another example worth noting is Denmark where local authorities are responsible for 'heat planning' at a regional and local level (Christensen and Jensen Butler 1982). In such instances the lobby for energy efficiency was incorporated into the planning structure (Baumgartner and Midturn 1987).

The creation of the Energy Efficiency Office (as a sub-division of the Department of Energy) and promotional exercises such as the 1986 Monergy Year did little to change things in the UK. The lobby for energy efficiency continued to be largely excluded from Government decision making and fragmented between over 20 trade associations and pressure groups. These represented a very underdeveloped and economically insignificant 'energy efficiency industry'. Even the environmental movement has only recently given energy efficiency a high priority in energy campaigning.

### Consumers

[In 1947] 'it never entered the heads of many Ministers and their supporters that the consumers might be in need of some protection from the Boards of these industries. Exploitation of the consumer was associated in their minds with the ways to make profits for shareholders.' (Sir Norman Chester, quoted in Electricity Consumers' Council 1982)

Before 1977 no national body existed to represent electricity consumers, only the twelve Area Consultative Committees established by the 1947 Act. Although after the Plowden Committee recommendation that the Electricity Consumers' Council (ECC) should be set up was implemented in 1977 consumers were able to make a coordinated response to Electricity Council policy, there remained serious difficulties (Electricity Consumers' Council 1982). Alone among the nationalised industry consultative councils, the ECC was not statutory. The Council found 'obtaining information and early and meaningful discussions on certain issues' difficult, especially with the CEGB, whom it described as 'unhelpful'.

In particular, the Council was aggrieved at lack of consultation with the industry on the annual setting of the Bulk Supply Tariff, and with Government when the financial targets for the industry were being set. Statutory status would make such consultations mandatory, and this was granted by the 1983 Energy Act. Although strengthened by this change in its status, the ECC remained underfunded, and no match for the CEGB.

### The Lawson doctrine

After 1979 there was shift in UK energy policy:

'But in general, as Secretary of State for Energy in the UK, I do *not* see the Government's task as being to try to plan the future shape of energy production and consumption. It is not even primarily to try to balance UK demand and supply for energy. Our task is rather to set a framework which will ensure that the market operates in the energy sector with a minimum of distortion and that energy is produced and consumed efficiently.' (Lawson 1982: 23 [italics in original])

Policy formation is almost always easier than its implementation. The failure to liberalise British Gas and the intractable problems of the coal industry have already been noted. In the same speech Lawson acknowledged that there was little scope to further liberalise the already market led British oil industry. But some measures were subsequently taken in these three areas. British Gas was sold, and BC subjected to a much harsher financial regime. In the oil sector British Gas' and the Government's stakes were gradually sold off. But for the ESI it was business as usual for the first two Thatcher terms, despite the liberalisation measures contained in the 1983 Energy Act. Supply-side pressures continued to dominate. Lawson noted the special features of the industry:

'Within this overall approach, electricity poses special problems. With the development of appropriate infrastructures, coal, oil, and gas can be stored, or traded, to a sufficient extent to provide market disciplines and supply flexibility. This is not true of electricity. For many of its uses, there are no acceptable substitutes and, except for insignificant amounts at the margin, there is no flexibility for dealing with under- or over-supply through trade.
So the electricity supply industry, unlike the coal and gas industries, has a duty to ensure that there will be sufficient plant available to meet the top end of the range of most likely demand requirements.' (Lawson 1982: 25)

Market forces alone could not be relied upon to ensure the investment necessary to keep the lights on ten years hence. The answer was for the ESI to plan to match capacity with likely demand, and for the Government to scrutinise their plans by comparing them against Department of Energy forecasts when approving capital investment programmes. The other conclusion that Lawson drew was that there existed a need for diversity in the types of fuel supplied to the ESI. Dismissing renewables as unlikely to make any sizable impact this century, he claimed that 'nuclear power is critical both to diversification and to reducing costs', citing the recent application by the CEGB to build Sizewell 'B' as based on both these criteria.

## The 1983 Energy Act

In his speech Lawson also noted the Government's intention to put the generating boards under competitive pressure by introducing legislation to encourage the supply of electricity by the private sector. This was the 1983 Energy Act. The electricity boards' statutory monopoly on generation was abolished, and area boards were required to publish tariffs showing the rates at which they would purchase electricity from private generators. In addition, the generating and area boards were henceforth to be obliged to allow private generators access to the transmission and distribution networks in order to supply large industrial customers on a contract basis. Removal of entry barriers in this way should, theoretically, have allowed generation outsiders (private firms using either conventional technology, renewables technology or CHP) to gain a foothold in the generating market, provided they could deliver electricity at, or below, the area board tariff price. In fact, there was barely any impact on either the total production of privately generated electricity, nor on the amount sold to the ESI. No generator made arrangements to sell electricity to a distant customer, using the transmission system, as envisaged by the Act.

There are two possible reasons why private generators chose not to compete: either they were unable to compete with the CEGB because this organisation was already operating either close to maximum efficiency or with substantial economies of scale; or, despite the Act's provisions, substantial barriers to competition still existed. A study (Hammond, Helm and Thompson 1989) concluded that both explanations applied to some extent. The productive efficiency of the CEGB was indeed high enough to deter competitors, and the threat of competition introduced by the Act would ensure that this situation continued. To this extent, the Act was not a failure. But real barriers to entry into the generating sector still existed.

These barriers were found in the pricing structure used by the CEGB (the Bulk Supply Tariff (BST) ). The response of the Electricity Council to the 1983 Act had been to re-adjust the balance between fixed and variable charges it made to the area boards – in effect a new standing charge, (the system service charge) based on the area's maximum demand, was introduced, and the charges per unit of electricity correspondingly reduced. Since the Act required area boards to base the private purchase tariffs at the avoided cost of electricity purchased from the CEGB this had the effect of reducing the potential returns to private sector generators. An independent review of the 1987–8 BST by the accounting firm, Price Waterhouse, found that, had the BST been based on the true marginal costs of the CEGB, unit costs would have been higher and fixed charges lower. This would have raised avoidable costs and, therefore, prices payable under the private purchase tariffs, by ten per cent. The other problem with the BST was the uncertainty associated with it. Potential entrants were entitled to be worried that, having changed the structure of the BST, presumably in order to deter competitors, the CEGB dominated ESI might resort to predatory pricing against entrants who, nevertheless, decided to compete. This prospect made projected income flows highly uncertain and precluded investment.

Whatever the potential of the 1983 Energy Act to keep the CEGB and SSEB on their toes, its actual impact on the day-to-day workings of the ESI was negligible, and its failure to promote competition was specifically acknowledged in the subsequent White Paper on electricity privatisation

(Department of Energy 1988a). Government policy was anyway moving away from liberalisation of the public sector towards privatisation. In 1987 the Thatcher Government was re-elected for a third term, with a dual manifesto commitment in respect of the ESI.

'Following the success of gas privatisation, with the benefits it brought to employees and millions of customers, we will bring forward proposals for privatising the electricity industry subject to proper regulation.'

'We intend to go on playing a leading role in the task of developing abundant, low cost supplies of nuclear electricity, and managing the associated waste products.' (Conservative Party 1987)

# PART II

The Government's approach to the ESI sale was in sharp contrast to previous privatisations of nationalised monopolies. The British Telecom, British Gas and water sales had been notable for the token amount of liberalisation that accompanied them. With electricity, such caution was thrown to the winds. The Government initially wanted the lot: a transfer to private ownership at a price that reflected the asset value of the industry; competition in generation; and the maintenance of certain strategic aims, such as the fuel diversity offered by the PWR programme and a guaranteed level of security of supply.

As was seen in Chapter 2, for any given sale of a nationalised monopoly the triple goals of privatisation, liberalisation and imposition of non-market objectives are mutually limiting. Over-ambition in pursuit of any one of these will adversely affect the extent to which the others can be achieved. The Government's original plans for the ESI failed to judge correctly where the boundary of possibility lay – the proposals were out of bounds.

In the central Part of this book we explore the translation of the Government's starting objectives into action, looking at the three agendas that forged the proposals – the open agenda, the hidden agenda and the absent agenda. Chapters 4 and 5 give a chronological account, from the first leaked draft of the White Paper to the flotation of National Power and PowerGen in March 1991. Subsequent chapters focus on three areas worthy of more detailed examination: nuclear power, renewable generating technologies, and energy efficiency.

# 4 The six principles

'In framing my proposals for privatisation, I have adopted six principles:

Decisions about the supply of electricity should be driven by the needs of customers.

Competition is the best guarantee of the customers' interests.

Regulation should be designed to promote competition, oversee prices and protect the customers' interests in areas where natural monopoly will remain.

Security and safety of supply must be maintained.

Customers should be given new rights, not just safeguards.

All who work in the industry should be offered a direct stake in their future, new career opportunities and the freedom to manage their commercial affairs without interference from Government.'

(Cecil Parkinson, Secretary of State for Energy, introducing the White Paper *Privatising Electricity*, House of Commons, February 1988.)

## The White Paper

In February 1988 the twin White Papers *Privatising Electricity* (Department of Energy 1988a) (dealing with proposals for England and Wales) and *Privatisation of the Scottish Electricity Industry* (Industry Department for Scotland 1988) were published. South of the border the main provisions were (see Figure 4.1):

- The division (70/30) of the power stations owned by the CEGB (except pumped storage) between two new companies (now known as National Power and PowerGen) prior to the privatisation of these companies. All of the CEGB's existing and planned nuclear capacity to be transferred to National Power.
- The sale of the 12 Area Boards, which would become licensed Regional Electricity Companies (RECs).
- The transfer of the National Grid to a new Company jointly owned by the 12 privatised RECs.

- The transfer of the statutory obligation to supply electricity from the generator to the RECs.
- A non-fossil fuel obligation (NFFO) on the RECs, whereby they would have to contract for a Government specified amount of capacity from either nuclear or renewable sources.
- The establishment of an 'effective regulatory regime', based on price control and policed by the Office of the Director General of Electricity Supply (DGES). This was envisaged as permanent for the monopoly distribution and transmission companies, but as playing a smaller part in generation as competition increased.

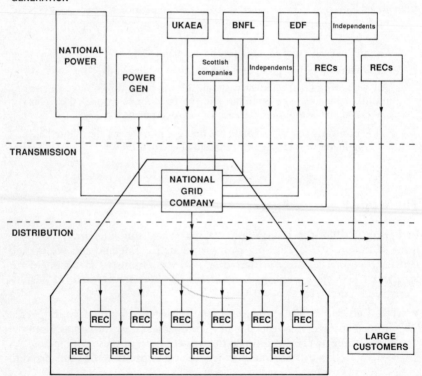

**Figure 4.1** The structure proposed for the privatised industry in the White Paper, *Privatising Electricity*

In Scotland the NSHEB and the non-nuclear assets of the SSEB were to be vested as separate public limited companies (plcs), with joint ownership of the nuclear stations previously belonging to the SSEB. Vertical integration of generation, supply and distribution was to remain. This was justified by the smaller size of the Scottish industry, which made fragmentation difficult if viable companies were to result, and by the transmission system, which was not a comprehensive grid (Hansard 1988a).

## The Energy Committee Report

The House of Commons Energy Committee had invited written evidence for its Report on the restructuring of the ESI the previous December, and started to hear oral evidence two weeks before the publication of the White Paper. The subsequent Report (Energy Committee 1988a), published in July, was critical both of the content of the White Paper and of the haste with which the Government was proceeding. In particular, the Committee:

- contrasted and criticised the protection offered to the nuclear industry with the proposed full exposure of British Coal to market forces.
- doubted whether competition would arise quickly between generators, and made several recommendations, including a time limit on the non-fossil fuel obligation, to enhance competition.
- recommended the imposition of statutory obligations on distribution companies to encourage energy efficiency by generators and by consumers, and to compare investment in energy efficiency as an alternative to new generating capacity. The Committee suggested that CHP and energy efficiency measures should be considered as a way of meeting the non-fossil fuel obligation.

The Government's response to this Report (Energy Committee 1988b) gave much more detail about the proposals than had been in the White Paper. While agreeing that there was a case to be made for time-limiting the non-fossil fuel obligation, the response rejected allegations that the Government was hostile to the coal industry. Energy efficiency measures were dismissed as a possible component of the non-fossil fuel obligation – the Government believed that competitive pressures would lead to increases in both the efficiency with which power stations converted primary fuel to electricity, and end-use efficiency.

## The Bill

The Electricity Bill, when published in December 1988, dealt with Scotland as well as England and Wales. The greater size of the ESI south of the border, and the increased complexity of the attempted restructuring in England and Wales, tended to focus attention away from the Scottish privatisation, which had its own very distinct problems. For the sake of clarity the following discussion applies to England and Wales only, unless Scotland is specifically referred to.

The Bill enshrined all of the White Papers' proposals. The major addition was a provision for meeting from Government funds the 'back-end' costs of privatised nuclear plants, up to a maximum of £1 billion (this sum was subsequently increased to £2.5 billion), in addition to the fossil fuel levy implicit in the non-fossil fuel obligation proposals.

This was primarily enabling legislation, and therefore much detail about how the proposed licensing, contracting and regulation would work was contained in secondary legislation, some of which was published as the Bill worked its way through its Parliamentary stages, and some subsequent to enactment. The room for manoeuvre that this gave was to prove invaluable to the Government once the going got tough.

## The open agenda

The six principles, identified by Cecil Parkinson as guiding the development of the proposals, formed the bulk of the open agenda of the ESI privatisation. These were the objectives that the Government decided to project as central to their plans. There was also a hidden agenda, as central to Government policy as the open agenda, but this was not made explicit for presentational reasons. The third group of issues relevant to ESI privatisation were those that were ignored by the Government, both explicitly and implicitly – the absent agenda.

The 'triangle' approach developed in Chapter 2 can be used to analyse Government objectives, by differentiating these into privatisation, liberalisation, and non-market objectives.

## Privatisation

In Chapter 2 progress along the P axis of the vector diagram was defined as the net proceeds in cash to the Treasury resulting from the transfer from public to private ownership, although timeliness was also an issue (Figure 2.1).

### Money

A good price for the ESI for the taxpayer was not among the six principles, but the initial intention was that a 'fair price' should be obtained, as Cecil Parkinson told the Energy Committee in January 1989. This had implications for the prospects for competition. If the generators were sold at a discount, they would be able to offer a return to investors on the basis of artificially low prices, therefore precluding market entry by independents – an example of a correspondence of interest, rather than a clash, between

privatisation and liberalisation. The English and Welsh ESI was not bur-
dened with debt, having invested little in recent years, and would not need
a cash injection. This contrasted with the Scottish industry, which was
heavily indebted as a result of building Torness AGR.

Although Ministers were careful not to put a specific price tag on the
industry, newspaper stories at the time, presumably the result of briefings
by Departmental press officers, were talking in terms of £20–25 billion
being raised.

## Timescale

The Government had made a commitment to complete the sale within the
lifetime of the Parliament. This can be taken to mean the transfer to private
ownership of a majority of the shares in all the nascent companies.
Legislation enabling the privatisation of water and electricity was introduced at the same time, at the end of 1988, but little restructuring was
needed to accomplish the water sale and the flotation took place in
November 1989 – despite the troubled passage of the Water Bill. The
reorganisation of the CEGB, which went to the heart of the institutional
arrangements necessary to keep the lights on, made the ESI sale an order of
magnitude more complicated and the proposed timetable for producing
detailed legislation was described by the House of Commons Energy
Committee as 'frighteningly tight' (Energy Committee 1988a: para. 176).

Despite this criticism the Government stuck to its guns, publishing the
Electricity Bill on time. By January 1989 it was planned that the new plcs
would be vested on 1 January 1990 and all would be sold by mid-1991.

# Liberalisation

The proposed restructuring, both of institutions and of responsibilities, was
radical compared with the BT and Gas sales. It would not have been
attempted had there not been a genuine belief that it would bring significant
liberalising benefits in its wake. The fact that five out of the six principles
were directly or indirectly to do with liberalisation demonstrates the
importance that the Government attached to this set of objectives.

No future role was envisaged for the Electricity Council, nor for an
alternative coordinating body (apart from the regulator) so the 'informal
vertical integration' (Yarrow 1986) of the past was to end. Horizontal
integration was also reduced, both on the generating and on the distribution
sides.

## The generation companies

The CEGB was to be cleft into three parts: National Power, PowerGen and
the National Grid Company. The split of the CEGB's generating assets
created a duopoly, but, unlike the BT – Mercury duopoly in the years

immediately following privatisation, this was not to be statutorily enforced. The limited existing competition from other generators was to continue, with the potential for further competition emerging as new capacity was ordered and built. A mixture of short and long term contracts were to be struck at the time of vesting the new companies. This would encourage competitors gradually to enter the market as these expired.

## The RECs

To the core activities of the ESI (generation, transmission and distribution) a fourth concept was added – that of supply. Defined as 'the bulk purchase of electricity and its sale to customers' (Kleinwort Benson 1990b), supply had previously been the responsibility of the area boards, except in a very few cases. Separate regulation of the natural monopoly of distribution and the potentially competitive activity of supply enabled the creation of a new market in electricity supply.

Ownership of the transmission system was to be transferred from the generating side to the distributors and the Grid was to be regulated to ensure fair access for independent generators. These arrangements were meant to ensure that private purchase tariffs would in future encourage independent generators, where this would result in savings to the distributors. The RECs were to be permitted to build and operate their own generating stations, but only to a maximum of 15 per cent of their total capacity. This limit was intended to prevent the post-privatisation development of regional vertically integrated monopolies. Generating stations owned by RECs would be financially 'ring-fenced', to prevent cross-subsidisation.

Furthermore, the generating companies were no longer to have a statutory obligation to supply sufficient electricity to meet current demand and to plan to meet future demand. Henceforth this was to be the duty of the Regional Electricity Companies. Although the bulk of generating plant would still be built by generating companies, not by the RECs, no generator would take the commercial risk of investing in a new plant unless a contract for its output existed, either with a REC, with an independent large electricity user, or with a combination of these. This implied that distributors, who were the customers in the generator/distributor relationship, and industrial users large enough to strike contracts directly with generators, would in future have far more influence on the investment decisions of the generators. These arrangements were in line with the Secretary of State's first principle: 'Decisions about the supply of electricity should be driven by the needs of consumers'; but the consumers referred to are, for the most part, not the ultimate users of electricity, but the customers of the generators, the RECs.

Competition was not to be confined to the generating side. The RECs, although natural monopolies, were also to be subjected to some competitive pressure, in line with the second principle: 'competition is the best guarantee of the customers' interests'. All large users were to have the choice of buying direct from a generator, and those near regional borders would have the additional choice of which REC to buy from. The fact that there were twelve companies enabled regulation by 'yardstick' comparisons – prices would be set to reward the more efficient, while penalising inefficiencies. In line with the third principle, regulation, including price control, would 'promote competition, oversee prices and protect the customers' interests in areas where natural monopoly will remain'.

## Nuclear power and liberalisation

The proposals were subjected to criticism from those who thought that they did not go far enough in the direction of liberalisation (e.g. Helm 1988, Robinson and Sykes 1988). Six generating companies were suggested as the minimum number if market power on the generating side was to be effectively curtailed. Duopoly, however, was forced on the Government following their decision to include the nuclear power stations in the privatisation. In evidence before the House of Commons Energy Committee (Energy Committee 1988a) Cecil Parkinson identified the ways in which the manifesto promise of further development of nuclear power had shaped the proposed structure of the generating side:

'That commitment to maintain a nuclear programme has had a very substantial impact on the chosen structure. . . . we felt it was very important to be able to have a clearly identifiable successor body to the CEGB to inherit its nuclear commitments and to carry that nuclear programme forward. We were also advised from a marketability point of view that, if nuclear was too big a component of any company, then it would be much more sensible to balance the nuclear component with a substantial fossil fuel range of stations.'

## Scotland

Nuclear power also pre-empted liberalisation proposals in Scotland. Shared ownership of the nuclear stations, was intended to ensure that the resulting companies were more nearly the same size. This, theoretically, would give competition between equals. In fact it would have bound the two vertically integrated companies together in a large portion of their activities, therefore ensuring as corporatist a structure after privatisation as there ever was before. The gross over-capacity in Scotland anyway precluded the development of competition in generation, as the White Paper reluctantly admitted:

'The Government has considered carefully the possible means of introducing competition into the industry in Scotland. . . . There is scope for competition in generation and the Government intends to provide a structural framework which will ensure competitive pressures are brought to bear on future investment decisions for generating capacity. The regulatory framework will be designed to encourage independent generators to enter the market on a profitable basis. However the present level of excess capacity on the Scottish system makes it unlikely that major new entrants into the generation market will be forthcoming in the short to medium term.' (Industry Department for Scotland 1988)

Yardstick competition 'by which means the customers of one company will be able to compare the prices and service they receive with those received by the customers of the other company' was the best that could be hoped for – a poor substitute for the real thing.

## Non-market objectives

Maintenance of the nuclear programme, in line with the manifesto commitment, was the most onerous non-market objective proposed by the White Paper and Bill. The constraints this imposed on the liberalisation of generation have already been noted. The open agenda justified this commitment to nuclear power as a means to achieve the first element of the 'security and safety of supply', pledged by the fourth principle.

Safety was not a difficult objective to ensure. An updating of the Electricity Supply Code, which was due irrespective of any privatisation plans, was promised. Adherence to this code would place the privatised ESI under no more onerous an obligation than any other private company subject to general or specific safety legislation.

### Keeping the lights on

Security of supply was far more complex. In his House of Commons statement introducing the White Paper, Cecil Parkinson emphasised the priority attached to this because of the lack of alternative fuels to substitute for electricity in many of its uses. The White Paper identified the main strands of the concept:

'There are three principal conditions for a secure supply of electricity:

Proper control of the generating and transmission systems, to ensure that power can be delivered to where it is needed.

Sufficient generating capacity to meet demand.

Protection against interruptions in fuel supply.'

(Department of Energy 1988a)

Maintenance of security of supply therefore demanded two major objectives: a system of statutory and contractual obligations to ensure delivery of present and future demand; and a mix of generating plant to give resilience in the event of disruption (either through price fluctuations or industrial action) in the supply of primary fuel. Although the Bill proposed that wide ranging authoritarian powers, mainly to be used in times of national emergency, were to be vested in the Secretary of State, it contained little detail about how these objectives were to be achieved in normal times. Secondary legislation, made under the Bill's provisions, was intended to set the correct framework, which would then be monitored and enforced by the Regulator, the Director General of Electricity Supply.

The first of these objectives did not present any serious problem in the short term. Although plant retirements and a premature closure programme had ended the situation of serious over-capacity that had existed in the early 1980s, the existing system, to be taken over by the new companies in early 1990, had (if moth-balled stations were taken into account) sufficient generating plant available to meet demand, with a statistical planning margin sufficient to preclude disconnections in all but nine winters per century.

The long term (in England and Wales) was more problematic. Projections showed an increasing capacity shortfall in the absence of new plant (CEGB 1988a). The consequence of the over-capacity of previous years had been a very limited construction programme during the 1980s and this had distorted the age profile of the CEGB's plant, a high proportion of which was now elderly or middle aged. In the privatised ESI investors would have to be convinced of the likelihood of a reasonable rate of return before parting with their money. Previous demand forecasts had proved unreliable. The regulatory framework in which the industry operated might alter, following a change in Government (or in Government policy), or an EC environmental directive. With such uncertainties prevailing, how could investment be induced, especially for peak load plant, which in years with mild winters might never be operated at all?

The imposition of a statutory obligation to supply on the RECs and the monitoring of their forward planning up to seven years ahead by the Director General was theoretically the solution to the problem of inducing investment. Under this obligation the RECs would strike binding contracts with generators, based on both unit charge and available capacity pricing. Apart from the technical problems of drafting licences and contracts in line with this system, however, it was suspected of having serious structural deficiencies. The legal responsibility rested with the RECs, who were prohibited from building more than 15 per cent of the generating capacity necessary to meet this obligation. No criminal sanction existed to use against generators who refused, for whatever reason, to fulfil their part of the arrangement. The two tiers of responsibility left a potential hiatus if the system broke down (Energy Committee 1988a). Such doubts were exacerbated in January 1989 when the draft of a speech by John Baker, the managing director-designate of National Power, was leaked, receiving wide publicity. The speech was to have been given to power station managers as part of the effort to re-orientate them towards life in the private sector. In the event, an anodyne version was read. The leaked draft, however, stated: 'Our task will not be to keep the lights on whatever the cost. It will probably pay us never to over-stress our plant.' (Hansard 1989a)

Apart from these structural difficulties, problems of practicality arose. RECs were to be both exposed to competition in the supply of electricity, and to be obliged to plan to meet demand. The problem, especially for RECs where the majority of demand came from large industrial users, lay in predicting future demand. If there was to be true competition, RECs would not know when contracting for new plant to be commissioned in, say, seven years time, how many of their existing customers would still be with them at that time, nor how many customers, lost to other generators subsequent to privatisation, would wish again to be supplied by the REC.

## *Diversity*

Nuclear power was unlikely to flourish in the privatised ESI without protection for economic and institutional reasons which are analysed in Chapter 6. Therefore the second objective regarding security of supply (a mix of generating plant to give resilience in the event of disruption of the supply of primary fuel) was to be met by the creation of a protected market for nuclear power and renewables, via the non-fossil fuel obligation. RECs would, each year, be legally obliged to contract for a specified amount of capacity from non-fossil fuelled sources. Because this was likely to be more expensive than fossil capacity, they would thereby incur a loss. The RECs would be recompensed for this by the Director-General, by means of a levy on all operators of fossil plant, including most independent generators.

A leaked draft of the White Paper, presumably put out to test the water of public opinion, had suggested a nuclear, rather than a non-fossil fuel obligation. In addition to the requirement to meet demand, the RECs would have been obliged to contract for a certain proportion of their overall capacity from nuclear stations. Refining this to a non-fossil fuel obligation in the eventual White Paper was entirely logical, and offered presentational advantages. Renewable sources of electricity also increased diversity and had a generally good public image, in contrast to the controversial nuclear programme. Combining the two technologies in the NFFO pre-empted somewhat charges of unfair treatment for nuclear power, while enabling the Government to claim that positive steps were being taken to promote renewables within the new industry structure. The NFFO, as originally envisaged, was therefore to serve three purposes:

- To ensure that the output of existing nuclear stations would find a market in the privatised industry.
- To oblige the RECs to strike contracts with National Power in order that new nuclear stations, specifically the planned programme of PWRs, would be built, in line with the manifesto commitment to continue the development of nuclear power.
- To give a degree of market protection to renewables.

Of these the second is undoubtedly the most important. The first could have been met by debt write-offs to improve the capital structure of the nuclear stations, together with grants towards decommissioning and back-end costs. By the time the Bill was published it was recognised that such grants would anyway be needed and Schedule 12 provided for up to £2.5 billion to meet such costs. The third purpose was probably an afterthought, tacked on for the minor political and presentational advantages that it would bring. But the second was vital in order that the momentum of the PWR programme, which had been considerably checked by the protracted Sizewell 'B' decision, should not be further impeded by the privatisation process itself. Following the March 1987 consent for Sizewell 'B', the CEGB had submitted an application in August of that year to build the second British PWR, Hinkley 'C'. The application had provoked massive opposition and a Public Inquiry into the proposal was due to commence in the autumn of 1988. In the early summer of 1989 applications were submitted for the third and fourth stations of the programme, Wylfa 'B' (on Angelsey) and Sizewell 'C'.

The CEGB were unable to argue the case for Hinkley 'C' on the economic grounds that had been used for Sizewell 'B'. The economic advantage of the PWR, which the Report of the Sizewell Inquiry thought highly probable (Layfield 1987), was becoming increasingly difficult to demonstrate. The world-wide price of fossil fuel had collapsed, and whereas Peter Walker, who was then Secretary of State for Energy, had been able to claim in his March 1987 decision letter that there was only a one in seven chance that a coal fired plant would be cheaper than Sizewell 'B', by December of that year his successor was taking a more cautious line. In a Parliamentary reply Cecil Parkinson made only a vague reference to the 'important contribution that nuclear energy is making and will continue to make to the strength of the British economy'. Diversity and capacity need were the rationales for the CEGB's application for Hinkley 'C' (Hansard 1987). The terms of reference of the Hinkley 'C' Inquiry explicitly said that consideration of the applicant's need was only likely to be relevant to the Secretary of State in the context of Government policy set out in this Parliamentary answer and the White Paper.

This was interpreted by the CEGB as removing economic comparisons, of Hinkley 'C' with fossil fuel and energy efficiency investment options, from the remit of the Inquiry. The case for Hinkley 'C' was therefore prepared on this basis (CEGB 1988b), and this relied for its mainstay on Government policy on diversity of primary fuels for electricity generation in general – and, more importantly, as expressed by the intended NFFO. Confirmation that the PWR programme provided the main impetus for the NFFO came from the Chairman of the CEGB, Lord Marshall, who stated that the primary objective of the NFFO was to enable the CEGB, now divested of its obligation to supply, to win the PWR Public Inquiries.

> 'If I didn't have the quota, I couldn't win a Planning Inquiry. . . . building nuclear power stations is always controversial in this country and in a Public Inquiry therefore, it is necessary for us to make some kind of national argument. Since we have lost our authority to make it we have to call upon the Government to make it and this is the way the Government is making it.' (BBC 1988)

*Miscellanies*

The remaining two principles posed comparatively few problems for Mr Parkinson. The fifth principle was that 'customers should be given new rights, not just safeguards'. These were the right to a supply of electricity, and the right to certain standards of service, backed by financial compensation if these were not met.

The sixth principle, that 'all who work in the industry should be offered a direct stake in their future, new career opportunities and the freedom to manage their commercial affairs without interference from Government', was very much in line with the philosophy and rhetoric of previous privatisations, and presented no practical impediment to the sale of the ESI.

*The electricity privatisation triangle*

Overall, the proposals envisaged by the White Paper and Electricity Bill were hopelessly over ambitious (Figure 4.2). The most obvious problem was the over-extension of the NMO axis, due to nuclear power. This was coupled with a modest extension of the L axis and an expectation that a sum approaching the book value of the industry (about £30 billion) could be raised by the sale. The boundary of possibility was well and truly exceeded by this combination.

## The hidden agenda

Some policy objectives were implicit in the White Paper and Bill, but not emphasised by the Government when promoting the privatisation. For example, the extension of share ownership was not among the six principles (apart from the commitment to employee share ownership) but assumed a somewhat greater importance in the ESI sale, scheduled as this was towards the end of the Parliament, than it did in the mid-term water sale.

*PSBR*

As has been noted, a fair price for the taxpayer was one of the objectives stressed by Cecil Parkinson, but one consequence of this, reducing the PSBR, was not. The effects on the PSBR of the water and electricity privatisations were very different. The net gain to the Treasury of the water authority flotation had been negative due to the capital restructuring that had been necessary to make the companies marketable. However, transfer to the private sector removed responsibility for the heavy future investment programme of the water authorities from the public purse.

With electricity privatisation the Treasury expected to gain both ways, with a substantial sum being raised by the flotation plus similar relief from the impact of the large future investment, which was due on the generating

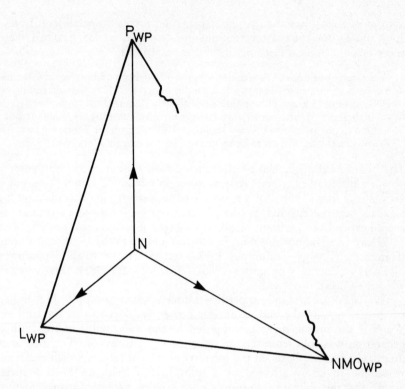

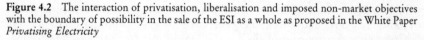

**Figure 4.2**  The interaction of privatisation, liberalisation and imposed non-market objectives with the boundary of possibility in the sale of the ESI as a whole as proposed in the White Paper *Privatising Electricity*

See Figure 2.1 for key.

side in England and Wales. The White Paper predicted a need for new plant by the year 2000 equivalent to a quarter of the CEGB's total 1988 capacity. This implied substantial investment in new power stations. As with water, of course, future ESI income streams would be lost to the public sector.

## The end of corporatism

A further implicit objective of the White Paper proposals was the destruction of the hitherto entrenched power of the CEGB and the break up of the corporatist ESI decision making caucus. The overall effect was a significant transfer of influence from the CEGB to the new RECs. In some ways the Board was an easy target – the exercise of its considerable political and monopoly power had made it many enemies, both within the industry and, widely, in political and economic circles. Allegations that the CEGB was so unpopular that this was sufficient explanation for its downfall (e.g. Bonner 1989 and Lyons 1989) are borne out, for example, by Dr. David Owen's speech on the Second Reading of the Electricity Bill:

> 'Yet when one thinks of the continual lies that have been told by the CEGB about the costs of electricity generation, I cannot understand how anyone can defend the status quo. I know of no public body that has distorted the truth over decades more than the CEGB. I experienced that in my own constituency when the Board wanted to put an oil-fired power station at Millbrook on the Tamar estuary. The Board's facts were shown to be incorrect, again and again.' (Hansard 1988b)

The Board's influence had been unsuccessfully mobilised in an attempt to obtain a different outcome. As was noted in Chapter 2, from the point of view of the management of a nationalised industry facing privatisation it is ideal to gain the advantages of freedom from Government constraints on capital expenditure, without the disadvantages of restructuring or liberalisation (Kay and Thompson 1986). In a memorandum to the Commons Energy Committee (Energy Committee 1988a) and informally to the Department of Energy (Energy Committee 1988a: evidence para. 981), this is exactly what the CEGB proposed.

The CEGB memorandum predicted interruptions to supply, higher electricity prices, and the end of nuclear power development in England and Wales if the management (as opposed to the ownership) of the bulk of generation was split from the management of transmission. The memorandum laid great emphasis on the interests of the consumer, which it claimed would be adversely affected by a split. In oral evidence Lord Marshall argued that the obligation to supply must involve integrated management of transmission and generation, which was also necessary for technical transmission reasons, and to enable generators to gain planning consents. He claimed that the division of the CEGB would not by itself provide competition, and that 'the real opportunity for competition is in the provision of new capacity'.

The White Paper seemingly signalled the end of the corporatist era of the electricity supply industry. By ignoring CEGB advice on the future structure of the industry, advice given both publicly and privately, it decisively broke the tradition of previous privatisations – where management advice had been relied on – and implicitly demonstrated the end of the leading role of the Board. This merely reinforced the liberalising effect of the explicit proposals. The dismantling of the Board, coupled with the double loss, of control of the grid and of the obligation to supply, represented a considerable defeat for the CEGB and a corresponding diminution of its political strength.

The dismantling of the CEGB's power base and of the corporatist caucuses in the various policy sectors related to the ESI was a deliberate and inevitable consequence of the restructuring proposals. Whereas the open agenda stressed the empowerment of RECs and the large customers, the negative effect this would have on the generating power base was not emphasised. The insider groups of the ESI, including the nuclear (examined in Chapter 6) and coal lobbies, were no longer to be protected from outside competition by the cosy arrangements of the past.

## Coal

The negative impact of the ESI sale on the coal industry was not spelt out in the White Paper, which merely noted that 'in future, generating companies will be free to purchase coal and other fuels from the most competitive sources', but this cannot have failed to have been assessed when the proposals were drawn up. The Government's presentation naturally emphasised the advantages of diversity and reduced reliance on indigenous coal supplies, rather than the negative consequences of this policy – pit closures and sterilisation of reserves.

The replacement of the joint understanding between the CEGB and BC with binding contracts between the generating companies and the Corporation implied a severe downward pressure on the price the BC received on the bulk of its product, and a concomitant retraction in output, as UK produced coal was replaced by imports. A foretaste of the difficulties that the coal industry would face, after electricity privatisation, was given at the expiry of the three year SSEB/BC contract in March 1988. The Scottish Board insisted that the old basis, whereby it had paid a price aligned to the CEGB price for 80 per cent of its coal, could not apply to future contracts. Partly this attitude can be explained by the commissioning of Torness AGR, which diminished the reliance of the SSEB on its coal fired stations. But, as the Energy Committee noted:

> 'There can be little doubt, however, that the prospect of privatisation, the "need to have credibility with investors", the desire and the ability to take advantage of an attractive world coal price, and the availability of suitable port facilities were all contributory factors.' (Energy Committee 1988a: para. 135)

This pressure on BC was reinforced by the very low price of internationally traded coal in the late 1980s. BC had little hope of competing at the margin; however, the limited port capacity and small volume of international traded coal provided some protection. Expectations were that the ESI would reduce its coal purchases from 70 million tonnes to 60 million tonnes as a result of privatisation and that this would force another round of pit closures.

Once a pit is closed and flooded, the reserves it contains are effectively lost for ever, along with the large capital investment that had been necessary to open up new reserves in the first place. There was therefore a case for strategic support in the short to medium term for the indigenous coal industry to keep pits open against the prospect of future rises in the international price of coal (Prior and McCloskey 1988), but the ESI privatisation proposals held out no prospect of this. The striking contrast with the protection offered to the nuclear industry was not lost on the Energy Committee:

71

'One of the most disturbing aspects of the Government's privatisation proposals is the uneven treatment it has given to the coal and nuclear industries. While the indigenous coal industry is left "wholly or largely exposed to short-term forces in international coal and energy markets, which often do not reflect long-term marginal costs", it is proposed to offer nuclear power a protected share of the electricity market.' (Energy Committee 1988a: para 155 [Emphasis in original])

Hostility to coal was denied by the Government in its response to the Committee, yet the comparison made by the Committee was a telling one. In line with the Lawson doctrine, coal was being forced to stand on its own two feet, yet every effort was being made to feather the intended private nuclear nest.

## The absent agenda

The items on the absent agenda are those that the Government had no intention of addressing by way of its privatisation of the ESI. The common factor shared by these issues is market failure: either externalities, or long term perspectives, or both, mean that markets alone are unlikely to meet adequately the challenge they pose. Including such non-market objectives in the privatisation proposals would have meant further lengthening the NMO axis, which was already unduly stretched by the commitment to nuclear power. The various exclusions were based on three lines of reasoning: the ideological, which argued that market forces would provide a better outcome than intervention; the practical, which argued that, as with the sulphur dioxide problem discussed below, other legislation was more appropriate to deal with the problem than the Electricity Bill; and the pragmatic, which quietly recognised that increased non-market objectives would adversely affect the privatisation and liberalisation objectives.

### Research and development

This was not a matter encompassed by either the six principles or by the White Paper. Responsibility for research in the nationalised ESI had been the collective responsibility of those within the particular corporatist caucuses, and had been coordinated by the Electricity Council. Thus nuclear research fell mostly to the UKAEA and CEGB. Research into new coal burning technologies, such as the fluidised bed project at Grimethorpe (see Chapter 9), was funded by the CEGB and BC. Much of this research was directed towards strategic, long term development, although some, into operational and safety matters, had a short term application.

Appearing before the Energy Committee in January 1989, Cecil Parkinson clearly differentiated between strategic and operational research. The former, he said, was the responsibility of Government, while the commercial self interests of the private ESI would guarantee the continuance of the latter. The distinction was clear and few doubted that research with short term applicability would continue. The prospect for research orientated towards longer term goals, however, was not good. The changed ethos of the ESI plcs meant commercial, rather than national interest, considerations would dictate industry spending, precluding long term strategic research. Moreover, there were serious grounds for doubting the Government's commitment to long-term research. The continuing pressure on public expenditure throughout the 1980s had taken its toll on many projects, and the survivors had been those which could demonstrate medium term paybacks. Short term orientation was too 'near-market' and therefore the responsibility of industry, while long term orientation was too far from commercial application to merit Government money.

Work by ETSU on renewables had been assessed along these lines in the early Eighties. The various technologies under investigation had been ranked in order of prospective commercial viability, and those at the bottom of the list, such as wave power, excluded. In July 1988 the Government contribution to the research and development budget of the Fast Breeder Reactor (FBR) programme at Dounreay was cut from £50 million to £10 million a year, with no commitment to further funding of the prototype FBR after 1994. The reason given was that there was no question of commercial deployment for 30–40 years. The Grimethorpe advanced coal burning research project ran into difficulties when the CEGB withdrew in 1988, and the Department of Energy, having withdrawn funding previously because of the willingness of the CEGB and BC to put their money in (Hinkley 'C' Inquiry 1988: 15.103–4), seemed reluctant to resume its participation, although the project eventually did secure sponsorship from PowerGen, BC and the Department of Energy.

## The power plant constructors

Protection of this industry was deeply at odds with the philosophy of the Thatcher years and was anyway doomed with the advent of the European single market, due to take effect in 1992. This, together with the privatisation of the ESI, left the industry to fend for itself, in both the home and export markets, in competition with the rest of the EC. Irrespective of privatisation there was the prospect of new power station investment after a decade in which only one station, Sizewell 'B', had been ordered, and this was very welcome to the industry, provided it could gain the orders. Restructuring and adaptation were likely to be necessary (Ince 1988). The Government objective was either a competitive power plant industry, or none at all.

## Not a green Bill

The environment was the most conspicuous absentee from the agenda set by the White Paper, by the Government's own admission: 'This is not an environmental Bill' (Under Secretary of State, Michael Spicer, Hansard 1989b). The operation of the ESI imposes substantial external costs on the environment, and pressure to limit these had been gaining momentum throughout the Seventies and Eighties. Despite this, the Bill contained few ameliorative measures.

*Acid rain*

Sulphur dioxide ($SO_2$) and oxide of nitrogen ($NO_x$) emissions from fossil fuelled power stations had become a matter of international concern. Although the Government had been very reluctant to instruct the ESI to invest in costly emission reductions, the phased installation of Flue Gas Desulphurisation (FGD) equipment at 6 GW of CEGB plant was announced in 1986. Subsequently, the EC Large Combustion Plant Directive, agreed by the European Commission in June 1988, imposed an obligation on the UK to cut $SO_2$ emissions from existing plant by 60 per cent of 1988 levels by the year 2003. Rather than give regulatory powers to achieve these cuts to the DGES, the Government decided to make emission control the responsibility of Her Majesty's Inspectorate of Pollution (HMIP). The necessary legislation was contained in the Environmental Protection Act (1990), not in the Electricity Act.

*The greenhouse effect*

Concern about the potential threat of global warming posed by $CO_2$ emissions (and other man-made pollutants) was sufficient by 1987 for this problem to merit a mention in the Conservative Party manifesto. Following the Toronto Conference on the Changing Atmosphere in June 1988 and Margaret Thatcher's speech to the Royal Society in September of that year, the hypothesis, that global warming due to greenhouse gases might have started, became widely accepted, despite the absence of positive proof.

A technical fix exists for $SO_2$, in the form of Flue Gas Desulphurisation (FGD), but economically viable technology to scrub the much larger volumes of $CO_2$ gas from power station chimneys is not in prospect. Other strategies to reduce both gases include increased energy efficiency (both at point of generation, during transmission, and at point of end-use) and fuel substitution (using low sulphur coal or other fuels as an alternative to high sulphur coal to reduce $SO_2$; substituting natural gas or non-fossil fuel alternatives to coal to reduce $CO_2$).

The UK had not adopted targets for $CO_2$ emission reductions at this stage, although the Toronto Conference had called for a global reduction of 20 per cent by 2005. In Chapter 9 it will be shown that by the end of 1988 the Prime Minister had realised that atmospheric pollution was an issue that the Government had to be seen to be addressing. But, despite the fact that in 1987 the ESI produced 36 per cent of total UK $CO_2$ (which is the most significant greenhouse gas) (Energy Committee 1989a), the Electricity Bill contained no mechanism whereby power station $CO_2$ emissions could be controlled.

The DGES was to be empowered to promote energy efficiency, but only by way of information provision, in lieu of action by the RECs, should they prove unwilling to do this themselves. The non-fossil fuel obligation was intended to maintain the present level of generation from sources which did not add to atmospheric $CO_2$. This was originally only a minor part of its rationale, security of supply through diversity being the main argument advanced in its favour (Energy Committee 1988b: para 47), but came to be used more by the Government as pressure increased for action on $CO_2$. But no regulatory incentive was proposed which would reward RECs who increased the efficiency with which electricity was consumed in their area. On the contrary, such action would diminish profits. The fewer the number of units of electricity sold, the smaller the RECs' income would be. Questioned in January 1989 by the Energy Committee, Cecil Parkinson suggested that the Bill would provide such incentives:

'At present the Area Boards have to accept on a cost plus basis whatever bill they are handed under the bulk supply tariff. In future . . . there is no great incentive for them to see too many stations built. They want the right number and they want the security of supply, but they are not in the business of electricity: they are in the business of distributing it. It may be better business, instead of buying more electricity, to encourage energy efficiency.'

He then went on to describe the strong position the RECs would be in to promote and sell energy efficiency improvements as 'potentially very profitable'. The message was that regulation in this area was unnecessary because market forces would automatically bring the optimum solution. Against CEGB projections which, having taken expected efficiency improvements into account, implied a 13–26 per cent increase in power station $CO_2$ emissions by 2005 (Energy Committee 1989a) never mind the 20 per cent cut proposed by the Toronto conference, this seems unduly optimistic. When it is remembered that the market for energy efficiency is renowned for its imperfections and that, far from being profitable, the firms already in the market were in despair at the lack of business, disingenuity, rather than optimism, suggests itself.

The attitude of Mr Parkinson's deputy, Michael Spicer, was more forthright and honest. Unwittingly echoing Tony Benn, who had been Secretary of State for Energy a decade before (Benn 1979: 90-1), he said:

'It is unacceptable . . . simply to tell people to turn off their lights, fires and electric kettles. . . . if they are honest, those who argue for conservation as the primary means of solving the problem of the greenhouse effect must accept that, if it is to have any impact, there must be a cut in coal fired production or, with economic growth ahead of us, a conservation policy must be imposed to make people turn off the lights to save energy.' (Hansard 1989c)

In ten long years the official line had not changed. Criticism that the proposals would not produce the institutional and regulatory framework necessary to reduce $CO_2$ emissions was to be expected from the Opposition and from environmental pressure groups, but it also found support in a very wide constituency. The Energy Committee believed that the new ESI structure could only encourage energy efficiency if the regulator was given powers to disallow tariff increases where generation investment had been undertaken without assessing investment in efficiency using the same criteria. The Chairman designate of PowerGen, Robert Malpas, complained that: 'As we in Britain are about to privatise electricity, the prime considerations are not about energy efficiency.' (quoted in the *Independent* 27 January 1989). He went on to advocate Government intervention 'through incentives, penalties, subsidies and taxes', as well as the strategies of information and promotion provided by the Bill, in order to bring about greater efficiency.

*Fuel poverty*
The exclusion from the Bill of greater incentives towards energy efficiency investment by the RECs was to the particular detriment of low income householders living in fuel poverty – 5.6 million households in 1988 (Boardman 1988). Lacking funds of their own to purchase either efficient heating systems or energy saving improvements for their homes, such households pay more, per unit of useful energy, than more affluent families and receive less delivered heat. Alleviation of this problem was not a Government priority.

*Rural customers*

The higher costs of connecting rural consumers to the electricity system had been met largely by cross-subsidy under nationalisation. Under the original provisions of the Electricity Bill there was to be no obligation on the RECs, or on the Scottish companies, to continue this practice. This was of particular concern to those in the NSHEB area, where the rural development obligations of the Board had traditionally accounted for a large proportion of its budget.

## The Passage of the Bill

Given the large Commons majority enjoyed by the Government the Electricity Bill had an unexpectedly bumpy ride through Parliament. After a two day Second Reading debate in December 1988 Labour failed in an attempt to have the legislation committed to a Special Standing Committee, with powers to take evidence, and the Bill was instead sent to Standing Committee E. Opposition to the Bill was coordinated by Tony Blair, the Labour Energy spokesperson, using the surprisingly unusual technique of concentrating on the most controversial clauses, rather than adopting a line-by-line blocking approach in order to provoke a Government guillotine motion (Kellner 1989). Labour's case against the Bill was pragmatic, based on the cost of the non-fossil fuel obligation and the neglect of energy efficiency incentives in the Bill (Elliott 1989), and even some Conservative Committee members were clearly uneasy about the latter point (Hansard 1989d). Much publicity resulted, aided by leaks from the disgruntled CEGB, but the Bill reached the Lords unamended in any significant way.

Not for the first time since 1979, the Lords proved more of an impediment to the Government's proposals than the Commons. The Bill was amended three times against the wishes of Baroness Hooper, Parliamentary Under Secretary of State, Department of Energy, who piloted it through the Upper House. The amendments:

- gave the Secretary of State the power to requisition nuclear power stations in the public interest.
- protected rural consumers from higher electricity charges.
- required each REC to promote the efficient use of electricity, on pain of refusal of tariff increases or capital investment approval.

Of these, the third was the most significant. It differed from the proposals in the original Bill, which merely placed an obligation to publicise energy efficiency on the RECs, by giving the DGES power to direct specific action in this field, backed up by financial sanctions. These sanctions, though, were its undoing. The DGES did not have the power to give capital investment approval and so could not refuse it. The clause was technically deficient.

By this stage back bench Tory unease about energy efficiency was growing. The Energy Committee Report on the greenhouse effect (1989a) had been published in July, and this stressed both the potential urgency of the problem and the primary role of energy efficiency in tackling it. In response to the Lords' amendment the Energy Committee issued a further Report (1989b), recognising the amendment as technically deficient, but recommending its replacement with a clause imposing a statutory obligation on the RECs to promote more efficient electricity use, backed up by penalties – including the refusal of tariff increases. Twenty-five Conservatives, including three PPSs, signed a Commons motion urging that the Director General of Electricity Supply be empowered to lay down energy efficiency standards for the RECs, and newspaper stories hinted at a back bench revolt on the issue. No such revolt emerged in the lobbies, although two Conservative members of the Select Committee, Peter Rost and the Chairman, Sir Ian Lloyd, abstained. The Lords' amendment was replaced with a Government alternative which enabled the Director General to set conservation targets for the RECs but gave him power only to monitor, not to enforce, these. The Lords did not insist on their amendment.

The Electricity Bill received Royal Assent on 27 July 1989. The legislative framework necessary to implement the White Paper, which had been framed by the six principles, was in place. But the problems of privatising electricity were only just beginning.

# 5 Spatchcock legislation?

'Spatchcock: A fowl split open and grilled after being killed, plucked, and dressed in a summary fashion.' (Shorter Oxford English Dictionary)

## Expedition and expedience

Parkinson's insistence on simultaneous privatisation and liberalisation created severe timing difficulties. Extensive restructuring was needed in advance of flotation and it was vitally important, both for the ESI and for the nation, that the result was a viable, flexible and efficient ESI. Yet the commitment to complete the sale before the General Election limited the time available for this mammoth task. The Energy Committee, alarmed by the lack of firm detail contained in the White Papers, had been horrified to discover, on examination of industry and Department of Energy witnesses, how little progress had been made on filling in the details by mid-1988:

'If the Government is intent on introducing a Bill – or Bills – in November 1988, it is faced by a frighteningly tight timetable. If at the same time it is discovering new problems, it runs the risk of producing ill-considered, spatchcock legislation. Electricity is too important an industry for the country to gamble that everything will come out right.' (1988a: para. 176)

How justified were these fears? This and the subsequent three chapters attempt to assess the successes and failures of the White Paper proposals in terms of their implementation, from the enactment of the Electricity Bill in July 1989 to the flotation of National Power and PowerGen in March 1991. The prospects for the ESI and related policy areas, now that the privatisation process is complete, are also discussed. Two layers of assessment are needed: potential and actual outcomes have to be weighed not only against the objectives which forged the White Paper and Bill, but also against the background of the absent agenda. The present chapter gives a general overview of the privatisation of the RECs and the English and Welsh generators, setting the scene for more detailed analysis of nuclear power, renewable sources of electricity and energy efficiency in Chapters 6, 7 and 8.

The task the Government had set itself was a hard one. There were many obstacles in its path. Although the Area Boards were, in general, well pleased with the proposals, CEGB management and staff were alienated and demoralised by the White Paper. Despite public reassurances that the matter was 'water under the bridge', and that the Government could henceforth expect full cooperation (Energy Committee 1988a: evidence para. 981) a series of unhelpful (to the Government) leaks and press briefings from the CEGB began with the publication of the White Paper. This lack of public cooperation was matched by a tough negotiating stance in private.

The objective of the National Power and PowerGen shadow management was not to fight a rearguard battle against the splitting of the CEGB – that battle had already been lost. To that extent the water was under the bridge, and both companies quickly developed a strong identity and competitive ethos once split into operational divisions of the CEGB in early 1989. The fragments of the fractured corporatist caucus found themselves adopting new attitudes in pursuit of newly defined interests. A new web of power relationships began to emerge. The bargaining card held by the shadow managements was the cooperation vital to a smooth privatisation, and this put them in a strong position.

Time was against the Government. The proposals involved not only restructuring the CEGB to a very tight timetable, but also devising the mechanisms by which the new market for electricity would operate. Licences and contracts needed to be drafted and then agreed by the various parties. The originally proposed vesting day of 1 January 1990 had to be postponed three months, and the first flotation, that of the RECs, by six months. Critics across the political spectrum (the Labour Party, Friends of the Earth, the Council for the Protection of Rural England, *The Independent*, *Financial Times* and free market economists) joined the Energy Committee in expressing strong doubts and urging caution. But the Government pressed on.

In the rush, the most important of the open agenda objectives were sacrificed bit by bit as expedition forced expedience. In addition, the electricity privatisation demonstrated yet again the paradoxical nature of 'rolling back the state'. To accomplish this, the state must initially roll forward – to increase intervention and bargaining in order to negotiate withdrawal.

### Nuclear fall-out

The most significant obstacle to privatisation, for economic and institutional reasons discussed in Chapter 6, was the inclusion of the nuclear power stations in National Power's portfolio. The Magnox stations were the first to go, withdrawn from the sale in July 1989 just as the Bill completed its Parliamentary stages, and they were followed in November by the AGR stations and the quarter-built Sizewell 'B'. A state owned plc, Nuclear

Electric, was created to own and operate these stations. The July announcement had coincided with a Cabinet reshuffle and the transfer of Cecil
Parkinson to the Department of Transport. He was replaced as Secretary of
State for Energy by John Wakeham, who, in the November statement,
effectively abandoned the PWR programme by announcing that the non-
fossil fuel obligation 'will be set at a level which can be satisfied without the
construction of new nuclear stations beyond Sizewell 'B'' (Hansard 1989e).

The abandonment of the privatisation of nuclear power was inevitable
from the outset – with all the time in the world this objective could not
have been achieved, as Chapter 6 will show. Other abandoned objectives,
however, might have been achievable, especially once nuclear power was
out of the picture, but were precluded by the rushed timescale of the
privatisation.

## Privatisation

### The RECs

One hundred per cent of the shares in the twelve regional distribution
companies were sold in December 1990. The price was £2.40, to be paid in
three instalments of £1.00 on flotation, 70p in October 1991 and 70p in
September 1992. A combination of advertising and customer incentives was
used, as in previous flotations of nationalised utilities, to tempt the private
investor. This strategy became, to some extent, a victim of its own success.
The sale was more than ten times over-subscribed – 5.7 million applications
were received from the public. No customer of a REC received more than
500 shares, and no non-customer more than 150. Applicants who asked for
over 5000 shares (or less in the case of some companies), received none at
all. Despite this, many unsuccessful applicants found that their cheques had
been cashed, and adverse weather conditions, combined with the Christmas
post and holiday, meant that partially successful and unsuccessful applicants
lost up to several weeks' interest on the value of the shares they were
unable to buy.

For those who intended to sell their shares immediately, the instant
profits from previous privatisations had fostered great expectations. There
was, therefore, bitterness amongst thwarted investors when they realised
that their expected large capital gains (the maximum first day premium was
76 per cent on the partly paid price) were in fact small losses (one to two
per cent, representing a month's interest foregone). Of those private investors who applied successfully the majority were allocated only 100 shares in
one or more companies, and dealing charges of up to £20 per holding took
a large share of this windfall. The comparison between the large potential
premium and the very modest actual proceeds is likely to have left even
those who did not end up out of pocket feeling disgruntled, albeit
unjustifiably.

The cause of popular capitalism was not significantly advanced by the REC flotations. Investors buying the shares as a long term investment will have been disappointed at the small size of their holdings. For customers who registered for incentives the combined return on their partly paid investment, of dividend (up to £11.38 forecast) plus £18 electricity voucher per 100 shares held continuously since flotation, is nearly 30 per cent over less than 11 months. However, the return is 30 per cent of very little. As no individual was allocated more than 500 shares the maximum return is £150, plus the capital gain on the shares. In the case of all but one REC, only those applying for 5000 shares received as many as 500.

The total value of the fully paid shares at £2.40 was £5.2 billion, and in addition the Government loaded a total of £1.9 billion of debt onto the twelve companies and £0.9 billion onto NGC. The overall gain to the Treasury was, therefore, £8.0 billion. Given the demand for shares this figure (and the share price) could have been higher, but several factors contributed to the decision to price at £2.40.

Iraq's invasion of Kuwait in August, and the subsequently fluctuating price of oil, cast a pall of uncertainty over the sale. The underwriters insisted that a *force majeure* clause be written into the prospectus, such that the share offer would be withdrawn should war in the Gulf break out before the commencement of dealings on 11 December. While removing some risk from the underwriters, this did not benefit either the small investor or institutions who planned to hold shares after this date. Neither did it protect the private investor planning to sell at a profit, and unable to do this without an interim certificate, from the possibility of a stock market crash due to war breaking out before the shares could be sold. A competitive price was necessary to persuade investors to take the risk. Another area of uncertainty was the Conservative Party leadership election. The price was set the day after Margaret Thatcher, challenged by Michael Heseltine, had failed to gain enough support in the first round of the contest to avoid a second ballot, and the day before she resigned. The humiliating possibility of her winning only after a second or third round and continuing in power to fight the General Election worried the markets.

These short term uncertainties were compounded by longer term issues. At the time of flotation the pooling and settlement system had yet to run for a complete year, and the REC's price controlled charges had been based on inaccurate forecasts of inflation. This resulted in a collective £240 million undercharging relative to what was permitted by the regulatory regime. This money was theoretically reclaimable in subsequent years, but trading conditions might have prevented this. The misjudgement drew attention to the lack of a profitability track record with which the companies were brought to market.

Because distribution price controls are based on the number of delivered units of electricity, rather than a mixture of fixed and volume related charges, the RECs' profits are vulnerable in the event of a downturn in demand. Such a fall is not improbable – it might be caused by such common events as warm winter weather, or a local or national economic recession. These circumstances will reduce the RECs' income, without correspondingly reducing distribution overheads, which are mostly sunk costs. Profitability is correspondingly vulnerable, as distribution accounts for the great majority and, in some cases, all of the operating profit of the RECs (Kleinwort Benson 1990a). One side effect of this is that the companies are under pressure to increase the number of units they sell, as this is their only way of increasing distribution income. Supply side pressure for increased electricity consumption is as great, if not greater, than it was in the days of the nationalised ESI.

A premium of 10 per cent on the fully paid share price (24 per cent on the part payment) was the aim of the Department of Energy and its advisors, Kleinwort Benson. The yield was set at an average of 8.4 per cent for the twelve companies, compared with British Gas and the ten Water Authorities, which were trading at the end of November 1990 with a forecast yield of 7.1 per cent and 7.6 per cent respectively. A post-flotation premium of 10 per cent would have reduced the RECs' yield to 7.6 per cent, while providing sufficient incentive to investors so that all the shares were sold (Thomas and Sychrava 1990). That the shares reached a much larger premium was largely a result of the huge public demand, which in turn was due to the privatisation bandwagon effect (as each sale results in windfall profits more members of the public are tempted to join in) and the hype of the advertising campaign. It was also in small part due to the rise in the FT index (about two per cent) that took place between the price being set and the commencement of trading.

The process of trying to assess whether the $NP_{REC}$ axis reached, or did not reach, the boundary of possibility (Figure 5.1) therefore uncovers a paradox: the short term demand for REC shares immediately after their flotation bore very little relationship to the long term prospects for the companies. By the end of one week's trading the forecast yields for the companies clustered at just above or below seven per cent in most cases. This slightly low level of yield is that typical of a safe and steady stock. Yet, as has been noted, major questions hung over the long term performance of the RECs. That the shares should trade at this level illustrates well the short-termism inherent in the private sector. The compromise price of £2.40 was too high, taking long term uncertainties into account, and too low, bearing in mind the short term demand. This is a kind of market failure – demand should be moderated by long term prospects. That it is not is partly due to the manipulation of the public by slick advertising campaigns. When style counts for more than substance the demand thus created is artificial. The most fundamental criticism of the REC privatisation is not that the companies were sold too cheap, but that they were sold too well.

Having said that, it must be concluded that the Government failed to match the demand it had created to the price of the shares. A good proportion of the 5.2 million private investors would have applied at almost any price, so great was their faith in the privatisation programme as a milch

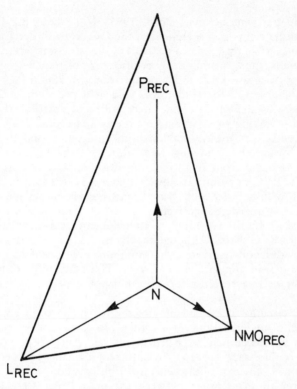

**Figure 5.1** The interaction of privatisation, liberalisation and imposed non-market objectives with the boundary of possibility in the sale of the twelve Regional Electricity Companies

See Figure 2.1 for key.

cow. Filtering out the more discriminating investors by raising the price by, say, 25p, would have meant larger individual allocations, less public discontent, and an extra £540 million in the Treasury's coffers. The institutions would also have paid the extra, as witnessed by their willingness to pay premia of 40–70p immediately after flotation. The boundary of possibility was artificially lengthened by the hard sell techniques, but $NP_{REC}$ was not sufficiently extended to take full advantage of this (Figure 5.1).

### The generating companies

The withdrawal of the nuclear stations from the remit of National Power transformed the 70/30 division of generating capacity into a 50/30 split (precisely 50.2:32.0 at the time of flotation). Sensitive to criticisms that the RECs had been sold too cheaply, and aware of the uncertainties caused by the continuing crisis in the Gulf, John Wakeham decided to float only 60 per cent of the companies. The Government pledged not to sell any of the retained 40 per cent before 1 April 1993. While retaining the right to exercise voting rights as a shareholder, the Government declared an intention not to exercise this. Sixteen per cent of the issue was offered for tender by institutions, thus ensuring a higher price for this tranche.

The offer price was £1.75 (100p on flotation and 75p in February 1992). The tranche reserved for tender was sold at a premium of 21p. In the interval between the setting of the share price and flotation, the Gulf War had ended – leading to a sustained surge in share prices. Thus first day trading premia were nearly 40p on both companies, and this price was sustained during the following week due to stake building by foreign investors. Demand from small investors was, however, substantially less than for the REC flotation. The generators were less than four times oversubscribed, with only 1.8 million applicants. As a result, all members of the public who pre-registered received some shares. This smaller response had been hoped for by the Government after the embarrassment caused by the stampede for REC shares. Although the flotation had been heavily advertised in the press and on television, the minimum investment had been set at £525 (£300 first instalment) as a deterrent. Those intending to invest larger sums might well have been put off by unhappy experiences with the REC sale.

In these circumstances, and despite the inevitable complaints from the Opposition of undercharging, it is difficult to claim that privatisation proceeds were not maximised in the generators' sale. The prospect of a first day premium is necessary to provoke sufficient demand to prevent undersubscription. In the case of the generators this premium was boosted by the strong surge in share prices between the price being set and the commencement of trading – had the Allied Forces' invasion of Iraq proceeded differently, the premium might have been less. As with the RECs, the possibility of a stock market crash due to hostilities was covered by a *force majeure* clause written into the prospectus. The 40 per cent stake retained by the Government acquired the 40 per cent premium on flotation.

Most innovatively, the tendering arrangements for institutions deprived them of over half the first day premium. The furtherance of popular capitalism does not require windfall profits for established City institutions and the tender scheme is likely to be used in future privatisations as a way of extracting more proceeds for the Treasury. If so, it will be unpopular with some sections of the financial establishment who have come to believe in an automatic entitlement to substantial profits every time a nationalised industry is brought to market. Indeed, one commentator went as far as to suggest that institutions should form a cartel in order to push down the tender price (Griffiths 1991).

By the time both instalments have been paid, £2.3 billion will have been raised. Debt loading onto the companies totalled £868 million, after long drawn out and acrimonious bargaining between the Department of Energy and the companies. The generators' privatisation axis reaches the boundary of possibility (Figure 5.2). This does not mean that the companies were sold at a price that reflected their assets' book value, only that, realistically, they could not have been sold for significantly more. By March 1991, total proceeds from the ESI privatisation stood at just over £11 billion, with 40 per cent of the generators' shares (worth about £1.5 billion at 175p per share) and the Scottish companies still to be sold. At the time of writing the flotations of Scottish Power and Scottish Hydro-Electric are expected to take place in May or June 1991. It is unlikely that they will boost the total ESI price to much more than half the £30 billion that was talked of when the White Paper was published.

**Figure 5.2** The interaction of privatisation, liberalisation and imposed non-market objectives with the boundary of possibility in the sale of National Power and PowerGen

See Figure 2.1 for key.

## Liberalisation

### Competition

Increasing competition in generation and supply was a primary objective of the ESI privatisation, but this was hampered at the outset by the duopoly structure chosen for the generating side. The considerable market power of the CEGB daughter companies is likely to limit competition arising between the component institutions of the newly privatised ESI and also to act as a disincentive to independent generators. Serious potential exists both for manipulation of the market by the giant generating companies and for collusion between them. The 70/30 split had been necessitated and justified by the need for a substantial company to inherit the nuclear power stations; however, the potentially greater share price that a duopoly would command (rather than, say, six generating companies) would have been taken into account in drawing up the proposals. Once the decision had been taken to withdraw the nuclear stations from the sale, the privatisation was too advanced to further break down the duopoly, apart from the hiving off of Nuclear Electric from National Power.

Paradoxically, the generating duopoly necessitated regulation to restrict competition even further. Limitations on short and medium term competition for supply to large customers were imposed prior to flotation to prevent the big generating companies from increasing their market share at the expense of the RECs and independent generators. Only customers with a demand in excess of 1 MW can be supplied by a company other than their own REC before 1994, and this restriction will stay in place, albeit at the lower level of 100 kW, until 1998. In addition: 'National Power and PowerGen are restricted until 31 March 1998 by their generation licences from meeting, in aggregate, more than a specified percentage of the applicable annual demand in any RECs authorised area without the DGES's consent' (Kleinwort Benson 1990a). This percentage was originally set at 15 per cent (from 31 March 1990 for four years) and 25 per cent thereafter, but in areas with a large proportion of industrial customers the quota was quickly reached. By the time of the flotation of the RECs in December 1990 the 15 per cent limit had been raised in the MANWEB, Northern Electric, South Wales Electricity and Yorkshire Electricity areas.

Competition was also deliberately circumscribed by the NFFO which imposed a guaranteed market share for nuclear power and renewable generation. As discussed in Chapter 4, the main aim of the non-fossil fuel obligation had been to induce the building of private sector PWRs at Hinkley 'C', Wylfa 'B' and Sizewell 'C'. The scope for market entry by independent generators was in the provision of new capacity, and this would have been correspondingly reduced had the NFFO been set at the level originally intended. CEGB evidence to the Hinkley 'C' Inquiry in the autumn of 1988 envisaged a need for new generating capacity of 11.8 GW by the year 2000, of which 3.12 GW would have to be non-fossil if the proposed obligation was to be met (CEGB 1988a). The combined capacity of three PWRs would have been 3.5 GW, 30 per cent of the total requirement. This obstacle to competition was removed with the abandonment of the Government's commitment to a PWR programme, but is a practical example of competition and non-market objectives in conflict.

Although compromised by these actual and potential barriers to competition, the restructuring of the ESI produced for the first time a market for electricity, the pooling and settlement system (Box 5.1), which is administered by the National Grid Company. Under the Electricity Act all generating stations with output capacity of 10 MW or above have to enter this system. The pool has been designed to eliminate the barriers to market entry that the Bulk Supply Tariff presented. The marginal cost basis is meant to ensure that the most efficient generators are called upon to produce power, subject to transmission and other technical difficulties. At the same time the capacity and uplift elements put the cost of measures necessary to maintain day-to-day security of supply (such as stations on standby against breakdowns elsewhere) into the pool price.

Price bids for each half hour period are submitted by generators to the NGC, which then allocates the lowest priced available capacity in any period to the demand on the system. Irrespective of their individual bid price, all generators delivering electricity to the grid receive the same SMP (Box 5.1) which is equal to the highest accepted bid in that period. The system is extremely complex, and it remains to be seen whether the big generators will be able to manipulate it to the detriment of their competitors. One possible strategy open to National Power and PowerGen is to bid baseload plant at low (or zero) prices, to ensure it is called, knowing that it will receive the SMP. With 50 per cent and 30 per cent of total plant, respectively, and detailed knowledge of the daily and annual demand curve from the days of the CEGB, this practice presents few risks for the two big generating companies, but is not available to smaller generators unless their marginal costs are genuinely low. There have been reports of zero bids in the first six months of the scheme (Fagan 1990).

Another potential anti-competitive practice is predatory pricing – bidding near to short-run marginal cost in order to keep the SMP low and deter new investment in plant by independents. In the long run this would not be a sustainable policy, but the threat of it presents a deterrence to market entry, although not to the same extent as it did in the days of nationalisation and the 1983 Act. The control of the CEGB was as good as absolute: the duopoly, while still powerful, cannot hope to equal the success of its predecessor in seeing off potential competition. In addition:

'In the period to 31st March 1993, the great majority of revenues in respect of National Power's and PowerGen's expected electricity output is substantially protected against, or is not exposed to, fluctuations in the pool price, as a result of contracts for differences and direct sales arrangements (Kleinwort Benson 1991: 11).

These contracts were arranged between RECs and the generators in advance of flotation in order that the risks and potential instability of the new system could be hedged. In an oligopolistic industry characterised by large capital sunk costs, such as the ESI, a system based on marginal cost pricing runs the risk that marginal cost may fluctuate greatly, leading to either excess profits or large losses to the various parties. Contracts for differences remove many of these risks by, for example, providing for the generators to

**Box 5.1**  The pooling and settlement system

On 31st March 1990, a new market was established for trading electricity between generators and suppliers. These new trading arrangements seek to reflect two principal characteristics associated with the physical generation and supply of electricity in an integrated system. First, with an integrated system it is not practicable to trace electricity from a particular generator to a particular supplier. Secondly, it is not practicable to store electricity in large quantities. A constant matching of generation of, and demand for, electricity is therefore necessary. For these reasons, and with limited exceptions, electricity generated within an integrated system is pooled to meet demand.

As a separate business from distribution, the RECs buy and sell electricity as suppliers. They buy electricity through the pool and, in establishing tariffs and contract terms for customers, aim to pass the costs involved in the purchase and sale of electricity on to their customers and to make a small operating profit.

*The pool*
Sales and purchases of electricity in the pool are made between participating generators and suppliers according to a set of rules which govern the market's operation and the calculation of payments due to and from each of them. The pool does not itself buy or sell electricity.

*Pool prices*
The pool prices payable by RECs for electricity are established on a half-hourly basis. Accordingly, for any REC, the combination of the level of its supply business demand and pool prices in each half-hour determines the costs of its purchases of electricity under the pool trading arrangements.

Pool prices have three components: the system marginal price (SMP), the capacity element and uplift. SMP and the capacity element taken together comprise the pool input price (*pip*), which forms the basis of payments to generators. *Pip* is affected by national demand levels for electricity and by the declarations made by generators in respect of the availability and offer prices of their generating plant.

The remaining component of pool prices is uplift, which covers certain of the costs associated with maintaining a stable integrated system.

The components of uplift include:

- the costs of ancillary services;
- payments in respect of sets scheduled . . . to provide reserve;
- payments in respect of the sets that are available but are not scheduled . . . to provide energy or reserve; and
- net payments related to the differences between the revised unconstrained schedule [based on lowest priced electricity necessary to meet demand] and the actual operation of sets [which may be different for technical reasons].

*Source:* Kleinwort Benson (1990a and b)

compensate the RECs during those periods when the pool price is high, in return for an initial payment in respect of the grant of the contract.

One of the statutory duties of the DGES, Professor Stephen Littlechild, is to promote competition in the generation and supply of electricity. Cross-subsidy between the generation and supply activities of the generators is proscribed by their licences, which also prohibit price discrimination between customers. But the regulator has no power to control generation prices and therefore prevent anti-competitive pool prices being bid by the large generators. Although the Electricity Act contains no specific provision to prevent such behaviour, it does bring the ESI within the scope of the Fair Trading Act 1973 for the first time. The DGES acts concurrently with the Director General of Fair Trading in exercising powers deriving from the 1973 Act and he has stated his willingness to do this should evidence of anti-competitive behaviour begin to emerge (Kleinwort Benson 1990b: 45). Extracting proof in such cases is, however, notoriously difficult, and enforcement will be problematic.

## Investment

Despite the small available market share, new entrants into generation have been coming forward. Some of these are proposing renewable projects covered by the non-fossil fuel obligation, and are therefore not in competition with the duopoly in the main market for generation, which is fossil fuelled. Out of over 50 independent generating projects proposed by March 1991 (totalling 15 GW), 95 per cent were gas fired, mostly combined cycle gas turbine plant (CCGT). The largest scheme for which contracts were signed during 1990 was a 1.7 GW gas CHP plant, to be built on Teesside by a consortium led by the American Enron Power Corporation and backed by four RECs. The size of the Enron plant is due to its proximity to a large ICI complex, which will take 15 per cent of the electricity and much of the heat. Other proposed plants are much smaller – typically under 500 MW. Apart from National Power and PowerGen, potential investors include RECs, BC and BNF plc, as well as companies completely new to the energy sector.

The shift to combined cycle gas turbines as the generation technology of choice is a result of the liberalisation of the industry. As late as the autumn of 1988 the CEGB had been planning three new coal fired stations based on twin 900 MW generating sets at Fawley, West Burton and Kingsnorth. For the reasons discussed in Chapter 3, nationalisation had favoured such large plant. These turbines represented a 36 per cent scaling up from the largest existing sets of 660 MW. The planned coal plant accounted for a further 46 per cent of the 11.8 GW capacity gap then expected by the year 2000, and taken together with the PWR programme, would have brought the CEGB daughter companies' share of this to over three quarters. Application to the Secretary of State for Energy for consent in respect of Fawley 'B' was submitted, but the application was suspended in October 1988. It had become clear that the area boards, in negotiation with the shadow managements of the nascent generating companies, were not prepared to sign contracts in respect of the capacity of these stations. Big was no longer beautiful – the area boards preferred to wait and see what other options were available before locking themselves into the large scale, inflexible solution the CEGB was offering.

Gas turbines, traditionally cheap to build and expensive to operate (and therefore used to meet peak demand), had become both cheap to build and cheap to run. Development of the combined cycle, whereby the exhaust gases from the turbine are used to raise steam for further generation, brought the thermodynamic efficiency to about 45–50 per cent, compared to about 30–5 per cent for coal fired plant. Even higher efficiencies (up to 80 per cent) were possible if the waste heat from the process was used to heat buildings or in industrial processes. The higher discount rates applicable to private sector investment also favoured gas turbines. With short construction times and low capital costs, interest charges were kept to a minimum. The short lead times and relatively small plant size offered flexibility in planning to meet demand, and were likely to be more attractive to investors than larger schemes.

By the beginning of March 1991 the duopoly's plans for CCGT were on the same scale as the CEGB's abandoned coal plant – 6.3 GW worth of projects either committed or planned (Kleinwort Benson 1991). Added to the independent sector's 15 GW this was substantially in excess of capacity need as forecast by the NGC, even if plant closures planned by National Power and PowerGen were taken into account (Martin 1991). North Sea gas was available in early 1990 at about 18p/therm, giving a generation cost of 2.2 p/kWh (Skea 1990), compared with 3.4 p/kWh for a new coal station (CEGB 1988a), using 10 per cent discount rate.

As the scale of the switch to gas became more pronounced questions about the strategic wisdom of this move were raised. The price of gas was likely to rise: in the medium term, if CCGT technology was widely adopted, as increased demand pushed up the price of gas; and in the long term, when UK gas fields became depleted, and supplies had to be sought from Norway, North Africa or the USSR. If in the meantime, domestic coal production was wound down as gas displaced coal fired capacity, the consequent sterilisation of reserves might mean future energy shortages. Such worries were vindicated in the week before the flotation of the generating companies when British Gas, to the outrage of the Gas Regulator as well as the prospective builders and operators of CCGT plant, announced a 35 per cent rise in the prices it would charge to electricity generators. BG claimed that it had taken the action in order to restrict demand in 1993 and 1994, as it would otherwise be unable to meet both the needs of existing customers and the planned increase in the electricity market. Trouble of this kind in the domestic energy market can doubtless be smoothed over. In the future, however, abrupt demands for large price increases may come from abroad.

## Regulation

The role of the DGES with respect to generation and supply is limited, as it is the Government's expectation that competitive forces will provide a significant spur to productive and allocative efficiency. The main regulatory constraints on the generators have already been mentioned: the limits on the proportion of supply business available to National Power and PowerGen in each REC area before 1998; compulsory pool membership for stations with an output greater than 100 MW; and the ban on cross-subsidy and discriminatory pricing. Other provisions affecting the generators are concerned with security and safety of supply. Levels of fuel stocks can be controlled by the Secretary of State, and generators must abide by the technical provisions of various Codes, which set out the rules necessary to maintain the safety and stability of the Grid and distribution systems.

Contracted supply by bodies other than RECs to non-tariff industrial or commercial customers is not subject to price control, as this market is competitive. But the supply of electricity by RECs, as well as the monopoly activities of transmission and distribution, is heavily regulated. Price control for distribution is based on a RPI + $X_d$ formula, with $X_d$ (which is specific to each REC) initially set between 0 and 2.5 (weighted average 1.1). Above inflation increases are allowed to RECs with large distribution investment in prospect. The formula for transmission by NGC is RPI – $X_g$, with $X_g$ initially set at zero.

Supply by RECs is price regulated at two levels. The overall price control applies to supplies by RECs in the aggregate tariff and non-tariff markets and is based on the formula RPI – $X_S$ + Y. $X_S$ has been set at zero initially for all RECs. The Y factor allows pass through of costs which are outside the control of the REC, including the cost of electricity itself and transmission and distribution charges, so the formula only applies to a small proportion of the cost components of electricity supply. However, the subsidiary level of control is more wide ranging – a price cap, limiting rises in the average price of electricity to the rate of inflation for all customers with a maximum demand of 1 MW or less. This cap is to apply until 1993, subject to a 'best endeavours' condition:

> 'If a REC suffers an increase in its allowed costs per unit supplied which results from circumstances which are unavoidable . . . the effect of which would be materially and adversely to affect the profits or losses of its supply business, then it may increase its maximum average charges per unit by more than that which would otherwise been permitted without breaching its licence obligation.' (Kleinwort Benson 1990b)

This price freeze is less onerous than might appear at first glance, coming as it does at the end of a period of successive prices which, while just below (1989) or only slightly in excess of retail price inflation (1988, 1990), were made at a time when the industry's major cost factor, the price of coal, was falling. It did not prevent an announcement of an 11–13 per cent increase in

91

the RECs' charges in early 1991 as the companies sought, on top of the RPI+X allowed by the pricing formula, to recoup the profits lost in the previous year because of the inaccurate inflation forecast used to set prices (see above).

## Customers

Liberalisation is intended to empower customers relative to producers. Customers of the ESI fall into four main classes: the RECs, who are the customers of the generators; large industrial users of electricity; small commercial and industrial users; and domestic consumers. As a result of the restructuring of the industry the first two groups have a more equal relationship with their electricity supplier than was the case in the past. For the latter two groups, the REC tariff customers, the situation has changed little.

The empowerment of the RECs, relative to the generators, was noted in Chapter 4. Industrial users in the 1 MW and above market had benefited from cross-subsidy under nationalisation – a cheap tranche of coal was dedicated to them by the CEGB, and their charges correspondingly reduced. Corporatism worked to their advantage. In the run up to flotation a one year price cap for this sector was announced, implying a continuing cross-subsidy into 1991. Beyond that, market forces would prevail. Whether competition will keep prices at the low level to which these customers are accustomed is questionable. Certainly, competition between the RECs, National Power and PowerGen in this market has been fierce in the run up to privatisation, as each seeks to increase market share. Despite the regulatory prohibition of cross-subsidy between supply to non-tariff customers and other spheres of the companies' business activities, such as generation and distribution, it will be tempting for the companies to weight their cost profiles towards less competitive activities, the better to compete in the industrial market.

The three year price cap for tariff customers has already been noted. With the phased introduction of supply competition into this market it might be argued that by 1998 all consumers would have a choice of electricity supplier. While technical advances in metering may, in fact, enable this, it is unlikely that suppliers will pursue the very small electricity user in the same way that Mercury is now extending its domestic telephony market share. The price to the consumer of a unit of electricity is roughly the same as a unit telephone call, but, proportionately, the marginal costs of supply are much greater for the electricity company. Duplicate telephone networks can be commercially viable – this is not so for electricity networks. Medium sized commercial consumers may eventually gain the benefits of choice, but these are unlikely to be extended to domestic consumers, who will remain customers of the monopolistic RECs.

## How much liberalisation?

Overall, the liberalisation of the RECs is modest, but significant. The companies remain highly regulated in the bulk of their activities, but exposed to competition in supply. This competition will become more open as the limits on supply to large customers are reduced in 1994 and 1998. As was noted in the previous section, this liberalisation (together with certain features of the regulatory regime) may be sufficient to compromise the long term profitability of the companies and, therefore, their value on flotation – $NL_{REC}$ therefore reaches the boundary of possibility (Figure 5.1).

Greater liberalisation occurred with the generators, with a buoyant independent sector emerging in the CCGT market at the beginning of 1991. How this will survive the attempts by BG to raise the price of gas remains to be seen. But even greater liberalisation could have been achieved had the structure of the generating industry not been determined during the mistaken attempt to sell nuclear power. A broken up duopoly would have necessitated much less regulation. $NL_{GEN}$ does, however, meet the boundary, as the slack in the triangle was taken up by the P axis. Six generating companies would have been worth less, in total, than two.

# Non-market objectives

## Security and safety of supply

The RECs' Public Electricity Supply (PES) licences contain provisions to meet the same generation security standard (of disconnections in no more than nine winters per century) as had applied in the last years of nationalisation, but only in respect of a REC's own customers. The Electricity Act put RECs under an obligation to continue supply to existing customers; to offer connection to the distribution system; and, if required, to supply new customers on request in most circumstances. The major exception concerned those customers already being supplied by a company other than the REC with the PES licence for their area. Should such customers wish, for whatever reason, to receive electricity from their REC they had no right to supply, only a right to connection to the distribution network.

If the new arrangements are successful in inducing sufficient investment to meet demand at the winter peak, this will prove to be no problem. Currently planned capacity is well in excess of projected demand. Privatised plant is more likely to be refurbished, if economic to do so, due to the higher discount rate used in the private sector (Fine 1989), although the duopoly is planning some premature plant closures. Projected demand might be further reduced by Government intervention in pursuit of further efficiency gains, with a consequent reduction in the need for new plant. While such intervention is at present unlikely, international concern and pressure over greenhouse emissions might, in future, prompt such a policy.

PART II

Against these factors is the risk that the generating companies might abuse their monopoly power by restricting output in order to put up the price of their product. This presupposes the failure of the independent sector to become established in competition to the duopoly, an unlikely prospect at the time of writing, due to the multiplicity of independent CCGT schemes planned. However, it is not impossible to contemplate, due to uncertainty about the future price of gas. In Chapter 1 it was seen that once a producer has so large a share of the market that it can alter the price by increasing or decreasing production, maximum profit is made at a level of production below that coinciding with allocative efficiency. Rather than refurbish or mothball old plant, the generators might instead close it down in the expectation of premium prices at times of electricity scarcity. As with anti-competitive pricing, collusion between generators may be tacit, and evidence of it may be hard for the DGES to identify. In a truly competitive market this behaviour would not be possible – restricted supply would give high prices and an incentive to market entry by independents. Generation is different. Scarcity will only occur at times of peak demand (typically winter afternoons) and the high prices it brings may be too uncertain to induce investment. In a colder than average winter, extra demand will provide excellent windfall profits for under-producing duopolist generators, while their profits in warmer years will be boosted by the need to carry less plant than is necessary to give supply security. New entrants at the margin of supply security cannot depend on the former of these advantages, and, by definition, cannot share the second.

The new market and regulatory arrangements are still in their honeymoon period, and there are many other uncertainties. Future electricity demand may rise by less than is now predicted; the long term response of investment capital to opportunities in generation is unknown; and there is increasing pressure (both in the UK and in the EC) for new regulatory measures to reduce atmospheric emissions by the ESI. For these reasons it cannot be concluded that security of supply will be jeopardised in the long term in the privatised ESI. However, given the potential hiatus in responsibility entailed in giving the statutory obligation to supply to the RECs in the first place (Chapter 4); the exacerbation of this by the creation of a second tier of electricity suppliers, to whose customers the RECs now have no supply obligation; and the institutional incentive to under-production represented by the generating duopoly that will dominate the generation side for many years to come, neither is it certain that the lights will stay on throughout January 2001.

## Non-market objectives and the boundary of possibility

The NMO obligations on both the RECs and on the generators are minimal (Figures 5.1 and 5.2). The price control regulation of the RECs is no more than is necessary in respect of a private natural monopoly. The obligations on the generators are only short term – after the expiry of the protective

94

coal contract with BC in 1993, the only burdens remaining will be compliance with general environmental and safety legislation. The fossil fuel levy will remain as a tax on coal, oil and gas generation until 1998.

## The hidden and absent agendas

### The coal industry and flue gas desulphurisation

The switch to gas further compounded the difficulties of British Coal. The proposed station at Fawley was perceived by the Corporation as a threat because, located on the Solent, it was to have been a coastal station, fuelled by imported coal. Its abandonment, in the face of pressures which culminated in the adoption of CCGT as the technology of choice for new generating plant, gave cold comfort to the domestic coal industry – particularly as the West Burton station, for which BC hoped to provide the coal, was abandoned at the same time. Then, in early 1989, a switch in the policies of the generating companies towards the reduction of sulphur dioxide emissions from power stations produced a new potential constraint on the output of British Coal. Compliance with the EC Large Combustion Plant Directive (Chapter 4) had been envisaged by the CEGB as requiring 12 GW of FGD retrofits to coal fired stations at a cost of £1.8 billion (Energy Committee 1990b). Substantial capital expenditure on middle aged plant is never an attractive option, and in addition the efficiency and operating costs of retrofitted stations are adversely affected. Not surprisingly, following the reorganisation of the CEGB, the shadow managements of the new generating companies re-assessed their commitment to FGD.

There are three ways of reducing $SO_2$ which are cheaper than FGD: importing coal with a lower sulphur content than the bulk of British production; replacing coal fired plant with CCGT; and increased efficiency in the end-use of electricity. Under the institutional and regulatory regime of the privatised industry only the first two of these would allow the cost savings to accrue to the generators. Energy efficiency (apart from the thermal efficiency of power stations) was therefore not on their agenda. In order to meet the $SO_2$ limit placed upon it under the Environmental Protection Act, National Power was committed by early 1990 to only 4 GW of FGD – it intended to use imports and CCGT further to reduce emissions. PowerGen was more equivocal. While telling the Energy Committee of an 'intention' (not a commitment), to retrofit two 2 MW stations by 1998, press stories were quoting PowerGen's chairman, Robert Malpas, as saying he would like to 'get away' with fitting FGD at only one plant (*Financial Times* 7 February 1990).

If any of the three alternatives to FGD is to have a significant impact on $SO_2$ emissions, it implies a large reduction in the demand for British coal. Department of Energy intervention in the negotiation of contracts between National Power and PowerGen on the one hand and BC on the other had resulted in a three year transition period when some protection would continue for the domestic coal industry. The generators agreed to buy 70 million tonnes of British coal in the first two years of the agreement and 65 million tonnes in the third year. Beyond that the scenario was one of increasing displacement of domestic supplies by imports and gas. By the EC's target date of 2003 for a reduction of 60 per cent in $SO_2$ emissions from existing plant, the generators speculatively assessed their likely combined purchases of British coal at 38 million tonnes. British Coal was more pessimistic, estimating maxima of 30 million tonnes if only 8 MW of plant was retrofitted as currently planned, or 50 million tonnes if a 12 MW retrofit was undertaken. A potential for 70 million tonnes would require 20 MW FGD (Energy Committee 1990b).

FGD is by no means a panacea: while reducing $SO_2$ by 90 per cent the technology results in an increase of 5 per cent in $CO_2$ emitted per unit of electricity produced. Substituting domestic for imported coal with a sulphur content half the UK average, however, will only reduce $SO_2$ by 50 per cent in that proportion of the coal fired generation sector. Gas substitution leads to virtually a one hundred per cent reduction, as would energy efficiency measures that reduced the demand for coal fired generation. The gas and efficiency options also reduce $CO_2$. Ideally a mix of all four options would give maximum flexibility to respond to future events, such as changes in the relative price of fuels, or curbs on $CO_2$ emissions. The transformation of the ESI, from nationalised corporatist caucus to privatised oligopoly, had increased the flexibility of response to the Large Combustion Plant Directive, by bringing CCGT and imported coal into the scheme of things in a way that the CEGB had been unable to do. The new structure, however, had its own built in constraints: short termism, induced by the market situation in which the generators expected shortly to be operating; and an institutional bias towards the supply side that meant that the potentially fruitful opportunity that end-use efficiency offered to the reduction of both $SO_2$ and $CO_2$ emissions was excluded from consideration.

Should more stringent reductions be required of the UK by the EC, more FGD might, after all, prove necessary. The 'comparable effort' basis on which targets had been set had resulted in comparatively low targets for the UK, particularly in the short term, because of the high sulphur of indigenous coal and, as the Government pleaded at that time, the need for expensive and time consuming FGD retrofits. Now that a less expensive reduction programme was envisaged, the EC might be less indulgent.

Many issues are raised by this very complicated story, but the overarching theme is the short sightedness that has resulted from an unbridled application of the Lawson doctrine. The pit closures that would follow such a sharp reduction in demand as now seems likely would, in the main, be irreversible – leading to a dependence on imported coal and, eventually, gas which has implications for both security of supply and the balance of payments. The attitude to this prospect of the Department of Energy and Department of Environment witnesses questioned by the Energy

Committee was *laissez faire* in the extreme. The only aspect of the generators' plans with which the Departments were concerned was compliance with the Directive. As long as the companies' plans were robust in this respect, the Government had no interest in the means by which compliance was achieved.

## The six principles revisited

This abdication of responsibility for strategic issues was an integral part of the philosophy of the ESI privatisation – the governing principle framing the absent agenda. Security of supply, research and development, the future of the coal and of the power plant industries were ignored because of ideology, defined by the Lawson doctrine, combined with the pragmatics of privatisation. Non-market objectives were ideologically distasteful and could practically only be imposed on the ESI as a whole at the expense of either privatisation proceeds, or liberalisation measures, or both.

But the absent agenda was not the only casualty. In the rush to market the three most important of the six principles got left behind: the first, second and fourth. Only the very largest of industrial customers will benefit from choice in the medium term, while the most vulnerable, domestic consumers including those in fuel poverty, are left as powerless as they ever were. Competition has been twice sacrificed: once upon the altar of nuclear power (which forced the duopoly) and secondly to the need to expedite the sale. With more time the duopoly could have been broken up. Future security of supply will depend on luck.

Compromise was to be anticipated when undertaking such a complex task. It would have been unrealistic to expect the six principles to be implemented in their entirety. Each individual trade off and sacrifice can, to some extent, be justified in the real, as opposed to an ideal, world (Veljanovski 1987). But such is the magnitude of what has been lost upon the way that, inevitably, questions as to the competence of those in charge are raised.

The spatchcock label suggested by the Energy Committee was appropriate. The ESI was indeed split open and prepared for privatisation in a way that was hasty and slapdash – but the haste is the inevitable companion of privatisation. With a maximum of five years between General Elections, sufficient time could not be made available to do the job properly. However, a realisation of where the boundary of possibility lay at the outset would have enabled the achievement of more of the Government's objectives, especially in the area of liberalisation. It does begin to look like carelessness.

# 6 Private grief: the nuclear fiasco

'We have made our argument, we have had our chance to have our say. That is all water under the bridge. We are now getting on with the job. But we will find out!' (Lord Marshall in evidence before the House of Commons Energy Committee 8 June 1988)

Thursday, November the ninth 1989, was the most momentous day in the history of post-war Europe. The opening of the Berlin Wall symbolised the end of state communism in East Germany. The end of border controls was sudden and dramatic, but surprising only in the speed with which events moved. The writing had been on the wall for several months.

Meanwhile, in Britain, a smaller empire also capitulated to pluralism that afternoon, again surprising most observers only by the speed with which the reverse was made. Officials at the Department of Energy will have welcomed the fall of the Wall as fervently as anyone; but they had an extra reason for doing so. Four hours before the gates in Berlin started to open, the new Secretary of State for Energy, John Wakeham, had announced one of the most humiliating policy reversals of the Thatcher Governments. British nuclear power stations were not, after all, to be included in the privatisation of the electricity supply industry, and the three pressurised water reactors which had been planned as successors to Sizewell 'B' would not now be built, at least until 1994. It was only two weeks since the resignation of Nigel Lawson as Chancellor of the Exchequer had thrown the Government into turmoil, and that events in Germany obscured the main domestic story in press and broadcast reports that evening and during the following few days must have provided some consolation to those who might otherwise have expected much more unfavourable publicity.

Four months earlier the Magnox stations had been withdrawn from sale. With consideration of the Bill virtually complete, the Commons winding down for the summer recess and the transfer announced of the Secretary of State for Energy, Cecil Parkinson, to the Department of Transport, the Government announced on 24 July that the Magnox stations were not, after all, to be transferred to private ownership, and that the £1 billion Schedule

12 provision to subsidise the back end costs of the nuclear industry would be raised to £2.5 billion. The reason given was that preparation for privatisation had brought new information to light.

> 'The costs for the Magnox stations, which have now become clearer, would represent major financial problems for the two [i.e. National Power and the Scottish Nuclear Company] nuclear companies. They can be paid for only by the customer or the taxpayer. The Government do not believe that this legacy of the past should be borne by customers in the future.' (Hansard 1989f)

The taxpayer, therefore, was to retain the liability for the Magnox stations, while the transfer of AGR and PWR stations to National Power was to proceed as originally planned. Despite the reiteration of the Government's intention to sell the AGRs and PWRs by the new Secretary of State, John Wakeham, speculation continued that National Power was not saleable due to the poor economics of nuclear power. By the end of October one source of this speculation was identified, in press stories, as National Power itself. It was rumoured that the price of the output of PWRs would be nearly three times as much as that from fossil fired capacity.

Then on 9 November, after weeks of escalating rumours, John Wakeham announced to the House of Commons the widely predicted decision to retain all nuclear capacity in the state sector. A third generating plc was to be created from the CEGB – Nuclear Electric – to be chaired by the then Chairman of the UKAEA, John Collier. Less expected was the announcement that:

> '. . . the non-fossil obligation will be set at a level which will be satisfied without the construction of new nuclear stations beyond Sizewell 'B'. . . . I am asking the CEGB to consider urgently what action it wishes to take with respect to its applications for my consent to build PWR stations at Hinkley Point 'C', Wylfa 'B' and Sizewell 'C'. The Government's statement is being communicated to the Hinkley Point 'C' Inquiry.' (Hansard 1989e)

Wakeham announced that the prospects for the civil nuclear programme would next be reviewed in 1994, when Sizewell 'B' is due to be commissioned. Malcolm Rifkind, the Secretary of State for Scotland, followed his English colleague with a similar announcement in respect of the Scottish ESI. As about 60 per cent of the assets of the SSEB were nuclear, the effect of the withdrawal on the Scottish privatisation was proportionately greater. The publicly owned Scottish Nuclear plc would dominate the ESI north of the border.

This was a considerable political reverse for the Government, but taking the belated decision removed the largest single obstacle to the privatisation of the ESI. The commitment was to complete the sell off during the life of the Parliament. The original timetable for vesting the plcs having slipped by three months, the revised programme was now achievable, despite the considerable remaining problems. The privatisation dropped from the headlines, leaks attributed to 'senior industry executives' dried up and complicated contract negotiations were eventually successfully concluded.

PART II

The nuclear power programme had been the exception to the abdication of responsibility for strategic issues noted in the previous Chapter. Its continuance was to have been assured by the non-fossil fuel obligation, coupled with the provisions for Government grants towards decommissioning and reprocessing costs contained in Schedule 12 of the Electricity Act. The constraints that this imposed on the introduction of competition to generation have already been noted. In the end the Government lost both baby and bath water. A truly competitive generating sector might have been created had nuclear power never been included in the sale, but by November 1989 it was to late to alter the duopoly structure, beyond the changes necessary to remove the nuclear stations from National Power. In addition, severe and irreparable damage had been done to the nuclear industry so that, despite ten continuous years of enthusiastic Government support, the programme of ten PWRs mooted in 1979 is effectively dead. Only Sizewell 'B' will be built, and the amount of nuclear electricity generated is in decline as Magnox stations reach the end of their lives.

In the immediate aftermath of the November 1989 decision most commentators concluded that 'the market' killed nuclear power. While economic factors were undoubtedly important, institutional factors also played their part. Just as the economics of nuclear power are incompatible with the private sector, so the fracturing, by privatisation, of the corporatist ESI caucus destroyed the political support on which the continuance of the nuclear power programme depended.

## Nuclear power and Thatcherism

The steadfast refusal of the Government to take account of the non-market strategic and environmental implications of privatisation in all other policy sectors (save for the failed attempt to guarantee long term security of supply) contrasts strongly with the attitude shown towards the nuclear sector. Why were the Conservatives willing to invest so much political capital in what proved to be a futile attempt simultaneously to privatise, and to secure the future of, nuclear power?

The public explanation given was the considerable strategic importance accorded to the industry. Nuclear power was valued as providing some diversity in generation fuel, which in turn gave enhanced security of electricity supply by providing protection against disruptions in the price or the supply of fossil fuels:

'. . . the Government has decided that it will have a nuclear programme. That is a distortion of the market, I freely accept that. That is why we will have to regulate its costs to make sure that the position is not exploited. It is a decision the Government takes because it believes that security of supply is very important, and that it would be quite wrong to be wholly dependent on any one source, any one primary fuel or any one source of energy. So we are just saying that we want to maintain a nuclear component. That was included in our manifesto on which we were elected.' (Cecil Parkinson: Energy Committee 1988a: Q. 429)

The perceived problem was the ESI's undue reliance on coal. Lessons from the fall of the Heath administration in 1974 had been well learned by the Thatcher Governments. Within six months of achieving office a Cabinet Committee agreed that the licensing process for the Westinghouse PWR should begin, with a view to an eventual 15 GW programme. The minutes of this meeting were leaked, and show the reasons for this decision:

'The Secretary of State for Energy said that a substantial nuclear programme of thermal reactors was essential to the nation's long term energy needs. In addition . . . the cost of nuclear power was likely to be significantly below that of the alternative fuels with the calculations robust against significant adverse movement in the assumptions. . . .

It was noted that such a programme would not reduce the long term requirement for coal, because of the likely decline in world oil supplies towards the end of the century. But a nuclear programme would have the advantage of removing a substantial portion of electricity production from the dangers of disruption by industrial action by coal miners or transport workers.' (Friends of the Earth 1986: 130-1)

Meanwhile the Government avoided conflict with the National Union of Mineworkers in the early years of office, during which time coal stocks at power stations were built up. Three AGR stations were commissioned in 1984: Dungeness 'B', Hartlepool and Heysham I. Although, due to design defects (especially at Dungeness 'B'), these stations' contribution to electricity supply was below their designed output, they potentially increased the total UK nuclear capacity from 6.5 GW to 9.5 GW (Hansard 1984).

March 1984 saw the beginning of the unsuccessful miners' strike against the impending pit closure programme. The 1974 strike had coincided with the winter and peak demand for both coal and electricity, and lack of power had led to widespread cuts and the three day week. In 1984 the lights stayed on. The timing of the strike, the NUM's failure to achieve a one hundred per cent stoppage, increased oil burn, large coal stocks at power stations, as well as the contribution from nuclear power, all played a part in the defeat of the NUM. By early 1987 the miners were back at work, with nothing to show for the bitter and tragic year they had endured, and the NUM had been permanently weakened and split by the emergence of the Union of Democratic Mineworkers.

Arguably, the miners were so comprehensively beaten that industrial disruption is no longer a serious threat to coal supplies. Nuclear power had fulfilled its function, albeit in a small way. Yet Government support continued undiminished. The strike had coincided with the end of the Sizewell Inquiry, where the CEGB's case for Britain's first PWR station echoed the Cabinet minutes of three years earlier. The primary justification for Sizewell 'B' was cost – CEGB evidence claimed that the savings the station offered compared with existing plant meant that it was cheaper to build it ahead of capacity need than to continue to operate those stations lowest in the merit order. This was backed up by three subsidiary arguments: diversity in primary fuel sources; establishing the PWR as a design option in the UK; and, as the consent process dragged on and on, capacity need. Belief that the PWR was much cheaper than fossil fuelled alternatives and that it offered an opportunity to lessen the CEGB's dependence on coal were therefore the overt reasons behind the Thatcher Governments' support for the PWR programme. Both these arguments became more difficult to sustain over the years. Falling fossil fuel prices damaged the economics of the PWR relative to coal. The diversity argument came to seem increasingly partial as non-nuclear alternatives offering supply security, such as renewables and end-use efficiency measures, continued to receive little official encouragement. Had diversity *per se* been a policy objective the Government would have embraced and promoted all the alternatives to coal.

The presumed cost and diversity benefits of a PWR programme are therefore not sufficient to explain the tenacious support given to the nuclear industry by the Thatcher Governments until 1988. Two other factors must also be taken into account: vested interest and the technocentric world view of the ESI managers, civil servants and ministers (especially the Prime Minister) who were contributing to policy formation. Support for the PWR went much further than the UK nuclear caucus described in Chapter 3. The drying up of orders for nuclear power stations in the USA in the Seventies had left Westinghouse and Bechtel, on whose design Sizewell 'B' was based, dependent on overseas orders if they were to stay in the market. Adoption of the PWR by Britain would act as a powerful endorsement elsewhere in the world. In addition, the UK, once PWR expertise was established, could be used as an export base to the vast Chinese market, circumventing the US Non-Proliferation Act which in the early Eighties prohibited such exports.

The 1982 appointment of the then Dr Walter Marshall to chair the CEGB substantially strengthened the PWR lobby. '. . . I have spent a quarter of a century trying to persuade this country to build light water reactors, and I am clear that I was appointed chairman of the CEGB to pursue that objective – amongst others' (Marshall 1990). Lord Marshall's advocacy of the PWR had led to him losing his post as Chief Scientific Adviser to Tony Benn in 1977 when Benn was Secretary of State for Energy. A 1983 *World in Action* television programme claimed that Marshall, Westinghouse, senior civil servants in the Department of Energy and Kleinwort Benson (coincidentally, the merchant bank selected by the Government to advise on the privatisation of the ESI five years later) were jointly promoting the interests of the PWR behind the scenes in Whitehall. Noting the Parliamentary denial of these allegations, O'Riordan *et al* conclude:

'. . . senior people in the UK nuclear industry are pro-PWR and pro-Westinghouse – in the UKAEA, in the NNC, throughout the upper echelons of the CEGB, . . . and in [the] Department of Energy. . . . The technology, its supporting organisation and the people involved were just too big, too powerful and too committed to be deflected.' (1988: 39)

The exercise of power by such PWR proponents was facilitated by the corporatist structure of the ESI. The PWR lobby developed into a sub-group within the nuclear caucus – a lobby within a lobby.

Technocentrism is based on belief in rationality and managerial efficiency, combined with optimism and faith in humankind's abilities (O'Riordan 1981). Technocentrics are 'cornucopians' (Cotgrove 1982), convinced that the onward march of technology will bring material wealth to increasing numbers of the earth's population. Those holding such a world view will tend to look kindly on nuclear power, admiring the scientific and technological achievement it embodies, while believing that the application of further technology will be able to ameliorate its associated problems, such as those concerning decommissioning and waste management. It is almost facile to describe Margaret Thatcher as a technocentric: the label can unerringly be applied to every Prime Minister, and probably every Cabinet Minister, who has held office this century. However, there are degrees of technocentrism. Harold Wilson was a particularly avid proponent of technological optimism, hoping that by harnessing the 'white heat of the technological revolution' the British economy could be transformed. Margaret Thatcher was as passionate as Wilson about the potential of technology. The first Prime Minister to be a trained scientist, her belief in the beneficence of the onward march of science was as great as her belief in the virtues of the free market. The attempted privatisation of the nuclear power stations was to expose the potential for conflict between these two creeds.

The then Prime Minister's optimism was evident when she opened Torness nuclear power station in May 1989, six months before the abandonment of the nuclear privatisation:

> 'Speaking to the 600 guests assembled at Torness, Mrs Thatcher said that she regarded the day as one of the highlights of her Prime Ministership. "It is most unlikely that one of Britain's most famous world acclaimed scientists, Lord Rutherford, who discovered fission, would have accepted the spectacular progress in scientific knowledge which marked the technological achievement in the construction of the giant nuclear power station at Torness", she said. "Even the great scientist himself expressed great doubts regarding the ability to harness nuclear energy for the provision of power. And yet, here we are celebrating the opening of Torness, a marvellous example of Scottish enterprise."' (*Atom* July 1989)

The message was clear – don't trust the faint hearts, no matter how eminent they be – scientific advance will always exceed your expectations. Thatcher's enthusiasm for nuclear power persisted to the end. In a speech on global warming at the United Nations on 8 November 1989, only hours before the Cabinet decision to withdraw nuclear power from the ESI sale and end the PWR programme, the Prime Minister highlighted the role that nuclear power might play in the world's efforts to cut $CO_2$ emissions.

Thatcher's third term of office was characterised by a general failure of policy implementation. The community charge, the Football Supporters Bill, the Prime Minister's unsuccessful resistance to Britain's entry into the

103

Exchange Rate Mechanism, are all examples of third term policy initiatives that proved impractical to implement. One common characteristic they share is Government neglect of expert advice, and the failed attempt to sell the nuclear power stations is an outstanding example of this. The Prime Minister's dual commitments, to financial liberalisation and to nuclear power, were both so firmly held by her that, despite warnings from political friends and foes alike, their mutual incompatibility was not acknowledged. The values we hold provide the framework with which we analyse information (Cotgrove 1979), and frames of reference have to change when they can no longer accommodate observed facts. This change usually takes the form of incremental adjustment, but the alternative is traumatic collapse. To an outside observer it would appear that the failed attempt to privatise nuclear power ended in just such a collapse on 9 November 1989. Nigel Lawson had resigned two weeks previously as Chancellor of the Exchequer, leading to widespread speculation about the judgement and political future of Mrs Thatcher. The Prime Minister's resolve to sell the nuclear stations might have continued even longer had her position not been temporarily weakened by this event.

The role of Cecil Parkinson, as Secretary of State for Energy, was also important. How was it that, confronted daily with mounting evidence that the nuclear privatisation could not be accomplished, he did not act sooner? Indeed, why break the tradition of previous privatisations in the first place by attempting both liberalisation and an onerous non-market commitment to nuclear power? Sharing the Prime Minister's political philosophy and technocentrism, Parkinson was therefore prone to the same inability to face up to the political impossibility of what was being attempted. He was no doubt encouraged by the example of the water privatisation, which, despite considerable legislative and other difficulties, had eventually been successfully accomplished. In addition, as a formerly disgraced Minister recently returned to Government, he was perhaps over-anxious to do well.

Parkinson knew that his political future depended on the success of the ESI privatisation and he therefore was ambitious to maximise gains along all three axes: privatisation, liberalisation and non-market objectives. In doing so he broke the boundary of possibility (see Figure 4.1). On the former matter, however, his judgement was absolutely correct – his transfer sideways to the Department of Transport (generally perceived as a demotion) in July 1989 was followed, sixteen months later, by his resignation from the Government on the day that his mentor, Margaret Thatcher, herself left office. It is unlikely that he would have survived the immediate reshuffle initiated by her successor, John Major.

It is the technology of nuclear power which determines its incompatibility with liberalisation, and this incompatibility is manifested in two dimensions: the institutional and the economic. Why this should be is now examined.

# Nuclear power and corporatism

## International lessons

Comparative research has shown that the institutional framework in which the civil nuclear industry operates is an important factor in accounting for its uneven international pattern of success. Nuclear power has characteristics which strongly distinguish it from other technologies (Table 6.1).

**Table 6.1**  The unique characteristics of nuclear generating technology

---

- *The cost structure*
  High capital and low running costs mean construction and availability targets are crucial to economic success.
- *Safety regulation and public influence*
  The risks of nuclear power and possible interaction with military applications pose unique problems.
- *The large number of institutions involved in design and construction*
  Utilities, vendors, architect-engineers, constructors, research institutions and regulators are involved in the design and construction of a nuclear plant, although in some cases one institution will fulfil more than one role.
- *The long product life cycle*
  Design changes may take up to ten years to be tested in an operational reactor, and generic faults may only emerge after longer times.
- *The difficulties of product proving*
  This is due, *inter alia*, to the small number of units and impossibility of destructive testing of complete systems.
- *The disincentives to design changes*
  These are the risk of unsuccessful changes proving expensive, and the difficulty of obtaining regulatory approval for such changes.

---

*Source:* Adapted from Thomas 1988a

These unique features mean specific institutional and political structures are necessary to foster the development of a national nuclear programme. Of all the institutions involved, the utility has the most important role in determining success or failure (Thomas 1988a). This is also heavily influenced by Government policies on such matters as centralisation, regulation, subsidies and competition. A centralised, authoritarian approach is most likely to lead to good economic performance of plant (ibid.; Rudig 1983).

Such an approach can guarantee the steady ordering programme that a healthy construction industry requires. France is the best example of the potential success of this. A political tradition of highly centralised administration, coupled with determined Government support for nuclear power, has enabled the largest (per capita) nuclear programme in the world. The state owned monopoly utility, Eléctricité de France (EDF), with the political and financial support of the state, has linked with a monopoly constructor, Framatome. The resulting programme has meant that benefits of scale and standardisation have been reached far beyond what has been achieved elsewhere. In contrast to France stands the US, with multiple, relatively small utilities, lack of Government support, and plurality of constructors and designs. Some US utilities have achieved excellent performance from their nuclear plant, while others have extremely poor records (Thomas 1988b). However, there has been a dearth of nuclear power station orders since the mid-seventies and some plants have been cancelled in various stages of completion. The adverse effects of the oil-shock recession were compounded by construction problems, regulatory delays and public opposition. The French avoided these problems by political will (the programme was not dependent on market judgements of relative costs of different forms of generation or likely demand); standardisation leading to production line techniques; incorporation of the regulator; and centralised control of siting (Thomas 1988a).

The relative success of the nuclear industry in the FRG is interesting, as a plurality of utilities (albeit well organised for efficient information exchange [Thomas 1988c]), combined with a federal political system, would seem to militate against success. The German Government has provided strong political support and the cost of German coal is high, compared to the US (Rudig 1983). The exceptional levels of economic growth the FRG has experienced in the last thirty years have meant the industry has been somewhat protected from the economic chills that stalled the US industry. Private ownership, however, is not synonymous with a liberal economic or institutional regime:

'All private sector nuclear utilities in other parts of the world are either integrated utilities or represent joint ventures between integrated utilities, thereby facilitating the passing on of costs (including unforeseen increases in costs) to the ultimate consumer.' (Energy Committee 1990c: para. 52)

Ownership matters less than structure and monopoly power. The abandonment of the Wackersdorf reprocessing plant in 1989 and of the Kalkar FBR prototype in early 1991, in the face of escalating costs and public opposition, shows that the German nuclear industry is, after all, vulnerable to the pressures experienced in the US.

The viability of nuclear energy depends both on active state support, and on the major actors of nuclear technology being involved in an integrated policy making structure – that is, corporatism. Where corporatist structures are absent, a successful nuclear programme is unlikely, unless economic conditions are stable and propitious. Even when such conditions exist, the technological features of nuclear power make the implementation of a programme prone to errors which are likely to have serious ramifications (Collingridge 1984).

## Corporatism – a model for the British nuclear policy sector?

To decide how well the corporatist model fits the civil nuclear policy sector in England and Wales it is necessary to examine separately two periods: 1955–1977, and 1977–1987.

### 1955 to 1977

Both the 1955 decision to proceed with a civil programme (based on Magnox reactors), and the 1957 decision (later deferred) to treble this, were taken by the Government on the basis of UKAEA advice. Neither the CEGB nor the construction consortia had much influence, beyond the most perfunctory consultation. The policy sector therefore was not fully developed as an effective corporatist system, as the vital utility and manufacturer interests were not properly represented. However, the closed policy system which had developed to administer the nuclear bomb programme after World War II (UKAEA/Government) had the potential to incorporate other interests, and this became inevitable as the civil programme got underway.

By 1962 there were disagreements between the CEGB and UKAEA over the choice of thermal reactor for the second programme. The UKAEA was pushing its design, the Advanced Gas Cooled Reactor (AGR), very hard, but the CEGB wanted to investigate American Light Water designs. To resolve this dispute the Powell Committee was established, consisting of representatives of both organisations, together with the Board of Trade and the Treasury. This was a typically corporatist response to inter-group conflict and was the first in a series of committees set up to resolve the thorny issue of reactor choice. In the early 1970s there was the Vinter Committee, and this was shortly followed by the Nuclear Power Advisory Board. The latter body had as additional members the area electricity boards, Electricity Council, and the recently formed monopoly constructor, the National Nuclear Corporation (NNC).

The construction industry had taken longer than the CEGB to establish itself as a major participant in this emerging corporatist system. The deliberate policy of fostering competition had initially led the Government to encourage five construction consortia to bid for nuclear power station contracts. This arrangement was more *dirigiste* than competitive, as, in the hope of maintaining the viability of all the consortia, contracts were awarded in rotation, not by tender. The initial multiplicity of consortia, and their exclusion from the Powell Committee, meant that by 1962 the nuclear power sector could still not be described as fully corporatist. However, the small number of orders and complexity of the technology led to mergers, followed by the spectacular bankruptcy of Atomic Power Constructions, the constructor selected for Dungeness 'B'.

The NNC, a monopoly constructor, created by merger in 1973 under Government pressure in the aftermath of the Dungeness 'B' fiasco, fits Schmitter's definition (given in Chapter 3) very well (Ward 1983). The definition also applies to the CEGB and UKAEA, both nationalised bodies, with respective monopolies on nuclear generation and research. Ward also suggests that the incorporation of labour into a consensual set of values, which is a feature of full corporatism, is absent from the nuclear policy sector. Given the strong pro-nuclear position of the unions involved in constructing and operating nuclear power stations, for example, the AEU, EETPU, GMBATU and EMA (Elliott 1988a), and their role in lobbying both the TUC and the Labour Party in support of the nuclear programme, this latter suggestion is surprising.

All the main official interests were brought together with the formation of the Nuclear Power Advisory Board in 1972 (Williams 1980) – the corporatist system had come of age. Why, then, was the industry in such disarray during the Seventies? The AGR programme had proved a costly mistake and the 1974 substitution of the Steam Generating Heavy Water Reactor (SGHWR) for the third programme ended embarrassingly in 1978. Thermal reactor policy created a series of 'crises' (ibid.), each mainly due to differences between the CEGB and UKAEA. Burn (1978) blamed the shortcomings of the UK programme on the 'restricting, centralised' approach with which it was developed, and claimed that economic and technological success would continue to evade the UK industry until more market orientated and pluralist arrangements were adopted, as in the US. The 1955/7 Magnox programme of several commercial size, but not commercially viable, reactors based on one technology (gas/graphite) was contrasted with the concomitant US development of multiple prototypes, followed by demonstration plants, by private firms with Government assistance. Analysing events up to 1976, Burn however notes that American arrangements were less successful in enabling commercial deployment. Like Thomas, he recognises that international experience shows the importance of the 'manufacturer-utility axis'.

Competitive forces have not produced, in the nuclear sector, the results that free market economists, such as Burn, expected. Strategic and military considerations have meant that some governments protect the industry, and those countries that do not tend to order from home suppliers. Long lead times mean that orders are often made without sufficient knowledge of the operating record of the design, and utilities fear technological exposure, and so avoid new or alternative designs. It is unlikely that the strategies advocated by Burn would have ultimately proved any more successful in the UK than they did in the US.

An alternative and, in view of the contrasting US and French experiences, more convincing explanation of the UK's problems would be that fully fledged corporatism developed too slowly. It was not until the mid-Seventies that the 'manufacturer-utility axis' was properly integrated into the system. Its earlier exclusion meant the CEGB had little input into the direction of UKAEA research (Select Committee on the Nationalised Industries 1963) and the UKAEA undue power and influence. The disarray of the UK nuclear programme by 1977 can be said to have been predicated on the relative weakness of the CEGB (and, to a lesser extent, the constructors) in the policy sector during the previous two decades.

## 1977 to 1987

Jessop (1979) has proposed a model which posits Parliamentarism and corporatism as parallel systems of representation that can coexist in a hybrid system. Pure Parliamentarism is based on participation via the exercise of political rights of citizens, both by voting and through organised interest groups. This is pluralism. Representation (voting, interest groups) and intervention (law and bureaucracy) are mediated through different institutions, linked by Parliament.

In a pure corporatist system representation and intervention are both mediated through the same institutions. Thus by the mid-Seventies those responsible for implementing the nuclear programme were those who were charged with devising the policy – the members of the Nuclear Power Advisory Board. Parliament had, on occasion, scrutinised the nuclear programme, but had not had a directing hand in its development (Williams 1980). By 1977 the autonomy of the corporatist system was becoming increasingly threatened by pluralist forces. The palpable failure of the AGR programme, coupled with growing public unease about the safety of nuclear power, meant that, although effective power was still exercised through the existing corporatist system, from this time there were attempts by outsider interest groups to exert influence through the parallel, pluralist mechanism. Just as the initial UKAEA/Government caucus had evolved to incorporate, first, the CEGB, and then the NNC, new ways had now to be found to legitimate nuclear decisions in the public arena.

If the developing corporatist framework had found it difficult to take decisions, accommodating the new demands for accountability produced a near paralysis. Although the Windscale Inquiry in 1977 allowed a reasonably expeditious resolution of the Thermal Oxide Reprocessing Plant (THORP) decision, the Sizewell 'B' Inquiry process meant five years elapsed between the application for consent and the start of construction. This delay, coming after a decade of indecision over thermal reactor policy, was damaging to the viability of the nuclear power station construction industry. It pushed up the capital cost of Sizewell 'B' by £98 million (CEGB 1988c). Most crucially, it occurred at a time when the political support previously enjoyed by the industry was eroding.

A watershed in this process was the publication of the Flowers Report (Royal Commission on Environmental Pollution 1976), which, though supportive of nuclear power, gave credibility to the nuclear opposition by echoing many of the concerns that it had raised. Criticism of the industry by establishment bodies became increasingly common, culminating in the 1986 Report of the Commons Environment Committee, which was highly critical of many aspects of nuclear waste management. Media interest in the issue was high from the time of the Windscale application and often unhelpful to the industry as it tended to emphasise sensational aspects. O'Riordan, Kemp and Purdue note the transformation of the civil nuclear issue, and the Pressurised Water Reactor (PWR) in particular, from a bipartisan to a party political issue between the announcement of the Sizewell 'B' project in 1982 and the Secretary of State's decision in 1987. The accident at Chernobyl in 1986 consolidated 'the final stage in (this) process' (1988: 3); a process linked to the concomitant growth of public opposition to nuclear power. However, as already noted, the Conservative Government's support for nuclear power was strong and constant throughout this period.

Despite this support of the programme, in 1987 after two terms of office, of the ten PWRs announced in December 1979 (one per year from 1982), plans remained for only four. Construction of Sizewell 'B' was at last able to commence, but consent procedures for the remaining three had not even started. The decisions on THORP and Sizewell went against the nuclear protestors, in each case after a Parliamentary debate – the pluralist system was weak compared with the corporatist, and outsider groups had little effect on actual policy. Implementation of that policy, however, became increasingly difficult. The anti-nuclear lobby had successfully frustrated some policy decisions, for example, the failures to mount site investigations at Luxulyan (for a nuclear power station) and Elstow and Billingham (for suitability for waste dumping) were largely due to locally organised protests. Each new delay undermined the viability of the PWR programme (Hinkley 'C' Inquiry 1989: 172:93C-94H).

Nuclear policy foundered in the industry's first two decades, due to the lack of an effective policy system. Once the system was established, the third decade was lost in countering challenges to its authority. It seems that civil nuclear policy cannot be implemented even in a hybrid system – virtually pure corporatism may be necessary. By the time of the 1987 election it seemed clear that the fate of the residual PWR programme depended on a Conservative victory. It is therefore ironic that the seeds of the programme's destruction were contained in the Government's manifesto commitment to privatise the ESI.

## Nuclear power and the privatisation triangle

The political and monopoly strength of the CEGB had to be destroyed if the industry was to be liberalised; yet the success of the PWR programme depended on a powerful nuclear caucus, especially at a time of restructuring, when scrutiny of the industry was intense. The White Paper proposals to privatise the existing nuclear power stations would have imposed an onerous non-market obligation on the industry due to the poor back end economics and short residual life of the Magnox stations and the operational difficulties of the AGRs. Ensuring the continuation of the PWR programme further extended the $NNMO_{NUC}$ axis (Figure 6.1). The Government had made some allowance for the special institutional requirements of nuclear power by opting for a 70/30 split, but the proposed structure of the industry was significantly more liberal than under nationalisation. The loss of monopoly power by the generators, inherent in the transfer of the obligation to supply to the RECs, was as significant a liberalising measure as the introduction of competition. $NL_{NUC}$ is therefore significantly extended. Because the line $NMO_{NUC} L_{NUC}$ is greater than twice the total length of the boundary of possibility, the nuclear stations are unsaleable at any price.

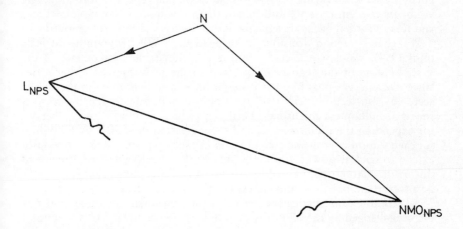

**Figure 6.1** The interaction of privatisation, liberalisation and imposed non-market objectives with the boundary of possibility in the proposed sale of the CEGB's nuclear power stations

See Figure 2.1 for key.

Even taking into account the subsidy implied by the non-fossil fuel obligation and the Schedule 12 provisions of the Electricity Act the presence and prospect of nuclear stations within National Power's portfolio would have lowered the share price, so $NP_{NUC}$ would have been substantially negative. But, given the inability of the boundary of possibility to stretch to the limits set by the liberalisation and non-market objective axes, this question is irrelevant.

## The collapse of policy

The purport of Wakeham's 9 November statement was three-fold: first he completed the withdrawal of the nuclear reactors from the sale of the ESI. This had been started by Parkinson in June with the withdrawal of the Magnox stations. Second, he abandoned Government support for the remainder of the PWR programme by lowering the non-fossil fuel obligation.

Finally he announced that, in order to increase the amount of non-fossil fuelled capacity available in the next decade, some Magnox stations might be life extended. Of these three decisions, the first had been widely predicted. The City was not interested in operating or building nuclear power stations. Due to the long term nature of the financial risks involved there was nothing a Government, elected only for a five year term, could do to persuade them that potential liabilities would be covered when they arose. This reluctance compounded the problems the Department of Energy encountered when trying to draw up contracts that reflected normal private sector investment criteria, rather than the protection of low discount rates and forty year paybacks that the nuclear industry had hitherto enjoyed.

Wakeham's second decision, to suspend the PWR programme (at least until 1994), was less expected – and not an inevitable consequence of the first. Because of the high priority given to the programme by the Tories since 1979, it was possible that it might have been continued in the public sector by Nuclear Electric. It is important to understand what the reasons for its abandonment might have been. These include an ideological distaste for expanding the public sector, and for increasing the PSBR by £2 billion for each station over the next eight years. As such purism did not previously extend to nuclear power (it did not prevent the openly admitted attempt to distort the market represented by the non-fossil fuel obligation) it can only be a factor and not the complete explanation for this decision.

A second reason might have been that the non-fossil fuel obligation was being challenged by the CPRE as an indirect state aid under EC competition law. Retaining nuclear in the public sector transformed this into a direct state aid, which was more likely to fall foul of the European Commission. The Commission was still deliberating in November 1989 and in the event did agree to the fossil fuel levy arrangements – but only until 1998, when permission to extend the levy will have to be sought. While this provides useful protection for existing reactors and forces the RECs to contract for the initial output of Sizewell 'B', it does not fulfil the original main purpose of the non-fossil fuel obligation, namely to induce the construction of further PWRs. Had Hinkley 'C' gone ahead as planned by the CEGB and National Power prior to Wakeham's decision, it would not have been due to be commissioned until 1998.

A third reason, cited by the Department of Energy (1990a), was a reassessment of 'the requirements for diversity of fuel supply in the light of developments in the electricity industry since the publication of the White Papers'. CCGT, own generation by industry, renewables and life extension of Magnoxes were all now perceived as having a role as substitutes for the diversity potential of the PWR programme.

### Economic factors

The third and most important factor behind the decision not to privatise the nuclear reactors was economic. In advance of the White Paper the advice of

Kleinwort Benson to the Department of Energy was that nuclear power was capable of being privatised provided that two conditions were met:

> 'They were first, that the costs had to be quantifiable. To the extent that they were not quantifiable it would be necessary to provide some cap for the costs. The second condition was that the costs had to be sustainable and supportable; by that we meant that the provisions that would have to be set up would be ones that the companies to be privatised could bear such that the financial viability of the companies was assured and would be recognised by investors.' (Kleinwort Benson, quoted in Energy Committee 1990c: para. 53)

This was the advice that gave rise to the non-fossil fuel obligation and Schedule 12. Kleinwort Benson maintained to the end that, had the Government been able to shoulder the burden of making nuclear costs quantifiable, sustainable and supportable, the nuclear privatisation could have succeeded (Energy Committee 1990c: evidence para. 165).

The specific circumstances of the July and November decisions were very different, but the common theme was the insuperable difficulties encountered in trying to meet these conditions. In a valedictory speech to the British Nuclear Energy Society three weeks after John Wakeham's announcement, Lord Marshall (1990) spelled out the economic difficulties he had faced, as prospective Chairman of National Power, trying to implement the privatisation of nuclear power. It was escalating cost estimates for decommissioning and reprocessing the spent fuel from Magnox stations that led to the first phase of the withdrawal of nuclear power from privatisation. CEGB provisions in the 1987/8 balance sheet for these purposes were £3.3 billion, but, by the time the much delayed 1988/9 accounts were published, this had risen to £6.8 billion. At one stage during 1989 the Department of Energy had received an estimate from National Power which suggested that eventual total nuclear provisions (not just Magnox) might be as high as £13 billion by 1990 (Department of Energy 1990a).

Marshall blamed several factors for this escalation: heavy pressure on BNF to reduce emissions from the Sellafield plant and to include the cost of Sellafield's decommissioning in their price structure; privatisation itself, which forced BNF to offer (for the first time) fixed price rather than cost plus contracts, in order that National Power would be sold with quantifiable liabilities; the short residual lifetime of the Magnox stations, which gave very little time to recover from consumers these extra costs; and reassessment of decommissioning costs, prompted by the closure of Berkeley Magnox station. Although these 'back-end' costs were the predominant factors in the withdrawal from sale of the Magnox stations, it was the capital structure of the PWR stations that forced the November 1989 U-turn. It was the custom of the CEGB to write off investment in generating plant over its entire working life. For the purposes of the Hinkley 'C' Inquiry a forty year station life had been used with an eight per cent discount rate. The assumptions on which this appraisal were based were of course challenged by objectors, but the result was a price for Hinkley 'C' electricity which was roughly comparable to new coal fired options. In his speech Marshall updated for inflation the CEGB's Hinkley Inquiry evidence to calculate a 1989 public sector price for electricity from Hinkley 'C' of 3.22p/kWh.

In the private sector, he claimed, matters were arranged differently. In order to reflect commercial rates of return National Power used ten per cent current cost accounting return (equivalent to 14 per cent discount rate) in the PWR calculations demanded by John Wakeham as soon as he took over from Cecil Parkinson as Secretary of State for Energy in 1989. This increase raised the unit price by 1.74p. Writing off the value of the station over a 20 year contract, as the lending institutions were insisting, rather than a notional 40 year lifetime, added another 0.75p. A further 0.54p was loaded on to allow for 'uncertainties' in reactor availability and reprocessing and decommissioning charges.

This adds up to 6.25p/kWh, nearly twice the original figure, but the assumptions it is based on are still favourable to nuclear power. It incorporates the Hinkley 'C' estimates, based on construction proceeding to time and cost, which were challenged at the Inquiry by CPRE, among others. Curiously, it omits interest payable on capital during the construction of the station, an assumption which the Energy Committee found unjustified. And a scheme predicated on these assumptions would still find it difficult to borrow the necessary capital. The cash flow of the station would be dominated by debt repayments in the first years, and Lord Marshall recognised that this would worry the banks. But the most fundamental criticism of Marshall's analysis is that it is based on a spurious differentiation between private and public sector investment criteria:

'The crucial question to be asked is, the price of electricity from these [PWR] reactors in the private sector and in the public sector. There is a distressing tendency for commentators to assume that there is only one answer to each of these questions. There is in fact an infinite series of answers to both of them.' (Marshall 1990)

To be fair, Lord Marshall was describing, rather than justifying, the current practice of the Government in assessing public sector investment. Since the 1967 White Paper on the Nationalised Industries (HM Treasury 1967), investment had been appraised using discounted cash flow techniques, using a single rate for all public sector projects. This was based on 'the minimum rate of return to be expected on a marginal low risk project undertaken for commercial reasons'. The justification for adopting a low risk basis was that the Government stood behind the nationalised industries and their debts. In 1989 the relevant discount rate had been raised from five per cent to eight per cent, due to the steep rise in interest rates that followed the 1987 budget. As evidence to the Hinkley 'C' Inquiry had shown (COLA 1988), this rate was still a long way below what a private sector company would use to appraise a PWR investment.

The Energy Committee found this differentiation completely unjustified: 'different rates of return in the public and private sectors for investments involving similar risk are an invitation to misallocate resources by spending money on relatively high risk, low return public projects . . .' (1990c: para. 30). Despite this, the Department of Energy used an eight per cent discount rate to justify to the Committee the continued construction of Sizewell 'B', by comparing the avoidable cost of continuation with investment in CCGT (Energy Committee 1990d).

## Institutional factors

This issue of risk was central to the failed attempt to privatise nuclear power, and had less to do with the transfer of ownership than with the proposed structure of the industry. Loss of monopoly power by the generators lessened their ability to pass on costs regardless to consumers and therefore created an acute awareness of the potential risks inherent in building and operating nuclear power stations. Tony Blair, the shadow Energy Secretary summed this up well:

'. . . where it used to be in the interests of the electricity board to tell us that nuclear power was cheap, it is now, short-term at least, in its interests to tell us that it is expensive, so that it can get more guarantees and more subsidies from the Government.' (Hansard 1989g)

A more anodyne explanation was given by the Government to the Energy Committee:

'. . . the detailed terms of any privatisation necessarily involve lengthy and detailed discussions between the Government and the industry concerned. The Government will have a variety of objectives such as the promotion of competition. Within this policy framework it will wish to maximise proceeds. The industry, however, will want financial, contractual and regulatory structures which give it the best possible prospects in the private sector and is unlikely to place the same priority on maximising proceeds. . . . It is hardly surprising that National Power sought to minimise any risk for its future shareholders while the Government sought the best deal for the taxpayer.' (Energy Committee 1990d: para 2.8)

Although substantial efforts were made to address the economic factors militating against the privatisation of nuclear power, institutional factors were not fully allowed for. Competition in generation was limited to a 70/30 split because of the inclusion of the nuclear stations in National Power, but even this amount of liberalisation was more than was compatible with the nuclear programme (see Figure 6.1). The collapse of political support for nuclear power within the CEGB – a direct result of the proposals – was also not allowed for by the Government.

Division of management structures in preparation for privatisation factionalised the Board, to the extent that a senior National Power executive could (half jokingly) suggest that PowerGen might be responsible for a press briefing suggesting Hinkley 'C' might not be built (Hinkley 'C' Inquiry 1989: 172:116G). In fact such briefings and leaks were widely attributed to John Baker, the managing director of National Power. As Lord Marshall pointed out, the primary responsibility of a private sector company is to its shareholders: if nuclear power was too risky an investment, nuclear power stations would not be built (BBC 1989). The Secretary of State's response eighteen months later, once the facts were inescapable, was as forthright: 'I am not willing to underwrite the private sector in this way' (Hansard 1989e).

Nuclear power had become a divested interest. While, obedient to Government policy, the CEGB pursued its case with vigour at the Hinkley 'C' Inquiry and submitted applications for Wylfa 'B' and Sizewell 'C', the success of these applications was not in the best interests of the nascent plcs. National Power wanted a substantial portion of the risks inherent in construction and operation covered before building and was unwilling to proceed on any other basis. PowerGen resented the subsidised competition that the non-fossil fuel obligation implied; and, similarly, the RECs would have perceived their best interests in as small a non-fossil fuel obligation as possible. Even the Government had lost interest. The pressing, short-term imperative of completing the ESI privatisation meant expedient measures were called for. The extra-Governmental members of the old nuclear caucus were no longer applying pressure in support of the PWR programme. With the UKAEA demoralised by cuts and reorganisation, nuclear power was a far easier sacrifice for the Department of Energy than the ESI privatisation would have been.

## The aftermath

After the event, recriminations of course abounded. Although the anti-nuclear lobby had made claims about the high cost of nuclear power for years, these were not generally believed by Ministers. The claim by Cecil Parkinson, later repeated by John Wakeham that: 'Privatisation is exposing the industry's existing costs, it is not the cause of them . . .' (Hansard 1989f) will have been greeted with mixed feelings by environmental groups such as Friends of the Earth and the Council for the Protection of Rural England, who could fairly claim to have drawn attention to the economics of nuclear power well in advance of the privatisation process.

The Energy Committee investigation into the cost of nuclear power was described by the *Financial Times* as 'One of the most damning accusations of incompetence in a Government department ever issued by a Commons select committee' (28 June 1990). The Committee criticised the CEGB for 'systematic bias' towards nuclear power during the years of nationalisation and for secrecy over the true costs during this time. The Department of Energy and the Scottish Office were criticised for not ascertaining much earlier from the Board what these costs were, and for a general lack of priority and urgency given to the problems of nuclear privatisation – extending even to the period when the Bill was in Committee. Kleinwort

Benson were accused of giving inadequate advice to the Department. Cecil Parkinson was singled out thus:

'Despite warnings from this Committee and independent commentators about the difficulties inherent in privatising nuclear power, and reservations expressed by the CEGB about the fragmentation of the electricity supply industry, he embarked on a policy for which it is now known inadequate preparation had been made, failed to obtain the information needed to ascertain whether the policy would work, gave insufficient priority to nuclear issues which were central to the whole privatisation scheme, paid too little attention to the two conditions for success laid down by the Department's financial advisers . . ., and allowed this major aspect of privatisation to remain unresolved until it was too late to revise the distribution of generating assets to which it had given rise. The conduct of this aspect of the privatisation amounted to the restructuring of one of Britain's largest and most strategic industries in an ill-prepared manner. The result has been the collapse of the present PWR programme and the creation of a structure for the generating industry in which it may be more difficult than it should have been for competition to become established.' (1990c: para. 107)

In response the Government robustly rejected criticism of the Department of Energy, Cecil Parkinson and Kleinwort Benson (Energy Committee 1990d), claiming that the haste with which the Committee had prepared its Report had led to a less than thorough investigation and unjustified conclusions. The Government claimed that the economic information that led to the 9 November decision was a by-product of the process of privatisation, and therefore could not have been foreseen. Indeed, Cecil Parkinson deserved credit for setting in train the disclosure process. Implied blame was laid at the door of the CEGB, for not anticipating earlier the increases in provisions and for delaying the calculation of a price for PWR electricity. The faint heartedness of the National Power shadow management was also criticised:

'The Government not only put forward Schedule 12 to the Electricity Bill, but offered National Power, in the form of the non-fossil fuel obligation, the "right to sell" its nuclear electricity under long term contracts with the distribution companies. The Government believes the Board of National Power consistently underestimated the significance of this "right to sell".' (Energy Committee 1990d: para 3.5)

Lord Marshall, for his part, firmly blamed the Government, not only for the privatisation fiasco, but for the accumulated blunders in the nuclear programme of forty years:

'I do not like this form of electricity privatisation, but the broad story of nuclear power in this country is the most powerful argument in favour of privatisation that I have ever seen. Over the last forty years Governments have interfered with this business so continuously, and with such appalling effects, that I am thoroughly convinced that it must be best to do everything that can be done in the private sector.' (Marshall 1990)

Interestingly, one quarter which attracted little blame (or rather credit) was the environmental movement, which had been waging a campaign against

117

the nuclear programme for nearly twenty years. Indeed, several 10 November editorials contrasted the perceived lack of success of this campaign with the efficacity with which 'the City' had ended the nuclear programme. What is ignored by this analysis is the crucial role that environmental pressure groups had played in exposing, but more importantly, increasing the cost burden of the nuclear industry.

Marshall's speech acknowledges the key role of pressure from environmentalists in three areas, when analysing the reasons for cost escalations in the back-end costs of the Magnox programme. The successful campaign to force Sellafield to reduce emissions into the Irish Sea, and to improve its own waste management and decommissioning procedures, forced up reprocessing charges to the CEGB and SSEB. Implementation of even exploratory plans for the disposal of low and intermediate level nuclear waste were continually frustrated by local opposition groups (backed up by national pressure groups) throughout the Eighties, leading to continued uncertainty and increased financial risk. The public distrust and fear of radioactivity had forced up CEGB decommissioning costs.

Although pressure groups' influence on the economic problems of the PWR programme was not as direct, the war of attrition fought at successive Public Inquiries looked set to continue and this added to the atmosphere of risk and uncertainty as to whether the programme could be implemented. As one participant at the Hinkley 'C' Inquiry put it:

> 'Our position . . . of high profile opposition will be saying to those prospective investors and the people who will be running the companies that wherever you go trying to build a nuclear power station there is going to be trouble and therefore you should be doing your damnedest to look for something else that's going to be less trouble.' (Roberts 1991)

The unlikely alliance of environmental groups, such as Greenpeace and Friends of the Earth, working with free market economists, both at the Hinkley 'C' Inquiry and in briefing MPs in connection with the Electricity Bill, was not unprecedented (a similar coincidence of interest is found with respect to, for example, the Common Agricultural Policy) but is certainly unusual. Greenpeace and Friends of the Earth jointly produced a newsletter (Greenpeace 1989) aimed at decision makers in the financial world, to coincide with the early months of the privatisation process.

## Baby and bath water

As was noted in Chapter 5, abdication of responsibility for strategic issues was an integral part of the philosophy of the ESI privatisation. Security of supply, research and development, the future of the coal and of the power plant industries were all ignored because of ideology – defined by the Lawson doctrine – combined with the pragmatics of privatisation. Non-market objectives were ideologically distasteful and could practically only be imposed on the ESI as a whole at the expense of either privatisation proceeds, or liberalisation measures, or both. Wise to this truth in all other areas, the Government was blind in the case of nuclear power. For Lord Marshall, quoted at the start of this Chapter, vindication brought no satisfaction, only 'a personal disappointment too large to describe in this formal document' (CEGB 1989).

With another industry (e.g. British Gas in 1986, or British Coal, or the Post Office) privatisation and meaningful liberalisation might have been achieved against the wishes of an incumbent management. Had the White Paper proposed keeping nuclear public, while selling the conventional stations, a multiplicity of generating companies might have been created. Had the CEGB been privatised as a monopoly, the goals of private ownership and continued development of nuclear power might have been achieved. But the ESI including the nuclear sector was the worst possible test bed for the hypothesis that liberalisation and privatisation were not mutually exclusive, because of the corporatist and distinctly un-liberal structures necessary to sustain a nuclear programme.

The legacy of this experiment was severe damage to two of the key objectives which the Government had sought from the privatisation of the ESI – the continuance of the PWR programme and a competitive generation industry.

# 7 'This is not an environmental bill'[1]

'I have noted the importance which Ministers attach to promoting energy efficiency.' (Prof Stephen Littlechild, Director General of Electricity Regulation [DGES 1990:11])

## Introduction

One of the items missing from the privatisation agenda was energy efficiency. This chapter examines why it was missing and why things may change in the future – but first, why is energy efficiency important?

The efficient use of electricity is important for several reasons:

- environmentally it is one of the most effective options for reducing pollution resulting from energy use. In particular it would reduce the carbon dioxide, sulphur dioxide and $NO_X$ emissions from coal fired power stations.
- economically, it can reduce consumption of an expensive fuel.
- socially, it could enable low income households to get more adequate energy services for a given expenditure.

These statements can be most readily backed up by reference to domestic electricity consumption and expenditure patterns. Electricity consumption represents a very inefficient use of primary energy, with typically under 30 per cent being converted into useful energy for the user. As a result, electricity is an expensive fuel both economically and environmentally. This can be seen by looking at examples of the comparative costs of domestic heating using various fuels (see Table 7.1). One of the environmental costs, the production of carbon dioxide, is shown in the table expressed in kilograms of carbon dioxide produced per useful kilowatt of heat used.

1. Hansard (1989b).

**Table 7.1**  Relative costs of fuels — economic and environmental

|  | Assumed efficiency of heating system (%) | Cost per useful kWh of heat (p) | kg of $CO_2$ per kWh |
|---|---|---|---|
| Direct electric fire | 100 | 7.01 | 0.83 |
| Electric storage heater on Economy 7 | 90 | 2.72 | 0.92 |
| Gas central heating | 70 | 2.09 | 0.28 |
| Coal open fire | 60 | 2.30 | 0.55 |

*Note:* The cost of a 'useful kWh' as used in this table is the cost of a kWh of heat produced by the heating system.
*Sources:* Sutherland Associates September 1990, Boardman 1990

Taken across all households, spending on electricity represents the largest part (50 per cent) of domestic energy expenditure even though many households use more energy in the form of gas or other fuels. The use of domestic electrical appliances alone accounts for around 30 per cent of an average household's fuel costs. There is a particularly heavy reliance on electricity in poor households, 4.8 per cent of the weekly expenditure of the poorest 30 per cent of households being spent on electricity, whilst in the average household only 2.3 per cent of expenditure goes on electricity.

**Table 7.2**  Household expenditure on fuel by income 1989

|  | 30% households with lowest incomes | | | average households | | |
|---|---|---|---|---|---|---|
|  | £/week | % fuel expenditure | % total | £/week | % fuel expenditure | % total |
| electricity | 4.18 | 50 | 4.8 | 5.27 | 50 | 2.3 |
| gas | 2.83 | 34 | 3.2 | 4.09 | 39 | 1.8 |
| solid fuel | 0.84 | 10 | 1 | 0.72 | 6.5 | 0.3 |
| other | 0.51 | 6 | 0.6 | 0.5 | 4.5 | 0.2 |
| total | 8.36 | 100 | 9.6 | 10.58 | 100 | 4.7 |
| total expenditure | 87.28 | — | 100 | 224.32 | — | 100 |

*Source:* Derived from Family Expenditure Survey 1989

The social differences in expenditure on electricity can be explained by the fact that poorer households are less likely to have central heating than more affluent households. If they do have central heating a greater proportion of these will have electric central heating than in more affluent households (Figure 7.1). It follows from this domestic expenditure data that improving electricity end-use efficiency has a big potential for reducing

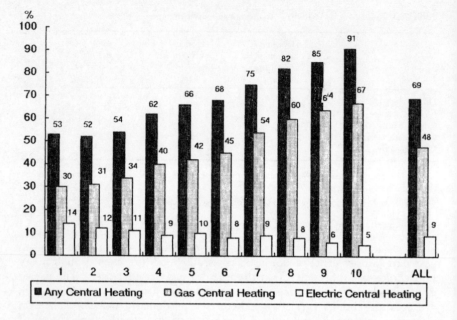

**Figure 7.1** Central heating ownership by income decile 1985

*Source:* Bradshaw and Hardman (1988)

**Table 7.3** Savings from energy efficiency measures in the home

| | Annual savings | | |
| --- | --- | --- | --- |
| *Measure* | *Costs (£)* | *kg of $CO_2$* | *kWh electricity* |
| replace 3 light bulbs with compact fluorescents | £13.50 | 158 | 190 |
| good housekeeping | £6.00 | 83 | 100 |
| switching to gas cooking | £29.50 | 360 | 1000 |
| replace old fridge/freezer with efficient fridge | £28.00 | 330 | 400 |
| replace old TV with efficient TV | £12.60 | 150 | 180 |
| insulation, and draught-proofing of electrically heated home | up to £175.00 | up to 2075 | up to 2500 |

*Source:* Friends of the Earth 1990

122

energy costs. In the case of low income households this could enable them to obtain affordable and adequate energy services such as warmth. Friends of the Earth have published a step by step guide to cutting electricity use in the home with the aim of achieving a 20 per cent reduction in electricity consumption. The measures listed are shown in Table 7.3. This quantifies the savings in costs to the consumer, costs to the environment, and in straightforward energy consumption.

In 1988 CPRE and Friends of the Earth produced a report (Skea 1988) showing the national potential for electricity efficiency measures and this again demonstrates their potential for curbing emissions from power stations. Three scenarios were set out:

- The TRAD scenario, took CEGB forecasts of electricity demand.
- the MOD scenario, assumed the achievement of modest and readily achievable energy efficiency goals, in line with EC policy.
- the TECH scenario, assumed the full take-up of all energy conservation opportunities.

The results of the analysis showed that only the TECH scenario would reduce carbon dioxide emissions and that it would also result in a 60 per cent reduction in UK electricity consumption by the year 2020. In the MOD scenario electricity consumption would increase by 18 per cent and in the TECH scenario by 50 per cent in the same period. At a time when global warming was becoming a key political issue this report was one of many showing the importance of energy efficiency in reducing $CO_2$ emissions. However, this was not recognised by the authors of the privatisation legislation.

## A tale of neglect

Since the Conservatives came to power, in 1979, they have consistently put forward the view that greater energy efficiency could be achieved by market forces with only minimal interventions from the State. It was, as a result, no surprise that the proposals for 'promoting' energy efficiency put forward in the Electricity Bill were very weak. This expectation has to be qualified by the recognition of the growing political importance of the environment in the period leading up to privatisation. The greening of the Conservative Party however came too late for electricity privatisation. It is also questionable whether energy efficiency for environmental ends could ever have been included in the primary legislation. As a non-market objective it would have further exacerbated the problems of the sell off and discouraged potential investors (see Chapter 4).

The other factor that mitigated against strong encouragement for energy efficiency in the legislation was the relative weakness of the 'energy efficiency lobby'. Though growing in strength, this lobby has always been a very disparate grouping and has no ready constituency in the Conservative Party. It was no match for the inertia of the supply-side dominated thinking within the ESI and the Department of Energy. Despite the David and Goliath nature of the conflict, the energy efficiency lobby was remarkably successful in getting its points across and caused some late nights for the civil servants at the Department of Energy. The result of the unequal battle is, however, an Act that is based on the principle that the price mechanism will ensure the optimum level of energy efficiency with only a little assistance from the electricity regulator.

This struggle between supply-side and demand-side views of energy policy is, however, an ongoing one. The Electricity Act 1989 does not signify that the supply-side viewpoint has won a permanent ascendancy in the field of electricity. The mechanisms set up by the Act could be used to very different ends by a government less wedded to market forces. As with the privatisation of gas, the form of regulation will change and evolve to suit the political climate of the times. Most significantly the Act gives the Secretary of State for Energy considerable powers over the electricity industry. Added to this is the growing influence of the European Community over energy and environmental policy in the UK. In Europe, energy efficiency is seen to have a significant role in policies to ensure security of energy supply and reduction of pollution.

## Government attitudes towards energy efficiency

'. . . the pursuit of energy efficiency is not, and can never be an absolute aim: the government's overall aim is to increase economic efficiency in the economy as a whole.' This statement appears in *Investment in energy use as an alternative to investment in energy supply* (Department of Energy 1983) which was submitted as evidence at the Sizewell Inquiry. It typifies the view of energy efficiency held by the Conservative Government throughout the 1980s. It was always assumed that if consumers were well informed and were receiving the correct price signals from their expenditure on fuel, they would want to invest in energy efficiency measures. The message was exactly the same five years later at the Hinkley 'C' Inquiry, when the Department of Energy's witness Mr C. Wilcock said, under cross examination: 'It is not our policy to curb demand . . . The entire policy is to encourage consumers to realise for themselves the steps they could take so that they carry out those steps for their own benefit.' (Hinkley 'C' Inquiry 1988:15:27 D). It was this policy that was carried over into the privatisation legislation, with the main requirement on the electricity supply companies being to provide information on energy efficiency.

In the run up to privatisation, the Department of Energy did not seem to recognise the concept of 'energy services' (such as heat, light or refrigeration). It is the price of these services rather than the price of a kWh of

124

electricity or a Therm of gas that is of most interest to the consumer. Thinking of energy use in terms of energy services automatically includes energy efficiency as it crucially affects the cost of any energy service. A company selling energy services would, therefore, be concerned not only about selling units of fuel but also about the efficiency of the appliance being used and the condition of the building in which it was being used, in order that the service it sold should be competitively priced. It is this way of thinking that underpins least cost planning (which is examined later) and many of the other proposals put forward by the energy efficiency lobby. For the Department of Energy and the Ministers involved in privatisation, this was quite simply a foreign viewpoint – an attitude which proved to be a fundamental stumbling block to more stringent requirements on energy efficiency in the legislation.

In a more general sense, energy efficiency was also neglected by Government. Despite the efforts of Peter Walker, who as Energy Secretary organised 'Monergy Year' in 1986, the Government's policy remained firmly focused on providing information to improve the operation of market forces. There was no question of intervention in the market whether with taxes or subsidies. The result of this was that throughout the Eighties and into the Nineties the Government paid little attention to the underdevelopment of the UK 'energy efficiency industry'. The energy efficiency industry is a disparate grouping of insulation, heat recovery and energy using process equipment manufacturers, companies offering energy management and auditing services etc. The message from all sources however was the same: 'The EEO's 1985 strategy review considered the poor development of the energy efficiency industry . . . a major barrier to improved energy efficiency in all sectors apart from transport.' (Comptroller and Auditor General 1989:18).

Unlike other members of the European Community, there are no tax incentives and little financial support for energy efficiency measures in the UK. In Spain, for example, the Government provides subsidies for industrial companies to invest in energy efficient technology (McGowan 1990:58). The Danes have also provided tax incentives for energy efficiency by raising the rate of taxation on fuels following the 1986 oil price crash. This is a counter cyclical tax, that is, it goes up if oil prices fall and goes down if oil prices rise. This provides a constant price message to consumers encouraging investment in energy efficiency measures. The Dutch also have a levy on fuel, some of the revenue from which is being used to finance energy saving measures – as is discussed in more detail later. However, in the UK, far from providing tax incentives the Government imposed tax disincentives such as VAT on energy saving measures – at a time when fuel was zero rated. This caused many complaints from industry. The Glass and Glazing Federation, for instance, said: 'The United Kingdom is now alone in the Common Market in applying VAT to the insulation of windows and not allowing a tax allowance, incentive or concessionary rate.' (Energy Committee 1985: 123).

At the start of the 1990s, with concerns over global warming high on the political agenda, it might be expected that the Government would be providing more encouragement to the energy efficiency industry. This has still to materialise. Expenditure by the Energy Efficiency Office (EEO) has fallen from a high of £24.5 million in 1986–1987 to just £15 million in 1989–1990. In December 1990, Andrew Warren, director of the Association for the Conservation of Energy (ACE) reported a 28 per cent fall in total UK spending on energy conservation over the previous two years.

The consequence of Government neglect was that the energy efficiency industry was demoralised and economically insignificant as the privatisation process rolled forward. It was therefore in a poor position to influence the legislation.

## The Pearce Report

A review of Government attitudes to energy efficiency would be incomplete without mention of the greening of the Conservative Party. This 'greening' was only in the rhetoric of Party spokespeople and was not marked by any major changes of policy. Many commentators point to Margaret Thatcher's Royal Society Speech as the beginning of this process, however a more significant step was marked by the publication of a report.

In August 1989 the then newly appointed Secretary of State for the Environment, Chris Patten, as one of his first acts published and gave his personal support to the report prepared for his department by Professor David Pearce, Anil Markandya and Edward Barbier. The report was labelled the 'Pearce Report' by the media and has since been published under the title of *Blueprint for a Green Economy*. Though many of the proposals put forward in the report were not new it was none the less a landmark. Pearce and his colleagues had put together a comprehensive statement setting out how sustainable economic development could be fostered by a mixture of market-based incentives. The merits of market-based incentives were set out earlier in Chapter 1, however, to many they could be just as well described as market interventions. Surprisingly the Report was endorsed by a Government renowned for its free-market ideology.

The Pearce Report was also significant in that it put environmental taxation on the UK political agenda. Underlying all of the Pearce Report's proposals is this statement about pricing:

> 'The economic principles underlying the 'proper' pricing of goods and services and of natural resources are the same. Prices should reflect the true social costs of production and use. Essentially this means getting the true social values of environmental services reflected in prices, rather than having them treated as "free goods".' (Pearce *et al* 1989: 170)

Coupled with this is the 'polluter pays principle' – that polluters should pay the price of clearing up the mess they create. In the case of electricity use 'the polluter' is both the generator and the consumer. The fact that electricity use in the home is virtually pollution-free does not release consumers from the responsibility for pollution created by the power station that produces their electricity (see Pearce *et al* 1989: 159).

The imposition of taxes or charges on polluting activities brings both of these principles together. The value of the environment is embodied in the charge so it is no longer free. At the same time the polluter is paying, and the revenue collected in the form of a charge or tax could be used for pollution abatement measures.

The translation of these ideas into real policies, such as a carbon tax, promised a bright future for the energy efficiency industry and some difficult times for the electricity industry. With Chris Patten's endorsement of the Pearce Report there was some expectation that the much awaited Government Environment White Paper would include some firm commitments to put Pearce's proposal into action. As the publication date drew nearer it became clear that the general problems with the UK economy would prevent this. In *This Common Inheritance*, the discussion of economic instruments such as carbon taxes is relegated to an annex. In the short section on this subject in the main text, the possibility of using carbon taxes is subordinated to the need to combat inflation (Department of the Environment 1990: 69). The section on energy efficiency was little better than a catalogue of existing programmes and research projects, with no substantial new proposals. The greening of the Conservative Party had come too late and was without substance, and so had no influence on the privatisation of the electricity industry.

Pearce's proposals, however, are still very relevant particularly since they present what are clear market interventions in a way that is acceptable to adherents of the free market. These have already been examined in Chapter 1. The type of interventions he proposes, such as environmental taxes, are being adopted in other European countries and are being examined by the European Commission. Given these developments, the electricity industry should watch out, while the energy efficiency industry should be patient.

## The energy efficiency lobby

'The energy efficiency lobby' in the UK is a very mixed bag of concerns. It encompasses pressure groups campaigning on environmental and poverty issues as well as the trade associations representing the energy efficiency industry. The messages put over by the various parts of the lobby have frequently contradicted one another, and there has been no convenient forum for co-ordination of lobbying efforts. It is therefore perhaps misleading to regard it as an entity at all. Its role in the privatisation of the electricity industry is best examined by looking at the activity of the separate parts.

As discussed above, the energy efficiency industry was in a very weak state. Represented by over twenty trade associations, it had no coherent voice except for the Association for the Conservation of Energy. ACE was very vocal throughout the passage of the privatisation legislation through Parliament. Its main message was about the virtues of least cost planning as practiced in the USA (as is examined later). This reliance on foreign examples was, however, a weakness. The failure to show in detail how this foreign experience could be applied in the UK made it easy for the proposals to be dismissed. ACE lobbied with the environmental organisations at various times, but kept its own independent position.

The views of the swelling ranks of the environmental movement were represented by Friends of the Earth (FOE) and the Council for the Protection of Rural England (CPRE). These two organisations worked very closely and effectively together. The increasing political importance of environmental matters was the main strength of this element of the energy efficiency lobby.

The fuel poverty groups such as the Child Poverty Action Group, Age Concern, and the National Right to Fuel Campaign wanted an increased emphasis on energy efficiency in order that the ESI would be required to invest in end-use efficiency measures in low income homes. However, they also had other more immediate objectives, concerning improvements to consumer rights, that resulted in their efforts being spread over several issues.

Early on there were some attempts to co-ordinate the lobbying efforts of the various groups by the National Council for Voluntary Organisations. This however proved to be ineffectual. Both the Labour Party and the Liberal Democrats were fairly reliant on the lobbying groups to provide relevant information briefings and proposals. The Labour Party's shadow Energy Secretary, Tony Blair, developed a close relationship with the environmental organisations. The possibility of conflicts between the objectives of the environmental movement and Labour Party energy policy was lessened by the weakened position of the NUM.

## The energy efficiency amendment

In Chapter 4 it was shown that the environment and energy efficiency were high on the 'absent agenda'. Many of the shortcomings in the legislation were apparent at an early stage and attempts were made by opposition parties to put in provisions which would have resulted in energy efficiency investment by the ESI. This was prompted by the energy efficiency lobby and by the recommendations of the House of Commons Select Committee on Energy which said:

'We assign the highest priority to the promotion of energy efficiency and we consider some form of institutional arrangements for comparing and balancing supply- and demand-side measures investments essential to transform the ESI's

128

claimed allegiance to energy-efficiency into practical action. This is a vital area for the Regulator's involvement.' (Energy Committee, 1988a: para 97)

This proposal was not taken up by the Government who continued to argue that 'competitive pressures' should be the main inducement to invest in energy efficiency. It was not until the legislation was debated in the Lords, however, that there was a successful attempt to introduce an energy amendment (Amendment 62 passed in the Lords 16.5.90). The amendment had all party support and it was proposed by three Lords, Shepherd, Ezra and Lauderdale. These three Lords had been members of the Committee which had examined electricity efficiency earlier in the year. The amendment encompassed the following principles:

- A clear requirement on the RECs to achieve real improvements in the efficient use of electricity.
- An established link between allowed tariff increases and the success of energy efficiency promotional activity.
- An assessment of supply contract investment programmes of the RECs to ensure that demand is met through the least cost route.

If this amendment had not been subsequently thrown out in the Commons, it is clear that these principles would have stimulated energy efficiency investment by the electricity industry. The wording of the amendment was:

'The Secretary of State, shall, after consultation with the Director, require each of the public electricity suppliers to make and produce evidence to the Director showing that he has made such arrangements as will promote the efficient use of electricity and may direct any public electricity supplier to take specific action in this area and, if appropriate, may refuse or amend any application for tariff increases or major capital projects.'

The amendment was, however, technically deficient as it would have required numerous other changes to the legislation to make it workable. This fact was used by the Government Whips to head off a backbench revolt in the Commons. The proposers knew the amendment was technically deficient but this had resulted partly through a lack of time when it was drafted and partly through an expectation that it would be thrown out anyway. It was none the less a significant achievement to have the amendment supported by the Lords. It was a clear signal to the Government that the proposed legislation was lacking in respect of energy efficiency. As a result, the Lords' amendment was removed but it was replaced by the Government's alternative.

'The Director may, after consultation with public electricity suppliers and with persons or bodies appearing to him to be representative of persons likely to be affected, from time to time –

a)  determine such standards of performance in connection with the promotion of efficient use of electricity by consumers as, in his opinion, ought to be achieved by such suppliers: and

129

b) arrange for the publication, in such form and in such manner as he considers appropriate, of the standards so determined.'

(Section 41, Electricity Act 1989)

Though this is a very weak alternative to the Lords' amendment, it does represent a considerable strengthening of the Director General's powers compared to those presented in the original Bill. As such, it was a small victory for the energy efficiency lobby. It also does provide some opportunities for a government which is prepared to intervene in the market. It would be quite possible for fairly onerous 'standards of performance' to be set, for instance requiring direct investment in low income homes.

## The supply licences

With the passing of the primary legislation, much of the lobbying effort fell away. There were however opportunities to influence the content of the licences that set out the specific requirements that would be placed on the generators, the National Grid Company and the Regional Electricity Companies. The most crucial were the supply licences which covered the activities of the RECs.

Friends of the Earth realised the opportunities and continued to lobby during the drafting of the licences. They had a face to face meeting with the Energy Secretary, John Wakeham, over the content of the licences, specifically proposing that the licences should be changed to allow the RECs to treat payments for energy efficiency measures in the same way as payments for energy supply. Though the arguments in favour of this were partially accepted by John Wakeham, Friends of the Earth failed to get it included in the licences. Time was against them as the deadlines for privatisation drew nearer and they did not have the expertise to draft a fool-proof framework to be included in the licence. On top of this, the RECs did not want any more changes to the licences – and they were in a powerful position to get their own way, as Wakeham was desperate to keep to the privatisation timetable.

## Electricity Industry attitudes to energy efficiency

In the run up to vesting and flotation there was some interest in the ESI in energy efficiency. There was a realisation in some quarters that constraints imposed by environmental concerns were going to increase and, therefore, the industry should be exploring what options it had to cope with these constraints.

Robert Malpas, the Chairman designate of PowerGen, was undoubtedly the most vocal exponent of energy efficiency from within the industry. However, he became increasingly isolated as the privatisation process progressed. His outspoken statements, saying that the industry should be investing in energy efficiency, were seen as direct threats to privatisation. His advocacy of energy efficiency undoubtedly played a part in his eventual downfall. However, even after his resignation, he appeared before the Energy Select Committee and continued to press for a vigorous campaign to promote the efficient use of energy in response to global warming.

More widely, the industry showed an initial interest in curbing demand but this soon faded. Several RECs started to investigate potential projects for load management and controlling demand through energy efficiency investment. However, as the details of the privatisation legislation and licences unfolded, it became clear that there was little incentive to follow through with these projects and the majority were shelved. The reasoning was quite straightforward – over 90 per cent of the RECs' profits and assets are tied to the distribution of electricity; under the RPI + X–Y price formula the more units of electricity they distribute the more profit they will make.

This assessment should be qualified by a few short term factors. There is the view that electricity demand will grow very slowly in the short term and in the long term will stabilise or fall. This view is supported by the very low growth forecasts put forward by the National Grid Company and the RECs, and the increasing penetration of energy efficient technologies. With this scenario it would be logical for RECs to take an active role in holding back short term demand growth by load management and direct investment in end-use energy efficiency measures. This would allow them to avoid investment in extra capacity in the distribution network that might be surplus to long term requirements. Though this runs counter to the message being given to the RECs by the regulation of prices, the advantages of this approach seem to be strong enough for RECs to be actively investigating various schemes along these lines. An additional short term factor is that the RECs were allowed to increase the element in electricity prices which covers distribution costs in order to cover investment in the distribution network. Any savings that can be made on this capital investment in the network will increase profits and shareholders' dividends.

On the generation side of the industry there are considerable concerns about the high cost of reducing acid emissions from existing coal fired plant, and worries about possible future measures to reduce carbon emissions. While investment in end-use efficiency measures is the most cost effective long term solution to both of these problems, it is an unappealing one to generators wishing to make money from selling electricity. However, these environmental worries have coincided with changes in investment criteria resulting from privatisation to produce a solution that is very attractive to the industry.

As was seen in Chapter 5, changes in investment criteria have resulted in the virtual abandonment of all plans to build large coal fired plant in favour of Combined Cycle Gas Turbines. These have the virtue of being very quick to build, giving a swift return to investors. CCGTs also (with current gas prices) produce very cheap electricity at around 2.5p/unit. This change will therefore be a downward pressure on electricity prices. In addition, CCGTs are much more efficient than other thermal generating plant, being capable of converting 45–50 per cent of energy contained in the fuel into electricity, compared to 30–35 per cent in most existing coal fired plant. Since they use natural gas as their fuel, acid emissions and carbon emissions are relatively low. Putting all these factors together makes CCGTs a very attractive option, and large numbers are planned.

As with the introduction of natural gas in the 1970s (see Chapter 3), we may be seeing history repeating itself with natural gas providing an easier alternative than end-use efficiency investment. It is also an alternative that maintains the status quo, with the supply industry maintaining its dominance.

## Least cost planning

Least cost planning was one of the main themes in the debate over the energy efficiency aspects of electricity privatisation. As such it requires some more detailed examination. It is also winning some important new adherents and, therefore, is still a factor that may affect the role of energy efficiency in the privatised electricity industry.

A definition of least cost planning was put forward by Roger Sant (Director of the Office of Conservation at the US Department of Energy): 'The "least cost strategy" . . . provides for meeting the needs for energy services with the least costly mix of energy supplies and energy improvements.' (OFGAS 1990:3). As such, it creates a level playing field for assessing potential demand-side investments and supply-side investments. It is practiced in many parts of the USA, the North Western states that come under the Bonneville Power Administration being a good example. It is closely linked with state level regulation of the fuel utilities by Public Utility Commissions or PUCs. PUCs have legislative, judicial and executive powers. In many states, it is the PUCs which have placed a requirement on the utilities to use least cost planning.

Least cost planning was advocated by several of the groups lobbying on energy efficiency in the run up to privatisation. Chief among these was the Association for the Conservation of Energy. ACE had already published a series of reports, entitled 'Lessons from America', which examined the use of least cost planning in the USA and advocated its use in the UK. During the Hinkley Point 'C' Public Inquiry, ACE again put forward its use and backed up its evidence on behalf of the Coalition of Opposed Local Authorities by bringing two witnesses over from the USA who had direct experience of using least cost planning (Hinkley 'C' Inquiry 1988: Day 31). Following the publication of the White Paper on electricity privatisation, ACE published another report *Regulating for efficiency* (ACE 1988) which summarised the case for American style least cost planning. However, as was acknowledged in this report, the UK government were not impressed with what they knew of regulation in the USA:

'American regulatory systems are too bureaucratic, being based on the regulation of profits, and involving interference at many levels. One lesson I have learnt from studying some parts of the United States is that the regulatory regime can in effect take over the running of the industry and stifle innovation.' (Michael Spicer MP March 1988, quoted in ACE 1988)

Least cost planning was seen by the Government as working against the liberalisation of the electricity industry. The Tories wanted light regulation through price control. Such views were of course welcomed by the industry who had no liking for the tight control on investment planning which would follow from the adoption of a least cost approach.

Friends of the Earth was the other main advocate of least cost planning amongst the lobbyists. They took it a step further by showing how this approach might be applied in the assessment of $CO_2$ abatement options. This idea was first put forward in their evidence to the Hinkley Point 'C' public inquiry and was followed by their publication of *Getting out of the Greenhouse* (Jackson and Roberts 1989). The methods used by Jackson have been criticised by advocates of renewable energy technologies as underestimating their cost effectiveness for $CO_2$ abatement (Toke 1990). However, even allowing for these criticisms, the message is clear enough – if a least cost approach to $CO_2$ abatement was adopted by the ESI, there would be a massive switch of investment to energy efficiency.

Despite the Tory Government's qualms about least cost planning, there is increasing support for this approach in some important quarters. For example the virtues of least cost planning in encouraging energy efficiency are also put forward in the European Commission's *Communication to the Council of Ministers on 'Energy and the Environment'* (COM (89) 369 final: 18). In proposals for a Community energy efficiency initiative called the SAVE programme, the Commission plans to support 15 pilot studies on least cost planning. The Commission explains the purpose of these studies as follows: 'These studies should establish the viability of this technique in the European context while giving companies supplying the public sector in the Community direct experience of planning mechanisms.' (COM (90) 365 final). With proposed Commission financial support of 2.25 million ECU these studies would be a significant step towards least cost planning in the Community, including the UK.

Least cost planning is also advocated by the Labour Party in its environmental policy document *An Earthly Chance* (Labour Party: 22). It is pointed out that there are difficulties in applying least cost planning when there are separate generation and distribution companies (this is not the case in Scotland). The Labour Party's solution is to renationalise the National Grid Company and '. . . require it to ensure security of supply, promote environmental objectives including the development of renewables, and ensure careful stewardship of our fuel reserves.' (Labour Party 1990)

There are also real problems in marrying British style price regulations with US style least cost planning. The Office of Gas Regulation (OFGAS) commissioned Ian Brown of ACE to examine the possibilities of applying least cost planning to the British gas industry. This was carried out in the context of a review of the 'gas tariff formula' which is the same RPI–X+Y formula used for electricity price regulation. Ian Brown produces no simple solutions but he does point out the main problem:

'. . . although customers as a whole could benefit from the efficiency and conservation programmes identified as cost effective in a least cost planning exercise, under the present tariff regime British Gas and its shareholders are unlikely to.' (OFGAS 1990)

This indicates that any move to least cost planning in the UK electricity industry would have to be accompanied by major revision of the current form of price regulation which lies at the heart of the present Government's privatisation philosophy.


## The Great Gonerby project

There is one small example of a least cost approach being taken by an English electricity company which is participating in a programme of energy efficiency measures in low income homes. This is a joint project between East Midlands Electricity, Neighbourhood Energy Action and South Kesteven D.C. at Great Gonerby near Grantham. This housing estate has a high concentration of low income households and they are being offered a package of energy saving measures and energy advice. East Midlands Electricity is financing the training of advice workers and is providing free low energy light bulbs to householders. Other measures are being paid for by the District Council (press release East Midlands Electricity 7.10.90).

East Midlands Electricity has been motivated to participate in the project because they will have to reinforce the distribution network if they do not curb electricity demand in the area. The scheme is an isolated example however – as yet, no other electricity company has been motivated to follow East Midlands' example. The reason for this is the strong disincentive for energy efficiency investment presented by the current form of price regulation. This highlights the challenge for the advocates of least cost planning – how do you integrate this approach with the current circumstances of the ESI in the UK?


## The European Commission, the Internal Energy Market (IEM) and energy efficiency

Looking ahead, a key institution that will affect the future of the privatised electricity industry is the European Commission. With the coming of 1992

134

and the Single Market in Europe, the Commission is becoming an increasingly influential body wielding significant powers. After 1992 it will be one of the institutions shaping energy policy in the UK.

From a UK perspective, the emphasis on increased competition and the play of market forces embodied in the creation of the IEM within the European Single Market would appear to be very much in tune with the philisophy behind the privatisation of electricity. However, most of our European partners are reliant on Middle East oil for a significant part of their energy supply. They have as a result pursued energy efficiency with greater vigour than the UK as a means of reducing this dependence. Several members of the Community have significant 'Green' lobbies in their countries, with representation in their parliaments. This too has resulted in policies for the promotion of energy efficiency as a means of reducing pollution. Both of these influences have fed through into European Community policy so that the objectives of the IEM are now being integrated with existing energy and environmental policy objectives.

In 1986 the Council of Ministers set out energy objectives for the period up to 1995 (OJ No C241, 25.9.86). These included the objective of improving the efficiency of final energy demand by 20 per cent. This was in direct contrast to what was happening in the UK where the Lawson doctrine resulted in the Government abandoning any attempts at energy planning. There is now considerable concern in the Commission that the objective of improving energy efficiency by 20 per cent will not be met because of a fall off in efforts to improve efficiency, resulting from low fuel prices. The Commission is therefore anxious to integrate this objective into overall Community policy on energy and the environment, and to renew efforts for greater energy efficiency in member states. The development of this integrated policy can be traced through a number of statements from various bodies in the Community.

Increased energy efficiency would have to be a central plank of any Community wide policy on transnational environmental problems such as global warming and acid rain. This is confirmed by Clive Jones, Deputy Director-General for Energy when reviewing likely policy developments after 1992:

> '. . . it is not unreasonable to expect that one of the key future constraints identified will be the impact on the environment of energy production and use. It will follow from that perception, I am sure, that two of the essential planks of future Community energy policy must be energy efficiency and the development of renewable energy sources.' (Jones 1989: 6)

Concerns about the environment also appear in the European Parliament's resolution on the IEM (OJ 89/C158/514). The importance placed on energy efficiency can be seen in documents coming from another influential body in the Community – the Economic and Social Committee – which is made up of representatives of member states and whose function is to advise the Commission. An example is this comment on a proposal for the directive on

135

the transit of electricity: 'The efforts to use energy as efficiently as possible in all its forms, including electricity, must remain a priority when the electricity market is integrated.' (OJ 90/C 75/23).

Last but not least, environmental concerns have been voiced by the Council of Ministers who, when commenting on the Commission's working paper entitled *The Internal Energy Market*, put forward the following aspiration:

'The achievement of a satisfactory balance between energy and the environment as an important goal under the Single Act and the Commission's intention to consider this field in greater detail and to prepare a coherent programme as soon as possible.' (Commission of EC 1988: 59)

With the messages about energy efficiency and the environment coming from all directions, the Commission put forward policy proposals in a communication to the Council, entitled *Energy and the Environment* (Com (89) 369 final). So, though rather late in the day, these matters are being integrated into a broader policy in preparation for 1992.

One of the measures put forward which has already had the approval of the Council is a Community Action Programme for improving the efficiency of electricity use (known as the PACE programme). This includes:

'Activities by electrical distributors and consumer organisations and Member State Governments to ensure that advice is available to consumers on the purchase, installation and use of the most efficient electrical appliances and equipment.'

and

'Efforts by electricity distributors and others to increase the penetration of more efficient appliances and equipment by more effective marketing, including examination of the potential of selective financial intervention.' (OJ No L157/32 9.6.89)

The co-ordination of the programme in each member state is the responsibility of each national government. In the UK, the Energy Efficiency Office has the co-ordinating role and presently has no plans for new initiatives. It is none the less another indication of the importance placed on efficiency of electricity use by the European Community.

## Initiatives in the Netherlands

The lack of new initiatives in the UK can be contrasted with efforts towards greater efficiency of electricity use in other member states. For example in the Netherlands the energy distribution companies have devised their own nationwide environmental action plan (MAP). This *preceded* the introduction into active government policy of the National Environment Policy Plan. In other words, this was the distribution companies recognising the increasing pressure for improved environmental standards and taking the initiative – in advance of Government policy. (This was the type of path that Robert

Malpas was mapping out for PowerGen.) There is a heavy emphasis on end-use efficiency and the use of CHP in MAP. The MAP programme has been made possible by the revenues from a levy on fuels, which is used for environmental programmes (Owens *et al* 1990: 7). This might be a model for the future use of the Fossil Fuel Levy in the UK.

The Amsterdam Energy Company has initiated a number of projects as part of MAP (European Commission 1991). These include a programme for the introduction of energy saving lighting. The company invited bids from lighting manufacturers to supply compact fluorescent light bulbs at a reduced price. Domestic consumers were provided with information leaflets promoting the use of compact fluorescent bulbs with tokens for 2–4 bulbs. These tokens could be exchanged for bulbs at lighting retailers and the cost of the bulbs would then be recovered from the consumer's electricity bill over a period of ten months. 150,000 bulbs were sold in the first six week campaign with only a minority of consumers using the tokens, most preferring to pay over the counter. This example is cited because, though motivated by environmental policy, it was discovered through the analysis of end-use data that the programme would also have positive effects on the distribution company's own costs. As can be seen in figure 7.2, lighting is a major contributor to peak domestic electricity demand in the City of Amsterdam. By reducing this peak, the Amsterdam Energy Company would reduce its capacity requirements for distribution and generation resulting in the more economic use of the system and reduced costs.

There are two lessons here for the UK distribution companies. First, that there are cost savings that they might accrue from efficiency measures and, second, that they will need comprehensive end-use data to identify where those savings can be made.

## The European Commission and energy policy in the UK

In November 1990 the European Commission published its proposals for a Community energy efficiency action programme – SAVE. This is a direct follow up to the communication *Energy and the Environment* discussed earlier. SAVE is designed to renew efforts to achieve the 1995 objective of a 20 per cent improvement in the efficiency of final demand and addresses the environmental objectives of reducing $NO_X$, $SO_2$ and $CO_2$ emissions. In putting forward the financial and taxation measures included in the programme this statement is made:

'Even though the price mechanism is well known to be a moving force in the search for better energy efficiency, it is clear that useful measures can be taken to promote the use of certain methods of financing.' (COM (90) 365 final)

In its proposals for third party financing, least cost planning and tax incentives, the Commission is clearly signalling that interventions in the energy market are needed to meet Community objectives on energy efficiency.

137

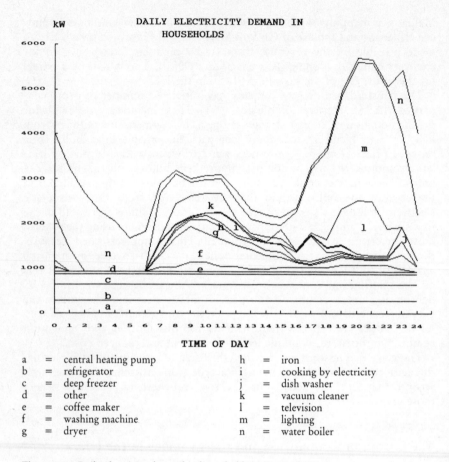

Figure 7.2    Daily electricity demand in households in Amsterdam

*Sources*: Commission of European Communities (1991)

However, with these moves being put forward within the context of the IEM and the Single Market, it follows that energy policy will have to be formulated increasingly at Community rather than national level. Clive Jones, Deputy Director General for Energy says:

> 'But will market integration necessarily mean that energy policies have to be integrated? In fact the inescapable logic is that one must progressively follow the other. Energy policies are, at the end of the day, marketing interventions, and such interventions by an individual country would obviously risk distorting trade and competition with other Member States.' (Jones 1989: 6)

This is recognised by McGowan as one possibility, with the Commission effectively taking control of energy policy as it attempts to see fair play between competitors in the market (McGowan 1989: 552). The implication of this scenario is that the privatised electricity industry is likely to face increasing pressures by the European Commission to become directly involved in the energy efficiency business. This would fulfil one of the main aims of the energy efficiency lobby at the time of privatisation – to transform the ESI into a supplier of energy services.

## Conclusions

In a market that is strongly biased towards energy supply, energy efficiency requires interventions in the market to be on a level with supply side options. This fact put energy efficiency onto the 'absent agenda' as it was incompatible with the political ideology of the Conservatives in the 1980s.

The initial struggle to strengthen the clauses on energy efficiency in the primary legislation was a very unequal fight. The Conservative Government had consistently failed to give any meaningful support to energy efficiency, and so there was no economic strength in this quarter when the time was running out.

While the energy efficiency lobby did make some headway, particularly on environmental matters, it was too late to divert the legislation. Any Government that took the time to examine the possible future scenarios for the industry, at that period in the Twentieth Century, should have recognised that environmental pressures would require a much greater involvement in end-use efficiency – and should have written this into the legislation. A great opportunity was missed.

To make a real impact on energy efficiency would have required strong interventions in the market. Instead, a form of price regulation was formulated that provided every incentive to the industry to sell more and to pollute more. It was not an environmental Bill.

The future of the industry as presented here, is very different. It is one where the European Commission takes a significant role in formulating energy policy in all member states. Energy efficiency has been shown to be of far greater political importance within the Community than it has been in the UK. It has also been shown that the Commission is ready and willing to make the necessary interventions in the market to foster greater energy efficiency, in order to meet environmental targets. So this presents a much more optimistic view for the future of energy efficiency in the privatised electricity industry. One where many of the objectives of the energy efficiency lobby may yet become a reality. Environmental taxes on energy, direct investment by the industry in energy efficiency measures, least cost planning – all remain real options for the future. All will be needed to combat the environmental damage resulting from electricity generation and use.

# 8 The renewable fig leaf

'It is perhaps a pity from the viewpoint of a technical innovation that Government funding had to be restricted at the point of demonstration, when funding overall normally has to increase quite dramatically.' (Dr F Clarke, ETSU, 1984)

'We as Members of the House of Commons, must rise above the merely technical arguments and try to fit the priorities into the overall policy structure.' (David Hunt, Secretary of State for Energy, October 1985, in House of Commons debate on renewables.)

## Introduction

Even if we make a major committment to energy conservation and the more efficient use of the fossil fuels, given the pressure on one hand of increasing demand and on the other of the greenhouse effect, we will need to develop new forms of generation. In the past nuclear power has been seen as the main option for the future. But increasingly that option looks less viable, while interest in renewable energy as pollution free and sustainable, is growing. The problem there, however, is that for the past four decades, nuclear power has been allocated the lion's share of Government R & D (Table 8.1), so that renewables are as yet relatively undeveloped. This does not mean that they cannot be fairly rapidly brought onstream, given the political will – one of their attractions is that the technology is often relatively simple and in many cases renewable systems can be deployed on a modular, incremental basis.

The fact that this has not yet happened in the UK, or happened only slowly, is rather surprising given that the UK has amongst the world's best wind, wave and tidal potential. In this chapter we explore how and why this potential has, so far, been marginalised and what the prospects are in the post-privatisation era.

**Table 8.1**  State funding for renewable R & D (£m)

| | Nuclear[1] energy | Solar energy | Wind energy | Tidal energy | Hydro[2] energy | Other renewables |
|---|---|---|---|---|---|---|
| 1976–77 | 110.0 | [3] | [3] | [3] | [3] | [3] |
| 1977–78 | 100.1 | [4] | [4] | [4] | [4] | [4] |
| 1978–79 | 127.4 | 0.2 | 0.3 | 0.0 | — | 3.1 |
| 1979–80 | 145.5 | 1.5 | 1.1 | 0.6 | — | 6.2 |
| 1980–81 | 186.2 | 1.2 | 1.4 | 1.4 | — | 9.1 |
| 1981–82 | 205.4 | 1.5 | 2.1 | 0.4 | — | 17.4 |
| 1982–83 | 214.8 | 1.7 | 4.6 | 0.0 | — | 12.2 |
| 1983–84 | 203.8 | 1.6 | 4.5 | 0.0 | — | 9.0 |
| 1984–85 | 196.1 | 0.8 | 6.6 | 0.3 | — | 9.6 |
| 1985–86 | 189.6 | 1.0 | 7.5 | 0.1 | — | 7.3 |
| 1986–87 | 174.5 | 1.0 | 6.0 | 0.1 | — | 7.4 |
| 1987–88 | 140.8 | 1.2 | 7.3 | 1.4 | 0.8 | 9.2 |
| 1988–89 | 159.1 | 1.5 | 8.5 | 1.2 | 0.8 | 9.4 |
| 1989–90 | 136.8 | 1.9 | 5.0 | 1.0 | 0.2 | 9.4 |

1 Nuclear expenditure figures are D Energy expenditure only: figures before 1986–87 include some non-R & D expenditure.
2 Hydro expenditure not separately identified until 1987–88.
3 All renewables 0.3.
4 All renewables 1.3.

*Notes:*
a  Figures for 1989–90 are forecasts.
b  The table incorporates expenditure on renewable energy by government departments, SERC, NERC, and CEGB.
c  Renewables expenditure for 1976–77 and 1977–78 includes energy conservation expenditure.

*Source:* Parliamentary question March 30 1990

## Renewables in the UK: the story so far

In 1980 Dr J.K. Dawson from the Department of Energy's Technology Assessment Agency, the Energy Technology Support Unit (ETSU), concluded (Dawson 1980) that, in principle, if all the UK's renewable sources were developed successfully up to their full potential, we might obtain a contribution of 'up to about 200 million tons of coal equivalent per annum' from renewables – about the same as we obtain from North Sea oil and gas, but, of course, on an indefinitely sustainable basis.

Clearly, it is a long way from 'potential' to actual delivered energy: there would be a whole range of technical, economic, social, environmental and institutional constraints, not least the level of financial support from government. Even so, there was evidently a significant and renewable resource of pollution-free energy, some of which could presumably be tapped if the need was there.

Enthusiasm for renewables had grown during the 1970s. In 1978 Glyn England, the Chairman of the Central Electricity Generating Board (CEGB), commented that 'in theory windmills could produce the equivalent of roughly a quarter of the CEGB's present output', while wave power systems could 'supply the whole of Britain with electricity at the present rate of consumption' (England, 1978).

Wave power became the front runner. By 1982 around £15 million had been allocated to wave research, and smaller amounts to solar, wind and so on, as part of an ongoing programme of assessment.

However, the incoming 1979 Conservative government had sought to rationalize the renewable R & D programme by focusing on the technologies most likely to be commercially viable. As was seen in Chapter 3, wave power (and active solar) was assessed unfavourably (Elliott 1987, 1988b). Despite protests from the wave research teams, who were claiming estimated (kilowatt hour) unit costs well below the initial 'target' of 10 p/kWh (and even below the new target of 5p/kWh), following a review by ACORD (the Advisory Committee on R & D) published in 1982, the programme was drastically cut back. Wind power then became the front runner, along with tidal power and, to a lesser extent, geothermal and passive solar.

ETSU's 1982 *Strategic review of renewable energy technologies* (R13), produced in support of the ACORD review, included the following estimates of long-term possible contribution ('maximum technical potentials') as percentages of current electricity demand: on-land wind 20 per cent; offshore wind 50 per cent; wave power 25 per cent; tidal power 15 per cent; geothermal hot rocks 10 per cent. Significant contributions to heat supply were also considered possible from solar, and biofuels. ETSU did stress, though, that these resource estimates did not take full account of economic or environmental constraints, and they did not see renewables playing a major role at least in the medium-term future.

Of course, this may be something of a self-fulfilling prophesy, which would inevitably become reality if the lion's share of R & D funding and capital investment continued to be allocated to nuclear power. By 1984 for example, some £2.2 billion had been spent on just one nuclear prototype – the fast breeder – while by 1987 only around £100 million (cumulative total) had been allocated to research on *all* the renewables. And as ETSU noted: 'all the technologies seem to need some sort of Government backing to help them get established' (ETSU 1982a).

The conclusion in ETSU's 1982 R14 report, *Contribution of renewable energy technologies to future requirements* (ETSU 1982b), was that, while 'the technical potential of the renewables is about half to two-thirds of the total UK energy supplied by oil, coal, gas and nuclear', in reality, given current priorities and the various economic and environmental constraints, by the year 2025 wind, tidal and geothermal power (the front runners) would be supplying at most, in the best scenario for renewables (assuming high fuel prices) only 5.8 per cent of Britain's electricity – with a maximum on-land wind energy installed capacity of 7.5GW and only 4GW offshore. This assessment was reinforced by the next ACORD review (and the parallel ETSU study, R30) in 1986, with wave power (and geothermal aquifers) finally being written off: 'the probability of achieving a cost lower than 9p/kWh [for wave power] is small' (ETSU R30 1986). This view was maintained despite the fact that the Norwegians had developed wave systems, albeit small coastal units, which it was claimed would generate power at 3p/kWh. As noted in Chapter 3, the debate on wave power has continued (Select Committee on the European Communities 1988).

*Wind power*

Meanwhile support for wind power continued, with significant projects underway – such as the £11 million 3MW Wind Energy Group (WEG) machine on the Orkneys. The emphasis was on private consortia led projects, with, however, the Department of Energy still providing much of the funding. There was also continuing CEGB involvement. For instance, it provided sites for the new wind turbine being erected at Richborough in Kent and the Carmarthen Bay Vertical Axis machine in Wales.

As a result of developments, in the USA in particular, it had become increasingly clear that wind power was going to be a significant option and proposals for wind farms in the UK began to emerge. In 1987, the British Wind Energy Association published a report (BWEA 1987) claiming that on-land wind turbines, on good sites, could generate reliable power at around 2p/kWh – making wind power one of the most economic sources of electricity.

In March 1988 Michael Spicer, then Minister with responsibility for renewables, announced a joint Department of Energy/CEGB plan for three 8MW wind parks, each with twenty-five 250-350kW wind turbines on sites in the South West (near Launceston), Northern Pennines and west Wales (near Cardigan), at a total cost of £8 million. A single 750kWh Howden wind turbine was also to be installed off the coast of Norfolk. This announcement was greeted with enthusiasm by the UK renewable energy community, since they felt that it indicated that the Government had accepted that new technologies like these needed public support beyond the research and development stage if they were to be deployed on a significant scale. Leaving it to the private sector was not sufficient.

In line with the Lawson doctrine, the Department of Energy saw the wind parks more as a 'demonstration' project, to be followed by private sector led full-scale programmes, with Lord Marshall, Chairman of the CEGB, talking in terms of 1GW of installed wind capacity in place by 2005, presumably based on private funding.

*The role of the private sector*

The Government's resistance to the idea of funding beyond the R, D & D (Research, Development and Demonstration) phase was made particularly clear in a reply by Spicer to a Parliamentary Question by Frank Cook MP

(Labour) as to whether the Government could offer grants to industry or to individual consumers to deploy full-scale renewable energy systems. Spicer pointed out that while there were funds for R & D (the baseline budget having reached £16 million/year) and for demonstration projects (under the EC's Energy Demonstration project scheme):

'. . . there are no grants available to industrial concerns which may wish to use renewable energy and we have no plans to introduce such measures and there are no grants currently available to members of the public who may wish to utilize renewable energy, and we have no plans to introduce grant aid for renewable energy . . . The renewable technologies would not be best served in the long term by distorting the market by grant aid or other subsidies for their use.' (Parliamentary Answer, 13 January 1988)

Given the fact that the Government provides various types of subsidy to other energy industries, most notably coal and nuclear power, this might seem a somewhat unfair and rigid insistence on the 'free play of market forces', especially given the fact that renewable energy systems were also having to face punitive local rates and very unattractive 'buy-back' rates from the CEGB for their electricity.

This policy met with some criticism. It was argued that, if we wanted the renewable options to be deployed on a significant scale, public support would be necessary, since the private sector was unlikely to want to face major financial risks with new technologies. It was also pointed out that this policy had *not* been applied to nuclear technology which had received and continued to receive lavish preferential treatment, including massive overt and hidden subsidies to supposedly 'commercial' plant, as well as support at the research and demonstration stage.

In June 1988 the Department of Energy published Energy Paper 55 which outlined a renewable R, D & D programme involving government expenditure rising to about £25 million/year around 1993, but thereafter falling off almost to zero by the year 2000 (see Figure 8.1). The Department's belief was that the private sector should and would take over an increasing share in R, D & D from 1990 onwards as the technologies approached commercialisation, with full-scale private sector investment in commercial systems then taking over from the mid-1990s. Passive solar and biofuels from waste were seen as 'economically attractive', while on-land wind, tidal and geothermal hot dry rocks were 'promising, but uncertain'. Overall, renewables could be generating up to 70TWh/yr of electricity and 20Mtce/yr of heat by 2025 (for comparison the UK currently consumes around 250TWh/yr of electricity, and a grand total of 330Mtce/yr of primary energy). While the renewable energy community was generally pleased to hear these projections, and with the news that the Department of Energy R, D & D funding would increase slightly in the short term, not everyone was convinced that the private sector could be relied on to pick it up after that. It rather depended on the terms under which the electricity supply industry could be operating after privatisation.

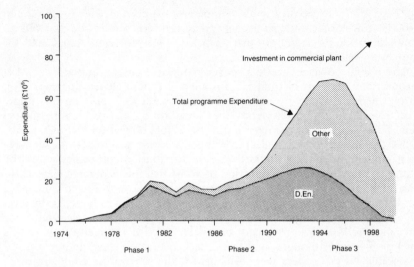

**Figure 8.1**   Profile of expenditure on renewable energy R, D & D envisaged, assuming that all the promising technologies succeed

*Source:* Department of Energy (1988b). Reproduced with the permission of the Controller of HMSO.

## Privatisation

In July 1988, the then Under Secretary of State for Energy, Michael Spicer, claimed, in an editorial in the Department of Energy journal, *Review*, that 'The climate for developing renewable energy technologies in Britain has never been more favourable; in particular privatisation of the electricity supply industry should boost the commercial prospects for these technologies as a free energy market is established.'

Initially, in the run up to the publication of the Electricity Bill in November 1988, there was certainly some enthusiasm for privatisation in the 'renewable energy' and 'independent generation' community, since it was felt that new market opportunities could be opening up. However, as the details of the privatisation programme, and its contractual arrangements in particular, emerged, this enthusiasm was converted into uncertainty and, in some cases, despair. In part the initial problem has been that the continuing uncertainty about the details of the contracts has made it difficult for innovators to obtain investment funds. And while the Government claimed to be trying to open up the field for competition, in practice what emerged subsequently, after a long period of wrangling, was a new (if temporary) form of quasi-monopolistic structure, with the interests of the two large generation companies formed from the CEGB (PowerGen and National Power) being protected – at least in some parts of their markets. Thus, while they could compete to supply the grid, to 'ensure an orderly transition', independent generators were not to be allowed to compete in the direct supply market below 1MW for eight years, and for four years below 100kW.

There was, however, to be a special renewable energy quota of 600MW (around one per cent of total UK installed electricity generating capacity), to be filled, in stages, by the year 2000. Generators supplying this quota would be able to benefit from the 'levy' to be charged on fossil-fuel generation – as part of the overall non-fossil fuel obligation (NFFO) established (for England and Wales) in the privatisation proposals. As we have seen, under this scheme the new private distribution companies would be obliged to buy in a fixed proportion of non-fossil fuel generated electricity, regardless of the price – the extra cost being passed on to the consumer via the levy on fossil fuel generation. The NFFO quota was to be set at the level of available nuclear generation (currently 14 per cent of electricity for England and Wales) so the major beneficiary of this arrangement would be nuclear power. Although, as we shall see, in practice separate nuclear and renewable NFFO orders were established, the renewables could, in principle, challenge nuclear for a place in the quota, as well as filling out the small 600MW renewable sub quota. Certainly, in principle and given time, they could mount a significant challenge – the CEGB had estimated that by 2005 renewables might generate eight per cent of the UK's electricity, rising to 18 per cent by 2030. Whether or not they could achieve these levels in practice, would depend on how much is invested in the meantime. And as we have seen, the Government's view was that future investment in renewables should come from the private sector.

### Private sector interest

The main sign of commercial interest prior to privatisation had been in tidal and wind power, although even there the level of interest in going it alone was not very high – most were hoping for State support, at least initially.

The Severn Tidal Barrage provides a good example of the problems facing the private sector if it seeks to go it alone with major projects, whether renewable, coal based or nuclear. The Barrage would be very front-end capital intensive, with a capital cost of £8.5 billion. The rates of return on this would make it very unattractive to private investors, even though the Barrage could generate reasonably competitive electricity for up to 120 years.

Windpower, by contrast, looks like a much more attractive short term investment. The technology, like many of the other renewables technologies, is smaller scale, modular and therefore more flexible, with lower front end capital requirements. The main signs of interest have been from the Wind Energy Group (Taylor Woodrow, British Aerospace) and James Howden, both having achieved significant initial export success in the USA. However, without a firm domestic base, the future for UK windpower is looking uncertain. Howdens, after some technical problems, subsequently decided to get out of windpower, with a spokesman commenting that 'privatisation has retarded the development of windpower' (SCRAM 71 July 1989). Their blade suppliers, Composite Technology, had already folded, while the pioneering wind turbine co-operative, the Northumbrian Energy Workshop had gone into receivership. An NEW spokesman commented that whereas initially privatisation was seen as 'an opportunity to sweep clean and get rid of the old ideas' in the end this had fallen foul of 'a political attempt to make it more attractive to shareholders' ('Wind Power Industry Hurt' *Sunday Times* 1.10.89).

Many of these industrial innovators argue that wind technology and renewable technology in general, needs public funding to get it established, in the same way as has been done in Europe (subsidies of up to 40 per cent have been provided for wind in Holland for example), and that at the very least they should have a fair chance to compete.

The main strategic priorities in the privatisation proposals as they have evolved, however, seem to be to protect nuclear power from market pressures via continued public subsidies, (including for example up to £2.5 billion set aside for spent fuel reprocessing, waste storage and plant decommissioning); to protect, albeit temporarily, National Power and PowerGen from some aspects of competition from independents; and to leave renewables more or less to survive unaided, with just a 600MW 'lifeboat' and a share of the fossil fuel levy to sustain them. In addition, when it came to trying to put up specific proposals within this framework, many renewable energy developers seem to have faced significant hurdles, not least in terms of continuing uncertainty about the details of the contracts that would be available.

Not surprisingly, some parts of the renewable energy and independent generation lobby became increasingly dismayed, a spokesman from the Association of Independent Electricity Producers commenting 'we feel betrayed by the Department of Energy because we received assurances from ministers that competition was the cornerstone of privatisation policy' (*Sunday Times* op cit). Evidently organisations like this have found it to be a continuing uphill struggle, at least in the initial phase, with the smaller new entrants in particular not being aided by the privatisation programme, and being faced, as they see it, by well-protected markets and uncertain contract arrangements.

## The next stage

Of course matters may improve as the details of contracts and institutional arrangements are sorted out. Certainly, some of the larger companies, like the new distribution companies, may find it both worthwhile and less problematic to invest in renewables, as may PowerGen and National Power. Indeed they have already indicated some interest in these new technologies. National Power and PowerGen are continuing to press ahead with the

CEGB's 8MW demonstration wind parks (although one was dropped in August 1990 following environmental objections), while the South Western Board (SWEB) and the North Western Board (NORWEB) have reviewed the regional options – with NORWEB estimating that renewables might meet 12 per cent of their requirements (NORWEB/ETSU 1989). Norweb subsequently put forward a number of project proposals as candidates for inclusion in the 1990 NFFO, including one for a windfarm. In addition, despite the uphill struggle, many smaller companies and even individuals, seem keen to try their hand in this new field. By the time of the initial December 1989 deadline for applications to be included in the renewable NFFO, the Department of Energy had received around 270 proposals, via the local area boards, from private companies, small and large; individual entrepreneurs; and land owners keen to develop wind, micro-hydro, biofuel projects and other similar projects – with a total installed capacity of around 1,500MW, about equivalent, in firm power terms, to the entire initial national 600MW renewable quota as set for completion by the year 2000. By March 1990, the total number of proposals had risen to around 370 (about 2GW worth), although that did include some duplication (e.g. rival projects for the same sites). Of course, not all these projects would survive the Department of Energy's assessment process (initially expected to be completed by March 1990 but delayed, as we shall see, at the last minute by an EC ruling), with funding no doubt being a major issue. But there was clearly a lot of local interest in renewables, stimulated in part by the availability of the NFFO levy.

Windpower was a major contender with around 300MW bid for in all, with the area boards well represented. For example, according to *Windpower Monthly* (January 1990), SWEB (the South West Electricity Board) received proposals for windfarms on over 40 sites, with a combined total installed capacity of around 160MW. According to *The Times* (11.12.89), NORWEB put in 40 proposals in all, including bids for landfill gas, windfarm and micro-hydro schemes; South Wales put in 20, predominantly for windfarm; Midland Electric 14, including micro-hydro and landfill gas; and Northern Electric, ten, including one for biologically digesting wood pulp. MANWEB (the Merseyside and North Wales Electricity Board) forwarded on the proposal from the Mersey Barrage Company consortium, of which it is part, for the proposed 700MW Mersey Tidal Barrage.

In general, however, most of the proposals came from individuals, local farmers, and small local enterprises and organisations, and many were no doubt purely speculative, with few of these likely to survive the Department of Energy's assessment process. But some were quite significant. For example, in Wales, Dr Brian John of Energy Parks UK, a small development company with strong local links, put up five windfarm proposals, while the Centre for Alternative Technology, the major independent demonstration/exhibition centre, put up four windfarm proposals. In the South West, the Cornwall Energy Project, a regional research and consultancy organisation which in 1988 did a detailed study of local renewable potentials, according to *Windpower Monthly* (January 1990), put in applications for windfarms on 15 sites, with a total capacity of 50MW.

Most of these independent projects, however, if proceeded with, would rely in practice on the technical backing and possibly financial support of industrial concerns, like the Wind Energy Group (a consortium backed by Taylor Woodrow and British Aerospace). For example, one local Cornish farmer, Peter Edwards, put forward a proposal for installing ten of WEG's machines, giving a total installed capacity of 3–4MW. According to *Windpower Monthly* (January 1990), WEG itself has applied 'for about six sites' in the South West, while National Power was said to be looking at two or three. According to WEG, overall it had applied for 100MW of wind energy projects.

Some of these industrial proposals may benefit from the prospect of significant funding from the European Community under the EC Energy Demonstration Scheme. For example, according to *Windpower Monthly* (February 1990), WEG has been granted 40 per cent EC funding towards the Edwards project mentioned above and for a joint project with Yorkshire Water Authority for a 1.3MW wind turbine powered reservoir pumping scheme, while the VAWT (the Vertical Axis Wind Turbine consortium backed by McAlpines) has obtained 30 per cent EC funding for a medium scale demonstration windfarm.

Finance was obviously not going to be the only issue; there was also the question of local environmental impact. Several of the wind projects ran into planning permission problems during 1990. However, given the nature of most renewable projects, it was the availability of the NFFO levy that was to prove the major problem.

## Renewable economics and the 1990 EC ruling

The economics of renewables, like those of most energy technologies, are very sensitive to the rates of return expected and the period over which the supply contract runs. Under public sector conditions, long contracts (often for the full lifetime of the plant) with low rates of return (traditionally five per cent, but more recently eight per cent) were the norm, but in the new private sector environment, at least a ten per cent rate of return on a current cost basis would be expected (this is about 14 per cent in real rate of return terms), along with shorter term contracts. Taking a typical wind-farm project as an example, Peter Musgrove from the Wind Energy Group (WEG) calculated that at a five per cent real rate of return over a 35 year lifetime, electricity could be supplied at 3.5p/kwh. However at 11 per cent over eight years, the unit cost would rise to 8.3p/kwh (Musgrove 1990).

The Department of Energy had set a cap of 6p/kwh for the 370 renewable projects under assessment as candidates for the fossil fuel levy. Many of the 370 or so applications assumed 15–20 year contracts, with unit costs therefore falling below 6p/kwh (e.g. 5.7p/kwh on WEG's figures for a wind farm over 20 years at 11 per cent rate of return), with the share that they assumed they would get from fossil fuel levy obviously helping to ensure success. On this basis the prospects looked quite good – and the 6p/kwh cap seemed reasonably generous.

But this assessment proved to be premature. Some area distribution boards evidently wanted shorter, more flexible contracts and, more importantly, the European Commission indicated that it considered that the UK Government's plan for the fossil fuel levy, as outlined in the privatisation arrangements (with non-fossil powered generation subsidized from a levy – the so-called 'nuclear tax' – on private fossil fuelled plants), might be in conflict with the EC's 'fair competition' rules. The main thrust of the EC's criticism was directed against what they saw as a proposed subsidy for nuclear power. The fact that renewables were also meant to benefit from the fossil fuel levy, and would suffer if the levy was blocked by the EC was incidental and, it seems, was not appreciated by the EC. But in the event an outright ban on the levy was avoided: at the end of March, just before vesting day for the UK's private electricity companies, and following strenuous lobbying by UK representatives, the EC accepted a UK Department of Energy compromise proposal – that the levy should only be allowed to run up to 1998, i.e. for eight years. This constraint would not seriously limit nuclear power, given that it was now back in the public sector and could expect 'internal' state subsidies. However the limitation to eight years had disastrous implications for renewables, with the consequent eight year contracts making it seem unlikely that more than a few of the proposed renewable energy projects could meet the 6p/kwh cap. The UK renewable energy community was seriously shaken by what many saw as a disastrous turn of events.

There was considerable debate over who was actually to blame – the EC or the UK Department of Energy. *New Scientist*'s claim (31.3.90) that 'the British Government has strangled at birth a large number of proposed projects for renewable energy' was underscored by the views it quoted from Peter Musgrove, who argued that there had been disagreement over the new contract time limits between the division responsible for renewable energy and that overseeing privatisation, the latter wanting 'the legislation to be as simple as possible without any consideration of what it does for renewables'. Certainly it seems that it was the UK side that suggested the eight year limitation – even though this might well have been as a compromise to head off an outright EC ban on the levy, with the renewable acting as 'fig leaf' which would then be sacrificed. Alternatively, it could be argued that the EC was basically 'set up' by the UK to act as the 'bad guy' – by wading in, as it thought, against a nuclear levy, without realising the implications for renewables.

But leaving speculations like this aside, it does seem clear that the UK Government's tie up of renewables and nuclear in the non-fossil fuel obligation and fossil fuel levy, had proved very unfortunate for renewables – with renewables being inadvertently tarred with the same brush as nuclear by those in the EC opposed to further nuclear subsidies. Of course there still remained the possibility, given that the EC favours renewables, that the UK's renewables could be given special status by the EC and be allowed to receive the levy over a longer period. Alternatively, the Department of Energy's 6p/kwh ceiling might be raised. So far, however, the UK Government has not sought an exemption for renewables from the EC ruling, but the Department of Energy tried to soften the 6p limit somewhat, by suggesting that the initial price could be higher, as long as it averaged out to 6p over the whole contract period. Even so, the overall mood within the renewable energy community was one of pessimism. For example, Peter Musgrove from the Wind Energy Group (WEG) commented at a BWEA conference: 'I cannot see how any wind farm can be funded in eight year contracts'. At one stage WEG threatened to withdraw 17 projects on the grounds that the financial terms in the contracts were too stringent.

With deadlines slipping and contract details in what seemed to many a state of permanent flux, the negotiations between the various intending generation companies and the area boards became increasingly complex, and at times confused. The Department of Energy was presumably facing pressure to get the first renewable NFFO arrangements finalised before the sell off of the Regional Electricity Companies, and this time pressure led to further problems – for example, at one stage intending suppliers were given just ten days (over the Easter holiday) to submit detailed information on their proposals. By late summer only 100 proposals remained on the table, with OFFER, the new Office of Electricity Regulation, then scrutinising them further.

The end result emerged in October 1990, with 75 contract proposals finally being accepted, the bulk of them being micro-hydro (25) and biofuel/waste projects including 25 landfill gas schemes. Only five wind farms (25MW in total) survived the contract negotiations, along with 2MW of individual stand alone wind turbines. The statutory renewable element of the 1990 NFFO was set at 102.25MW declared net capacity (taking into account the intermittency of wind), to be attained by April 1995, with this level of capacity then running until 1998, when the levy would end. The 75 projects themselves, if all successful, were expected to result in the installation of some 170MW of capacity (or around 150MW declared net capacity) so there was a small safety margin. But the difference between this figure and the total of around 2000MW initially bid for, from the original 370 or so projects, was widely remarked on.

Friends of the Earth commented: 'The Government has squeezed out viable projects by continually changing the rules. The pathetically low and unambitious target sums up the Government's attitude to the future of renewables', while the British Wind Energy Association saw the wind allocation (less than 30MW in total) as 'embarassingly small' compared with countries such as Denmark, the Netherlands and Spain (*New Scientist* 29.9.90). The point was regularly made that the NFFO levy scheme did not cover Scotland – which was by far the largest wind energy resource of any area in Europe. For its part, the Government tried to shift part of the blame

151

onto the renewable energy community, with for example Colin Moynihan, the new Minister responsible for renewables, suggesting that the wind operators were 'too poorly prepared'. This was hotly denied by Jim Halliday, President of the British Wind Energy Association, commenting that it was the way the contracts had been devised and then constantly revised that had been the problem. 'The technology is ready to be harnessed, but the Government has sometimes suddenly changed the goal posts. It is not surprising that prospective wind operators have been unwilling to sign.' (*The Times* 24.8.90).

Recriminations and special pleading apart, it does seem clear that the 1990 renewable NFFO exercise had not gone smoothly, especially in relation to some of the more novel options like windpower. In part this was due to the haste in which the whole process was carried out, as determined by the need to complete negotiations in phase with the overall privatisation process. The Department of Energy was evidently somewhat surprised by the number of proposals that came forward and, given that this was the first such exercise they had been involved with, it is perhaps not surprising that there had been some delays and confusions. In this situation, from the Department of Energy's point of view, successfully selecting 75 projects might be seen as something of a triumph.

The administrative situation will hopefully be improved for the subsequent rounds of the NFFO, following a Department of Energy review of the 1990 exercise. To try to ease the situation, arrangements were made for additional protected renewable tranches, with separate sub tranches for each renewable, to be made available in 1991 – in part to support projects that were not ready for the 1990 round. But the more substantive problem of finance, and in particular the 1998 levy limitation, seems likely to remain.

### Where next?

It could be argued that the renewables were sharing the same fate as the Pressurised Water Reactor, and indeed the Fast Breeder Reactor, the nuclear industry's other main 'new technology' – both of which have, in effect, fallen foul of the privatisation process. Following the Government's announcement in November 1989 that the nuclear element was to be retained in the public sector and the PWR programme (Sizewell apart) halted, Lord Marshall, then Chairman of the CEGB, complained that the nuclear industry had been 'compelled to abandon it (the PWR) because of the nature of the privatisation process which forces short term commercial judgements on a project whose value is primarily long-term and strategic' (Marshall 1990). Clearly nuclear power has suffered some retrenchment in its role as the Government's chosen 'strategic energy technology'. But, renewables have, as yet, not been targeted as its replacement.

That is not to say that attitudes are not changing. The Government clearly hopes that the private sector will follow up some of the renewables, with the Department of Energy committed to promoting renewables via a process of 'technology transfer' – the transfer of the research results from the various relevant Department supported research, development and demonstration projects, to industrial concerns. Essentially this involves the diffusion of information, via publications, reports, conferences and so on, and certainly there is a wealth of research data now available – for example via the Department's extensive publications and the Energy Technology Support Unit's Renewable Energy Inquiries Bureau at Harwell.

This approach is, however, inevitably somewhat passive. Although the Department of Energy regularly implores private sector interests to take advantage of the potential of renewables, the 'take up' has so far been rather slow. At times there is something of an air of desperation in the Department's entreaties, presumably fuelled by the need to try to breathe life into the Government's policy of letting the private sector take over responsibility for renewables. Thus, for example, Issue No. 7 of *Review* (the Department's quarterly Journal of Renewable Energy), called on industry 'to play a stronger role both in the R & D phase and in its commercialisation', (Editorial *Review* Spring 1989) but Issue No. 8 simply asked for 'patience to withstand the necessarily slow process of change and adoption of new ideas and vision to see beyond the short to medium term', coupling this with a warning that the Japanese 'will surely not be slow to exploit renewables options' (Editorial *Review* Summer 1989).

What is missing in this 'hands-off' approach is, clearly, the availability of significant funding, other than for providing information to stimulate interest from the market. Quite apart from R, D & D, and public investment in full scale projects, a serious 'hands-on' support programme would involve measures to develop the necessary industrial support structures and technical infrastructure – not least in terms of training provisions in the new specialisms. That certainly was done by other Government Departments when awareness of and expertise with information technology was perceived by the Government to be strategically important. While there are some welcome indications of interest in such projects within the Department, it may not be in a position to consolidate these developments. Subsequent to the completion of the privatisation process and the winding up of public energy research, it could well be that the Department of Energy will be significantly slimmed down, or perhaps absorbed into another Department, its main residual functions being taken over by the new regulatory bodies like OFFER, the Office of Electricity Regulation.

A change of Government could alter this – with the Labour Party for example being committed to regulation as a major new tool of intervention – as well of course to significant public funding for renewables. But for the present the Conservative Government remains wedded to privatisation as the main tool for stimulating renewables, with the Department of Energy's Renewable Energy journal, *Review* (Issue 9 August 1988) commenting that: 'privatisation legislation, with its non-fossil fuel obligation, is arriving at a time when the technologies are ripening toward exploitation'.

Few renewable energy advocates would now accept that a free market approach will be sufficient, and indeed many would argue that, if renewables are to make a significant contribution, there is still a need for further state support, at least for a few years, as is happening elsewhere in the EC.

Clearly the potential is there, but it remains to be seen what the impact of the UK's market led approach will be. While some of the currently more cost-effective renewable projects may get private funding, research on more advanced systems may be reduced, with the result that the UK may ultimately have to import technology from abroad. Commenting on the CEGB wind parks, Dr. Philip Surman, the project co-ordinator, told *Windpower Monthly* (8 August 1989) that while 'it is unlikely that we will go outside Britain for the first windfarm . . . all sorts of options are open after that'. Japan, following Denmark's initial success, is already pushing ahead rapidly with wind power exports, with major windfarm drives in the USA and elsewhere. Japan has also been developing wavepower systems, as has Norway – this being a field which the UK once led. A familiar pattern could thus be re-emerging, with the UK unable or unwilling to capitalise on its research strengths.

## Conclusions

The above analysis is inevitably based on incomplete data – the privatisation process has only just been completed. But the preliminary phase has done much to expose some of the contradictions and uncertainties within UK energy policy. So far the privatisation arrangements seem to have blocked, as much as stimulated, the strategic development of renewables.

For its part the Government has tried to rescue the situation to some extent – but at the cost of further undermining one of the basic tenets of privatisation, namely enhanced competition. Step by step, more and more market protections have had to be introduced. First nuclear and renewables were protected by the NFFO. Then came the separate 600MW renewable quota, with, subsequently, Peter Morrison, the Minister responsible for Renewables, commenting in Issue 11 of *Review* that 'emerging technologies need some market protection as they move out of the R & D and demonstration stages into the competitive commercial world'.

However, within this protected renewable 'ring fence', within the NFFO ring fence, renewables were meant to compete with each other. Indeed *Review*'s editorial commented that the NFFO 'has a major advantage over initiatives in other countries in that it takes the whole range of renewable technologies capable of being applied for electricity generation. It neither encourages nor discriminates against any one particular technology: all pit themselves against real market conditions' (*Review* 11). But, this 'free market' rhetoric will have to be modified somewhat given the plan proposed by the Secretary of State for Energy in January 1991, to introduce a series of 'bands', or sub-quotas, within the 1991 renewable NFFO, for each renewable. Although it would not be finally confirmed until the autumn, the overall 1991 NFFO was expected to be set in the range of 50–200MW, with bands of 25–50MW for wind, 5–10MW for hydro, 30–60 for landfill gas, 50–100MW for municipal and general industrial waste incineration and 15–30MW for others such as sewage gas, and combustion of special wastes. Thus each renewable would have its own share of the NFFO, in effect protecting them from competition from each other. The overall aim was to give projects which were left over from, or not ready for, the 1990 NFFO round a second chance, as well as to cater for new projects.

Originally there had been talk of introducing just a protected tranche for windpower, presumably following its poor showing in the 1990 NFFO, in order to protect it from competition from some of the other more immediately deployable renewables, like refuse burning. In the event, however, the multiple 'band' idea emerged, and within this concept a concession was made towards competition, with the ranges of the band implying that there could be trade offs at the margins between the bands, as well of course as competition within bands (with a complex new 'blind price' tendering process replacing the 1990 price ceiling).

Even so, the arrangements that have emerged seem a far cry from full competition, with designated bands within a protected renewable sub-quota within a protected NFFO and with, in practice, the NFFO having separate nuclear and renewable sections – eliminating any direct competition between nuclear and renewables. Basically, at each stage, the initial concept of competition has had to be watered down, with protected quotas, ring fences and cross-subsidies – all in an *ad hoc* way. As Professor Ian Fells from Newcastle University put it: 'All these are interventionist elements, and piecemeal intervention is no good when we need a strategy' (UK Electricity Supply Conference, London, July 1990, *The Independent* 5.7.90).

This question of funding for renewables had taken on an extra dimension following the events in the Gulf from August 1990 onwards, with, for example, a *New Scientist* editorial (18.8.90) calling for a rethink, and linking this to the criticisms of energy R & D policy that had emerged from the House of Commons Energy Committee which had concluded: 'we doubt that an R & D programme which involves spending three times as much on nuclear R & D as on all other energy R & D put together is a good reflection of the UK's future energy needs and opportunities' (Energy Committee 1990a). In particular it lamented the 'tiny or declining' R & D budgets for renewables. Perhaps in response to criticisms like this, on August 23 1990 Colin Moynihan, the new Energy Minister responsible for renewables, indicated that the Government was considering providing support to help strengthen the UK wind energy industry. With Howdens already out of the race, and the Wind Energy Group threatening to pull out, that was seen by some as 'too little, too late', especially given that the detailed announcement on these proposals was not to emerge until the following year – by which time there might not be a UK wind industry to support.

The Labour Party had already made it clear that it saw support for renewables as essential. In June 1990 Rhodri Morgan, a Labour energy spokesman, commented:

> 'the Government has dangled all sorts of carrots in front of renewable energy in 1989, but 1990 has been a year of betrayal' . . . [and called for] . . . 'an effective scheme to ensure that renewable energy projects with long payback periods can proceed' . . . [arguing that] . . . 'we need 1–2GW of wind power, with a further 1–2GW of biomass wastes and landfill gas . . . by the end of the century'.

Frank Dobson, Labour's front bench Energy Spokesman, put Labour's criticisms even more forcefully. Speaking at a Combined Heat and Power Conference in June 1990 he commented that: 'the history of the renewable energy programme over the past two decades has been a disgrace to governments' and proposed the establishment of a new Renewable Energy Agency, independent of the UKAEA, to oversee research.

The political battle lines have thus been relatively clearly drawn. Both sides, and those in the middle, wish to be seen as 'green' and as keen to support renewables. Labour has the advantage of being able to enter the situation fresh, although it will presumably be short of cash for renewable projects. The Conservative Government will have to rely on its record and, as we have seen, so far the Government's privatisation programme has arguably hindered as much as helped the development of renewables. Indeed the influential Watt Committee on Energy, a professional association of British energy experts, claimed in a major report on renewables published in November 1990 that: '[The] new institutional and financial factors would seem to positively harm the prospects of increasing the proportion of electricity supplied by renewable sources' (Watt Committee 1990). The practitioners evidently felt similarly, with Peter Musgrove from WEG quoted in *New Scientist* (18 August) as beginning to doubt 'whether they really want renewables to happen' and a *Wind Power Monthly* editorial talking of 'duplicity'.

Renewables were marginalised by the nationalised ESI, and this situation looks likely to continue under privatisation. In the next two chapters we set a new context for ESI policy making, based not on ideology, but on the real and urgent changes in the way we generate and use electricity that will be necessary in the Twenty-first Century. Within this policy context, neglect of the potential of renewable technology will no longer be a viable option.

# PART III

The coming decades will set unprecedented challenges for energy policy, both on the resource and on the environmental fronts. How well will the restructured ESI be able to respond? In Chapter 9 we look at the specific case of the greenhouse effect, a concern which was emerging onto the political agenda at exactly the same moment as the plans for electricity privatisation were being formulated. The impact that the greenhouse phenomenon had on Government rhetoric is contrasted with the effect it had on the Electricity Bill.

Chapter 10 casts a wider net. Starting from scratch, what should the objectives of energy policy be? Having formulated these, we ask what kind of ESI is needed if they are to be achieved? And finally we answer the question set in the Introduction: was the privatisation of the electricity supply industry a step from bad to worse?

# 9 Turning down the heat

'A Hunter, not very bold, was searching for the tracks of a Lion. He asked a man felling oaks in the forest if he had seen any marks of his footsteps, or if he knew where his lair was. "I will", said the Woodman, "at once show you the Lion himself." The Hunter, turning very pale, replied, "No, thank you. I did not ask that; it is his track only I am in search of, not the Lion himself."

The hero is brave in deeds as well as words.' (Aesop c. 570 BC)

## The greenhouse effect and the UK ESI

Without the warming effect of certain atmospheric gases, such as carbon dioxide and methane, life on earth would not be viable. It is not the greenhouse effect *per se* that poses a threat to the future security of humankind, but its enhancement by the activities of our species. Since the Industrial Revolution, and particularly in the last fifty years, the cycles by which naturally occurring greenhouse gases are both produced and absorbed have shifted out of equilibrium. In addition, synthetic greenhouse gases, the chlorofluorocarbons (CFCs), some of which are extremely persistent, have been released into the atmosphere in quantities which are, theoretically, large enough to alter significantly the balance of global temperature. CFCs are also implicated in stratospheric ozone layer depletion, which, while being an issue of immense importance in its own right, is a separate phenomenon and does not contribute to global warming.

Although carbon dioxide ($CO_2$) is a weak greenhouse gas, the large increase in its atmospheric concentration (due mainly to fossil fuel burning, although deforestation has both released biomass $CO_2$ and slowed its photosynthetic capture) means that $CO_2$ is responsible for over half of global warming. Methane, emitted from boggy land (including rice paddies), ruminant animals, and fossil fuel extraction, ranks roughly equal to the CFCs behind $CO_2$ in warming potential. Minor contributors to the problem are nitrous oxide and tropospheric (lower atmospheric) ozone.

The generation of electricity contributes to global warming through the burning of fossil fuels to produce $CO_2$, and, to an unknown but lesser

159

extent, through the release into the atmosphere of methane gas during the extraction and distribution of fossil fuels. Small quantities of nitrous oxide and ozone are also produced by fossil fuel combustion, but the rest of this chapter will discuss $CO_2$ emissions only – mainly because $CO_2$ is the major culprit as far as the ESI is concerned, but also because, as yet, no realistically priced technical fix exists to scrub $CO_2$ from smoke stacks, and therefore production of all four gases is, and will continue to be, very roughly in proportion to the use of fossil fuel by the ESI. Measures to reduce ESI $CO_2$ will, to a varying extent, also reduce methane, nitrous oxide and ozone.

In 1987 UK power stations emitted 202 million tonnes of $CO_2$, 36 per cent of total national emissions. Most of this (32 per cent) was from CEGB stations. The other major emitting sectors were industry (25 per cent), transport (17 per cent) and domestic (15 per cent) (Energy Committee 1989a). As the UK share of global $CO_2$ emissions is three per cent, it can be seen that the ESI accounts for about one per cent of the world total. It is in this context that this Chapter examines the privatisation of the ESI and the greenhouse effect. A fully developed policy response would extend much further than the electricity, or even the energy sector. The small, but significant role the ESI can play as part of a coordinated response to global warming merits an examination of the ramifications of electricity privatisation for global warming.

The different fossil fuels produce different volumes of $CO_2$ when burned to produce electricity. One unit (kWh) of primary energy from coal, oil and gas combustion produces $CO_2$ in the ratios 1:0.82:0.56 respectively (Energy Committee 1989a). When primary energy is converted to electricity the advantage of gas over conventional coal stations is increased if the gas is burned using CCGT, due to the greater thermal efficiency of this technology. CHP plant of any fuel type, although slightly less efficient in terms of $CO_2$ per unit of electricity, is much more effective overall in curtailing $CO_2$, due to the additional savings represented by the $CO_2$ avoided by not having to generate the heat by other means. As was noted in Chapter 5, plant fitted with FGD to reduce $SO_2$ suffers the penalty of decreased thermal efficiency, raising $CO_2$ emissions by up to five per cent.

## Nuclear power and $CO_2$ emissions

The operation of nuclear power stations produces some $CO_2$, through fossil fuel burned in order to construct the station and manufacture fuel (Friends of the Earth 1989). Construction and manufacturing emissions of about one to two per cent of equivalent coal capacity are also attributable to renewable sources such as hydro, wind and tidal, and of less than half of one per cent to energy efficiency measures such as insulation and low energy lighting. Emissions due to current nuclear power stations are about four per cent of the equivalent coal fired capacity, but, if a large number of nuclear stations were constructed world-wide, this figure would rise. As the richer uranium reserves became depleted, poorer grades would have to be used, and correspondingly greater volumes of fossil fuel burned to recover these. Eventually the 'point of futility' is reached when the operation of further nuclear power stations will result in greater $CO_2$ emissions than coal. A programme with the target of generating 50 per cent of the world's electricity by 2020, based on thermal reactors, such as AGRs and PWRs, would exhaust proven uranium reserves of a quality above the point of futility by about 2035 (Donaldson and Betteridge 1990).

These conclusions represent the common ground between the nuclear establishment and its critics (Donaldson and Betteridge 1990; Mortimer 1990, 1991). The implications to be drawn from them for nuclear power and global warming are, however, controversial. There are two main areas of dispute: the status of speculative uranium reserves of an ore quality above the point of futility; and the potential of the Fast Breeder Reactor (FBR) to increase the efficiency with which uranium is used. From the UKAEA it is argued that: 'Realisation of only half the speculative estimate would double the existing resource base and would obviate any need to use extremely low grade ores on a short time scale.' (Donaldson and Betteridge 1990). Mortimer's riposte is that the definition of speculative reserves precludes their use in planning nuclear programmes. On the potential of the FBR to increase the energy available from uranium, Mortimer is pessimistic and the UKAEA more optimistic, while also admitting that: 'It is probably true to say that the FBR will not make any *significant* contribution to ameliorating the greenhouse effect for several decades.' (Donaldson and Betteridge 1990 [italics in original]).

*Climate change*

Scientific knowledge of the greenhouse phenomenon is not adequate to predict the effects on climate of a continuing change in the composition of the atmosphere, although there is a consensus that such changes are likely and that they are far more likely to be deleterious than benign. Changes in continental weather patterns and rises in sea level are among the possible effects. During the period 1987–9, a flurry of activity led to significant advances in understanding, yet it was not until January 1991 that the UK Meteorological Office was able to state that there was more than a 50 per cent chance that observed rises in global temperatures throughout the 1980s were due to pollution.

# The greenhouse effect and the UK Government

Less than twelve months after the enactment of the Electricity Bill, the then Prime Minister, Margaret Thatcher, suggested that it might be necessary to stabilise emissions of carbon dioxide in response to the greenhouse effect. Whether or not this is a sufficient response, it is ironic that the Bill, which offered a golden opportunity to facilitate such reductions, mostly failed to address this question.

Political interest in the greenhouse issue waxed as scientific understanding became disseminated. As this process coincided with the genesis of the electricity privatisation White Papers, and the Parliamentary progress of the Electricity Bill, it is interesting to chart the changes in attitude displayed by Conservative and Government pronouncements over this period, and to see if this had any influence on the framing of the ground rules for the privatised ESI. Although the mechanism by which global warming occurs had first been postulated last century, it was during Margaret Thatcher's second term of office that the publication of research by the US Department of Energy (1985) and the United Nations Environment Programme (Bolin *et al* 1986) had set the first official alarm bells ringing, albeit rather faintly.

By 1987 concern was sufficient for the issue to feature in the Conservative Party Manifesto, although it was cited as a rationale for the continued nuclear programme rather than as an issue in its own right, demanding a fully developed policy response. The nuclear dog was wagging the greenhouse tail:

> 'Coal will continue to meet much of the steadily rising demand for electricity. Renewable sources of energy can make some contribution to the nation's energy needs, which is why Government-sponsored research has been increased. Nevertheless, to reject, as our opponents do, the contribution of nuclear energy to supplying reliable, low-cost electricity, and to depend on coal alone, would be short-sighted and irresponsible.
>
> The world's resources of fossil fuels will come under increasing strain during the 21st century; so may the global environment if the build up of carbon dioxide – the so-called greenhouse effect – significantly raises temperatures and changes climates.
>
> After the most careful and painstaking independent assessment of the safety case for a new pressurised water reactor at Sizewell, therefore, the Government has decided to proceed with the next phase of our nuclear programme.' (Conservative Party 1987)

## The Toronto conference

The event that put global warming firmly on the political agenda was the Toronto-based World Conference on the Changing Atmosphere, convened by the Canadian Government in June 1988. The conference, of scientists and policy makers from 48 countries, issued a sombre statement, guaranteed to make front page news around the world, which began:

> 'Humanity is conducting an uncontrolled, globally pervasive experiment whose ultimate consequences could be second only to a global nuclear war. The Earth's atmosphere is being changed at an unprecedented rate by pollutants resulting from human activities, inefficient and wasteful fossil fuel use and the effects of rapid population growth in many regions. These changes represent a major threat to international security and are already having harmful consequences over many parts of the globe.

Far reaching impacts will be caused by global warming and sea level rise, which are becoming increasingly evident as a result of continued growth in atmospheric concentrations of carbon dioxide and other greenhouse gases. Other major impacts are occurring from ozone layer depletion resulting in increased damage from ultra-violet radiation. The best predictions available indicate potentially severe economic and social dislocation for present and future generations, which will worsen international tensions and increase the risk of conflicts among and within nations. It is imperative to act now.'

The Conference went on to demand internationally coordinated action to grapple with this threat. Recognising that stabilisation of atmospheric $CO_2$ concentrations would require a 50 per cent cut in global emissions, the conference call was for an initial target of a 20 per cent cut (relative to 1988 levels) by the year 2005. It was envisaged that half this reduction would arise from efficiency measures and half from 'modifications in supplies', i.e. switching from high to low $CO_2$ emitting energy sources.

For the UK Government, Lord Caithness, Minister of State for the Environment, sent a message to the conference. This displayed a simultaneous awareness of the potentially catastrophic consequences of global warming, and a marked reluctance to take any ameliorative measures beyond those to which the Government was already committed (such as the Montreal Protocol controlling the production of CFCs) and those that were either market led (such as energy efficiency and realistic energy pricing, incorporating externalities) or involved building nuclear power stations. Whereas the Conference statement called for concomitant research and action, the UK Government believed that, in general, the first should precede the second.

This policy was presented as cautious: waiting for firm evidence before taking action. Given the scale of the possible effects of global warming it might have been thought that *pre*caution, acting in advance of firm evidence, might have been advisable. Even at this stage scientists were pointing out that time was of the essence. Models predict a time lapse of the order of about fifty years between the rise in atmospheric concentrations of greenhouse gases and a rise in global temperature. The earth is already committed to some warming due to past emissions – 'business as usual' now may necessitate more draconian action later. As the Energy Committee put it:

'We believe the *risks* of not adopting targets such as these are so great, and the insurance premia required to achieve them so modest, especially when expressed as a percentage of GDP, that it would be irresponsible to avoid the challenge.' (1989a: para. 147 [italics in original])

## Global warming and the Electricity Bill

The Caithness statement implicitly excluded the adoption of a UK target for the overall reduction of $CO_2$ emissions such as had been suggested by the Toronto conference. This exclusion operated on two levels. The first was a refusal, in the short term, to set a target and a date for its implementation.

More serious was the second level, which was a refusal to plan for the eventual adoption of such a target, in particular by adopting a structure for the privatised ESI that would facilitate a reduction programme.

By the time that the implications of the Toronto conference were sinking into the consciousness of the world's population, the White Papers had already been published and the drafting of the Electricity Bill (under the direction of the Department of Energy, not Environment) was well under-way. Given the complacent attitude of the Department of Environment (the lead Department on the greenhouse issue) it is superficially unsurprising that it was thought acceptable by the Department of Energy to restructure the ESI with no thought of $CO_2$ emissions beyond an ultimately unworkable set of proposals to maintain nuclear generation at its 1988 level by the year 2000. As was seen in Chapters 4 and 6, these proposals sprang much less from a desire to curb global warming than from the prejudices of the politicians and civil servants involved.

Yet, the restructuring of such a major industry will happen only once in a generation. The effect of the Toronto conference was such that no-one could seriously believe that the greenhouse effect was going to fade from the political agenda as quickly as it had arrived. Why was it not realised, when drafting the Bill, that, just as had happened with $SO_2$, action to cut emissions was going to be demanded, if not domestically then internatio-nally, sooner or later? Indeed, the impact of the Toronto conference on UK public opinion was considerably reinforced by the speech that it inspired the then Prime Minister to make at the Royal Society in September 1988. Claiming that international and Government action to protect the environ-ment was one of the greatest challenges of the late Twentieth Century, Mrs Thatcher linked the health of the economy to the health of the environment to make the point that the cost of environmental protection was 'money well and necessarily spent'. The speech, however, contained no proposals as to specific funding for specific projects. As rhetoric it was highly significant, raising the profile of environmental issues across the board in the UK. As far as specific action on global warming was concerned, however, the speech signified nothing.

The mindset behind the 1987 manifesto (nuclear dog with greenhouse tail) was still uppermost in Government thinking. This was demonstrated, not only by the publication of the Electricity Bill in December 1988, but also by the extraordinary outburst of the Secretary of State for the Environment, Nicholas Ridley, in October. Speaking on BBC 1, Mr Ridley claimed that a massive increase in nuclear generation would be required to combat the greenhouse effect as 'the nuclear programme is the only serious way of reducing our carbon emissions'. Plans for such an expansion were, however, rapidly denied by Whitehall sources. Ridley's gaffe was attributed to his over-enthusiastic interpretation of a Department of Energy brief, which had suggested that the White Paper proposals to protect nuclear power could, in part, be justified by pointing out the environmental prob-lems caused by coal burning, such as acid rain and the greenhouse effect.

By early 1989, while the Bill was in House of Commons Committee, the Energy Committee had started its investigation into the greenhouse effect. Department of Energy evidence showed that, despite the increased profile given to the greenhouse issue by ministers, the Government was still clinging to the Caithness policy, as given to the Toronto conference. The Energy Committee Report (1989a) noted that market mechanisms alone will not produce an adequate response to global warming, and advocated that the Government should encourage the ESI incrementally to invest in all energy production systems which reduce greenhouse emissions. The Committee noted the willingness of the Government to provide such encouragement for nuclear power and urged that the non-fossil fuel obligation should be expanded to cover energy efficiency and combined heat and power. To reinforce the seriousness of these recommendations the Report concluded:

'It would be inexcusable if pusillanimity and the inability of the Governments of the world to plan long-term allowed irreversible and disastrous global warming to occur for want of the means or the political will to take effective action to curb it.
   It would be irresponsible not to adopt targets for reducing greenhouse emissions, especially when the costs of doing so are modest.'

The role of this Report in the reversal by the House of Commons of the Lords' amendment on energy efficiency was noted in Chapter 4. Resisting considerable pressure, partly engendered by the Report and emanating even from its own backbenchers, the Government rejected the amendment. In its response to the Report the Government reiterated, yet again, the Caithness line. Despite the Committee's recommendation, that a $CO_2$ emission target should be set, the Government refused and justified its stance by reference to the then impending report of the InterGovernmental Panel on Climate Change (IPCC):

'. . . more data is clearly needed, and it is expected that the preliminary work of the IPCC, in which the UK plays a major role, . . . will provide further and expert assessment of impacts and possible responses to allow future policy to be more soundly based than is possible at present.' (Department of Energy in Energy Committee 1989c: para. 1.3)

As far as the privatisation of the ESI was concerned, the IPCC report (eventually published in May 1990) was irrelevant. By this time the Electricity Bill had been enacted for eleven months, and the new plcs were vested with a regulatory and contractual framework in place. All of this had taken place against the background of a growing rhetorical recognition by the Government that global warming was an issue of the utmost international importance:

'We have unwittingly begun a massive experiment with the system of this planet . . .' (Margaret Thatcher 27 September 1988 in speech to Royal Society).

165

'The Government has been at the forefront of those who have identified global warming, and associated climate changes, as one of the most important issues facing the world today. . . . These changes could, at the worst, have devastating effects on the world's geography and ecosystems, and on human economic, social, and cultural life.' (Department of Energy in Energy Committee (1989c))

'Of all the challenges faced by the world community in the last four years, one has grown clearer than any other in both urgency and importance – I refer to the threat to our global environment.' (Margaret Thatcher 8 November 1989 in speech to United Nations)

## A target for CO₂ emissions

The IPCC report, when it arrived, did not make these statements seem at all exaggerated. The panel's 'business as usual' scenario, in which current trends of fossil fuel use continue, gave a predicted rise of 3°C in global mean temperature by 2100, leading to a rise in sea level of 65 cm. In response the Government made its long awaited commitment on $CO_2$ emissions. As a contribution to international action the UK would reduce by up to 30 per cent *projected* $CO_2$ emissions by the year 2005. The effect of this would be a stabilisation of emissions over 15 years, as the proposed reduction equalled projected increases.

The target was criticised as displaying the very pusillanimity against which the Energy Committee had warned ten months before. The limitation of $CO_2$ control to stabilisation, rather than reduction, and the length of time anticipated to meet even this limited objective, were widely derided – even before the dubious basis of this target was exposed. It emerged that the Department of Energy computer model used to predict 'business as usual' $CO_2$ emissions was defective, and that a growth in $CO_2$ emissions of as much as 30 per cent by 2005 was unlikely. Stabilisation by this date was correspondingly less of a challenge than Mrs Thatcher had claimed when announcing the target. International comparisons were also made. Despite the impression, given by the Government since the Toronto conference, that Britain was at the forefront of international action on global warming, and the insistence by Thatcher that the UK would not set a unilateral target, many of our EC partners had already made commitments to stabilise, or even cut, their $CO_2$ emissions by the year 2000.

### The Environment White Paper

Whatever the merits of the target, how was it to be implemented in an energy sector modelled on the Lawson doctrine? Targets imply Government intervention and planning, concepts hitherto anathema (at least rhetorically) to the post–1979 Conservative Government. This mystery was somewhat resolved with the publication of the Environment White Paper (Department of Environment 1990) in September 1990. The

166

'demanding target of returning emissions of carbon dioxide, the dominant greenhouse gas, to 1990 levels by 2005' was reiterated, coupled to action on methane and CFCs which would reduce the overall warming potential of British emissions by 20 per cent by the same date.

The ESI privatisation legislation was hailed as helpful to meeting this target:

> '. . . the changes being brought about by the Electricity Act 1989 are likely to have a beneficial effect in reducing electricity $CO_2$ emissions. The Act will introduce competition among electricity generators, giving a strong incentive to generate energy more efficiently, and encourage electricity generation from non-fossil fuels. Indeed the two major non-nuclear electricity companies in England and Wales (PowerGen and National Power) believe that their intended installation of high efficiency gas-fired plant, and greater use of renewables, will hold their $CO_2$ approximately constant for the foreseeable future, whereas the Government's earlier projections for the electricity supply industry assumed some growth.' (Department of Environment 1990: para. 5.23)

The remainder of this chapter will analyse these claims in an attempt to predict how easy it will be for the ESI to meet, not just the current UK $CO_2$ target, but the more demanding cuts that lie on the horizon as international concern and action on global warming grow. Two issues underlie this analysis: planning and flexibility. The potential of the privatised ESI to respond to global warming illustrates its potential responsiveness to other pressures, both economic and environmental – the specifics of which are currently unforeseen – which are very likely to arise between now and the end of the century.

## Competition

The Environment White Paper's claim that competition would bring increased efficiency in generation was not novel – it had been the standard Government response, during the Parliamentary debates on the Electricity Bill, to criticism that the cause of energy efficiency would not be moved forward by that legislation. It is true that private ownership may give an impetus towards productive efficiency above that which is found under public ownership, but this effect is limited in the absence of competition (Kay and Thompson 1986). Thus, in existing, say, coal fired plant the efficiency with which heat energy from the combustion of coal is transformed into electricity may improve slightly. This improvement, if it occurs, is likely in reality to be marginal as the recent CEGB record of improving thermal efficiency may have left little further scope for further increases.

New plant offers much larger potential efficiency gains. In as much as privatisation has provided the spur to investment in CCGT it can be held responsible for the stabilisation in $CO_2$ referred to in the White Paper. In part, however, this is fortuitous. The higher thermal efficiency of CCGT gives it an economic, as well as an environmental advantage, and thus competitive pressures lead directly to $CO_2$ reductions. However, the greater part of the forecast reduction in $CO_2$ is due, not to efficiency gains, but to the switch from coal to gas. This is almost entirely coincidental: had gas produced more, not less $CO_2$ than coal, investment in CCGT would still have proceeded apace. Concern by investors about future $CO_2$ emission limits would have operated at the margin of the investment decision, but would not have outweighed the clear economic advantage.

The CEGB was dependent on coal for 78 per cent of the electricity it supplied in 1988-9. Although the quantity of coal burn in power stations must decline, if emissions of $CO_2$ are to fall, this large dependence means that coal will remain an important fuel source for the ESI for many years ahead. Carbon dioxide emissions per unit of coal fuelled electricity would be significantly reduced, however, by the development of advanced coal burning technologies, such as fluidised bed combustion (FBC) and integrated gasification combined cycle (IGCC), or a hybrid of the two known as topping cycle plant. A research facility into these technologies is based at Grimethorpe in Yorkshire.

These novel coal burning techniques offer large efficiency gains (sufficient to reduce $CO_2$ emissions by up to 25 per cent compared with conventional coal plant [Energy Committee 1989a]) combined with the flexibility of small plant size. As such, it might be thought that this technology would be rapidly deployed in the privatised industry. However, the research funds necessary to bring the technology to commercial fruition are in short supply. British Coal, having pledged £11.5 million of the £27.5 million required to continue the Grimethorpe project, is unable to offer more because of Government pressure to show an operating profit. Despite £5 million raised from the Finnish Ahlstrom Corporation, and expressions of support from the Department of Energy, the Treasury seemed reluctant to commit further public funds, believing that more private money should be found (Energy Committee 1989a). The short-term availability of cheap gas, however, means that private sector interest is not high. The announcement in early 1991 of a £3.7 million grant from the Department of Energy will tide the project over for a further year, but future funding is still uncertain.

Innovation is often a casualty of undue reliance on competition: in this case market failure has perhaps been narrowly avoided. The paucity of the sums of money, quibbled over by the Government, which were needed to secure the future of a most promising technology, both economically and environmentally, is striking. This is especially so when they are compared to past and present subsidies to nuclear power. The Grimethorpe example demonstrates that, although in some ways competition enhances the prospects for $CO_2$ reduction, this is not an automatic correlation. If short-termism stifles beneficial technological developments, competition may act to the detriment of reduction programmes.

*Non-fossil generation – nuclear*

As we have seen, the potential role of nuclear power in reducing $CO_2$ emissions is contentious. The most vociferous lobbyists for $CO_2$ reduction are the environmental pressure groups, whose total opposition to nuclear power is long standing. Some see this stance as contradictory:

'I found one of the most depressing aspects of the Hinkley Point inquiries was that when an issue of such momentous potential importance as global warming arose an obvious contribution to a solution to that problem, increased reliance on nuclear power, should be resisted as a matter of principle by organisations genuinely concerned with the environment.' (Barnes 1990: para. 32.68)

The groups are able to defend themselves by citing the potential for energy efficiency to reduce $CO_2$ emissions more rapidly, and at less cost, than nuclear power. In their view, to build nuclear power stations as a response to global warming is a gross misallocation of resources (Keepin and Kats 1988; Toke 1989). For the purposes of the present analysis the question of whether or not a programme of nuclear power stations in the UK would be a worthwhile contribution to the amelioration of the greenhouse effect is somewhat irrelevant. What matters is that, at the time that the foundations of the ESI privatisation were being shaped, the Government believed that it would be. The Caithness statement demonstrated this and, as the Secretary of State's letter giving permission for the Hinkley 'C' PWR demonstrated, this belief continued beyond the time when the PWR programme was abandoned:

'There are . . . potentially substantial advantages to the global environment from the displacement of fossil fuel combustion by nuclear power. It is the Government's policy not to approve investment in further PWR stations unless they are assessed as being economic over their life taken as a whole, having regard to these wider factors.' (Department of Energy 1990b)

This is an oblique reference to the new approach that is being developed for 1994, when the moratorium on nuclear power station construction will be reconsidered. The nuclear balance sheet will be redrawn, by crediting the technology with its external benefits. The two main areas of credit will be environmental ($CO_2$ and $SO_2$) and diversity (protection against fossil fuel price volatility and supply interruptions). The methodology used will be regarded with the utmost suspicion by the anti-nuclear power movement, who fear that undue weight will be given to the benefits, and too little to the disadvantages, of nuclear power in this analysis.

Such suspicions may be justified, since the nuclear industry is institutionally very well placed to make a come-back in 1994. The creation of Nuclear Electric, in the state sector, as a single purpose nuclear generator, backed up by BNF and UKAEA, has streamlined the nuclear caucus. Nuclear Electric plc will obviously have a strong institutional interest in seeking future development. Their bullish attitude was signalled by the decision of John Collier, in the aftermath of the November 1989 decision, not to withdraw the application for consent for Hinkley 'C', despite the fact that no capital investment sanction will be granted by the Government until 1994, if then. Consent by the Secretary of State for Energy was subsequently granted.

British Nuclear Fuels, its structure and ownership unaffected by the current round of privatisation, is expending much effort on promotion and public relations, and has announced that it is developing proposals, which will be ready in time for 1994, to build new PWRs to replace its ageing military Magnox stations at Calder Hall and Chapelcross. The UKAEA is under threat of reorganisation, and is diversifying as quickly as it can into non-nuclear areas, but can still be counted a significant nuclear supporter. Support from the industry's trade unions is undiminished.

The industry is taking the 1994 review extremely seriously: as well as developing the new methodology for assessing the cost of nuclear power, the operation of existing plant is being subjected to an efficiency review. The ambition of John Collier, the Chair of Nuclear Electric, is to reduce the subsidy to nuclear power represented by the fossil fuel levy, if possible to zero. However, despite expectations of a steadily declining levy, the 1991–2 percentage rate is 11 per cent, 0.4 per cent higher than the previous year's. This increased rate is due to lower than expected electricity prices and high levels of non-leviable non-fossil electricity imports, rather than a rise in nuclear power costs.

However, the levy is a clear indicator that nuclear power is not currently competitive, and it is obviously in the interest of Nuclear Electric to minimise this stigma. The exemption granted to this State aid by the European Community expires anyway in 1998. Using public sector investment criteria, which reduce the cost of capital, will help Nuclear Electric in this task. The poor performance of the AGR stations will be improved if the on-load refuelling, for which they were designed, can be made to work. Other areas for improvement in the profit and loss account lie in back-end costs. Storage of AGR fuel, rather than reprocessing, is increasingly being seen as an option. Plans to decommission reactors to a green field site are now being seen as unnecessarily ambitious. A cheaper option is permanently to entomb the reactor after demolition of peripheral buildings (Passant 1990).

Even if costs can be reduced to the extent necessary to enable a political decision to revive the UK nuclear programme, it would take decades to build this programme up to a size where it could displace enough fossil fuel burning to have a significant effect on $CO_2$ emissions. For the UK the question of whether nuclear power has any potential as part of a strategy to curb $CO_2$ emissions is irrelevant in the short and medium terms. As a result of the privatisation fiasco, the nuclear industry is not in a fit state to meet the challenge of prospective $CO_2$ reduction targets in the early years of the next century.

*Non-fossil generation – renewable*

Deployment of renewables would be vital whatever the prospects for nuclear power, in order to displace as much fossil generation as possible. Because of the inability of nuclear to make a meaningful contribution, the role of renewables becomes more significant. The Environment White Paper set a target of around 1 GW by the year 2000, whereas many observers feel that much more could be achieved given sufficient funding, perhaps as much as 4 GW.

The case for treating the development of renewables as a strategic supply priority within an overall policy of $CO_2$ reduction rests on both short and long term arguments. In the short term, several of the renewables are already economically competitive with conventional and, of course, nuclear generation. Even given the tight financial conditions so far imposed in the renewable NFFO, micro-hydro, refuse as fuel and, to a lesser extent, wind power are all moving ahead. A 'least cost' approach should favour these options. In addition they are quick to install.

The longer term case is based on the simple fact that these are *renewable* resources – indigenous and sustainable – with no threat of unexpected price increases or disruption. If assessed using the methodology which is currently being developed for the 1994 nuclear review, these advantages would be costed in so that some of the currently less economic options, such as wave power, might become competitive. Both nuclear power and renewables, if used to displace fossil fuel combustion, reduce $CO_2$ emissions. The major advantage that renewables hold over nuclear power rests on the resource base. As long as the sun shines onto planet Earth, renewables will be able to harness that energy. In contrast, as was seen earlier, a thermal nuclear reactor programme large enough to impact on global warming would exhaust all proven uranium reserves in a matter of decades.

As was seen in Chapter 8, present Government policy is not greatly facilitating the deployment of renewables, which is likely to be slow in the privatised ESI. The only glimmer of light is the non-fossil fuel obligation which offers some scope to achieve greater progress, particularly if the EC will allow an extension of the 1998 time limit. As with nuclear, the technical possibilities of renewable technologies become irrelevant if political and structural obstacles frustrate their development. The choices that lie ahead will be made on both the technical and on the political levels. In this context it is interesting to note the promotion of renewables as the natural companions to nuclear by some of its advocates. This thinking has been echoed by the Secretary of State: '. . . renewable and nuclear generating capacity should not be regarded as competitors: both have a part to play.' (Department of Energy 1990b).

History has shown that renewables tend to be marginalised by the nuclear industry. Given the very different technological characteristics of these two options, and the different institutional structures they require for their development, this is not surprising. Should a nuclear programme ever get off the ground again in the UK, it is likely that the development of renewables would suffer as a result.

*The absent agenda*

Interestingly, the Environment White Paper only claimed that the Electricity Act will give incentives for supply side efficiency: the claims in respect of end-use efficiency that were used to defeat the Lords' amendment were not thought to be worth repeating. Yet there is universal consensus on the potential efficacy that improvements in energy efficiency currently offer as cost-effective means of cutting $CO_2$ emissions:

'Fuel substitution and new technologies of fuel use offer only limited and often contentious means of curbing $CO_2$ emissions. In contrast, *the most striking feature of our Enquiry has been the extent to which improvements in energy efficiency – across all sectors of the economy – are almost universally seen as the most obvious and most effective response to the problem of global warming.* Energy efficiency investments offer multiple attractions: many are inherently economically attractive at present energy prices, whilst others are relatively low cost; they are environmentally benign, and they are capable of speedy introduction, thereby ensuring an early reduction in $CO_2$ emissions. The Government through the Secretary of State, one of its Ministers and the Department of Energy; the electricity supply industry as represented by the Electricity Council, the CEGB and the UKAEA; other major energy supply interests such as BP, BG and BC; environmental interests as represented by FoE, Greenpeace and the World Wide Fund for Nature (WWF); and research institutions such as ETSU and the Open University as well as, more predictably, ACE, the pressure group funded by the energy efficiency industry, were in rare agreement, all seeing enormous and inherently attractive scope for a reduction in $CO_2$ emissions through energy efficiency investments.' (Energy Committee 1989a: para. 102 [emphasis in original]).

Unlike the Environment White Paper, the Energy Committee did express a view on the impact of ESI privatisation on the prospects for efficiency improvements. Having noted the nature of the market failures which currently block the implementation of cost-effective improvements, the Committee quoted the CEGB: 'significant reductions in (energy) consumption would require direct or indirect intervention by Government across all forms of energy use, whether by regulation, pricing or subsidy.' (para. 111). Such interventions, in the opinion of the Committee, would be more difficult after privatisation, although Chapter 7 shows that there is potential to manipulate the regulatory framework set up by the Act in ways that its drafters did not intend.

*Carbon taxation and the non-fossil fuel obligation*

In spite of the approval given in the Caithness statement to the principle of incorporation of external costs into fuel pricing, the Government remained sceptical about carbon taxation in practice:

172

'Long term measures affecting the relative price of energy can only sensibly be taken when competitor countries are prepared to take similar action. Unilateral action by Britain would do little to influence global warming. It would have a damaging impact on activity and employment in the energy intensive sectors, relative to our competitors, to little purpose. In the immediate future the reduction of inflation is of overriding importance. Given this, and our best assessment of how long it will take to achieve an international consensus, tax or other measures directly raising the relative price of energy outside the transport sector will not be introduced in the next few years.' (Department of Environment 1990)

Yet one of the measures introduced by the Electricity Act, the fossil fuel levy, used to finance the non-fossil fuel obligation, might be thought of as a carbon tax. The Government has chosen not to present it in this way: the Environment White Paper, a comprehensive review of Government thinking on green issues in 1990, makes no linkage between the two.

Partly this is because the main justifications for the NFFO were, at the outset, diversity and security of supply. The greenhouse effect was used only as a supplementary and superficial justification, never a main defence. Also the crudity of the fossil fuel levy, looked at in terms of carbon taxation, would leave the Government open to ridicule if it did attempt to present the levy in this light. The levy does not differentiate between the different fossil fuels: gas, with its much lower $CO_2$ to primary energy ratio, is taxed at the same rate as coal. The levy applies only to the electricity industry in England and Wales, leading to intranational, as well as international market distortions.

The Energy Committee recommended, rather than a carbon tax, a system of comprehensive energy taxation by the EC to take into account the transboundary externalities of energy production, the proceeds to be applied to investment in energy efficiency (Energy Committee 1989a: para. 141). This chapter has shown that the Government record on rhetoric is much better than its record on action, as far as the greenhouse effect is concerned, so the prospects for such a tax are distant. Yet again, a contrast with the favouritism shown towards nuclear power has to be drawn. Carbon taxation must wait for consensus abroad and economic recovery at home: yet the fossil fuel levy is acceptable as a way of subsidising nuclear power. Whatever the problems raised by carbon taxation, and there are many (Owens et al 1990), a whiff of double standards is in the air.

Forms of carbon taxation are widely used by our European competitors. In Holland and Denmark the proceeds of fossil fuel taxation are used for environmental purposes. Germany is planning to introduce such a tax, while, outside the EC, Finland and Sweden have already implemented one. In this context the UK's refusal to act 'unilaterally' does not stand up.

## Markets – incomplete solutions

As well as the unanimity on energy efficiency, the Energy Committee found a second area of widespread consensus:

'Our witnesses were virtually unanimous in conceding that *market mechanisms unaided would not produce an adequate response to global warming.* . . . This is not to say that market forces will have no part to play: . . . However, as we have explained in the section on energy efficiency, we should like to see these market forces in favour of moderating demand fortified by the fiscal system, regulatory measures and incentives.' (Energy Committee 1989a: para. 134 [emphasis in original]).

Atmospheric pollution by greenhouse gases is the tragedy of the commons (Chapter 1) written on a global scale. The untrammelled pursuit of self interest, on an individual and on a national level, will lead to disaster. A collectively, rather than an individually, based response is vital, and this accounts for much of the Government's paralysis even once the scale of the problem had been grasped – hence the rhetoric. Collective solutions were anathema to the Thatcher Governments. As a result of this ideological blindness, the ESI has been reshaped with scant regard for what is likely to become the most important energy policy consideration of the Twenty-first Century: the greenhouse effect.

# 10 From bad to worse?

'As international diplomacy faces the problems of CFCs, carbon emissions and acid rain, as the world faces the prospect of new crises of hunger and disease, the monotonous invocation of the market as an all-embracing solution is simply not credible.' (Gordon Brown *The Independent* 27 July 1990)

## A new agenda

The analysis of policy in this book has focused on two levels: the level of political choice, where objectives are set and individual decisions are made, and the structural level. Institutional structure can either facilitate or constrain choices – just as the development of nuclear power was fostered by the corporatist nationalised ESI, so it was precluded in the privatised, liberalised industry.

The description of ESI privatisation in previous chapters has been more descriptive than prescriptive. Although inconsistencies in, and absences from, the Government's agenda have been noted, there has been little attempt to present an alternative set of coherent energy policy objectives. In moving, as we do in the first half of this chapter, from mere criticism to advocacy of alternative approaches, recognition of the relationship between structure and choice is vital.

Political choice traditionally has been circumscribed by the structure of the ESI. Chapter 3 showed how insider groups flourished at the expense of outsiders. Many rational political options were precluded: action to improve national energy efficiency; development of renewable sources of energy; and CHP. None of these received more than marginal and grudging support from a Government and industry caucus intent on preserving the status quo.

Consideration of the crucial role of structure reveals the extent to which ESI privatisation was a missed opportunity. A rational restructuring of the

ESI would involve, first defining a coherent set of policy objectives, and then, deciding on the structure best suited to facilitate these. Structure would then be subordinate to choice, rather than the other way around. Indeed, it can be argued that, to some extent this is what the Government did – but not in a coherent and sustained way. Fostering competition necessitated the break up of the CEGB: but the limitation of this break up to a generating duopoly was predicated on the narrow policy objective of sustaining and privatising the nuclear power programme. Because of this ultimately futile ambition much wider policy objectives (competition and liberalisation) will be constrained in the privatised ESI.

Talk of 'rational decision making' can attract the charge of utopianism. Change always starts from a status quo which itself determines the boundaries of choice. Choice and structure, means and ends, facts and values cannot easily be separated. Policy implementation is an iterative process, as unexpected consequences arise and have to be allowed for (Ham and Hill 1984). The ESI privatisation has shown this very clearly. Idealised models of whole societies, let alone the UK ESI, can be drafted on paper, but there they will remain. Yet one very positive lesson of the Thatcher years is that wholesale reshaping of entire policy sectors *is* possible. Corporatism can be picked up by the scruff of its neck and shaken out. Restructuring into an ideal type cannot be achieved, but substantial incremental change in line with policy objectives can be viable.

The question which this book set out to explore is in fact two questions. Was the nationalised ESI 'bad'? And will the privatised ESI be 'worse'? These two questions then beg many others: bad for whom? Worse in which respects? By defining what the objectives of energy policy in the late Twentieth Century should be, past, present and potential future structures can be evaluated for suitability in achieving these. The policy objectives here advocated for the UK ESI are more comprehensive and fundamental than those with which the Government embarked on its privatisation. Common elements between the two sets of objectives are, however, to be found. The potential for achievement of these objectives is limited by a host of factors, not least the now accomplished transfer of the industry into private ownership. Yet progress towards implementation of this new agenda is possible, given the political will.

## The four essential objectives

### Sustainability

The four essential objectives of energy policy are sustainability, equity, efficiency and flexibility. Of these, sustainability is paramount. The objectives interact: gross inequity, inefficiency or inflexibility preclude sustainability – just as inflexibility tends to preclude efficiency. Indeed Pearce *et al* include equity as one of the three key characteristics of sustainable development:

'a substantially increased emphasis on the value of natural, built and cultural environments; . . . a concern both with short- to medium-term horizons . . . and with the longer-run future to be inherited by our grandchildren, and perhaps beyond; . . . emphasis on providing for the needs of the least advantaged in society ("intragenerational equity") and on a fair treatment of future generations ("intergenerational equity").' (1989: 2)

The energy (and therefore the electricity) policy sector is one where the issue of sustainability is particularly acute. The dependence of human societies on energy is matched by the pervasiveness of the environmental impact of energy use. No method of generating electricity exists which does not create environmental damage. This damage may be, *inter alia* to the atmosphere, ($CO_2$ and $SO_2$), to rivers and the sea (thermal and radioactive pollution), to landscape (wind farms and nuclear power stations) or to complex eco-systems (tidal barrages). Some technologies are less malign than others, but all have a substantial environmental impact.

Similarly, medium and long term horizons are of considerable importance in electricity policy. There are several reasons for this. The environmental damage caused by electricity generation may be transient, as with the eyesore caused by a windmill during the time it is on site. More often the damage has medium to long term ramifications, as with $SO_2$ and $CO_2$ pollution. In the case of some large scale projects, such as hydro-electric dams and barrages, effectively irreversible damage to habitats may occur.

Depletion of fossil fuels is in excess of their replenishment by geological processes by many orders of magnitude. Although the 'doomwatch' scenario posited in the late 1960s, of oil shortages due to exhaustion of reserves, has not yet materialised, it is a simple fact that consumption in excess of production will, one day, create scarcity. In this context the sterilisation of coal reserves by pit closures which are justified by conventional economics, seems questionable when measured against the longer-term criterion of sustainable development.

The technical characteristics of the ESI, including the non-storability of electricity and the long lead times for consent and construction of new generating stations, also show the importance of making ESI decisions with regard to the longer, rather than the shorter, term. Security of supply is one aspect of sustainability. An energy policy that is truly sustainable will need a decision making structure that takes account of the long term.

Unfettered free markets are inadequate to this task, as was seen in Chapter 1. Corporatist institutions are better able to take a long view – thus the CEGB was able to implement a nuclear power programme in a way that the liberalised industry was not. However, the long term view taken by such bodies will be very heavily coloured by institutional self interest and, therefore, is likely to be resistant to change. In addition, corporatism leads to producer domination and consequent inefficiency, inflexibility and inequity. A decentralised industry, with the Government discharging its responsibility for long term planning through a flexible regulatory system would seem to be best suited to deliver the sustainability objective.

## Equity

Energy policy poses several questions of equity. Intergenerational equity is one of them. The philosophy of sustainable development suggests that each generation should bequeath its successors at least as much capital stock (including environmental capital stock) as it itself inherited. This has many implications for energy policy. It means that, as fossil fuels are depleted, there rest obligations upon this generation, not only to adopt prudent and frugal depletion policies, but also to develop alternatives, so that future generations will not be starved of energy as a result of present day activities.

Furthermore, many of the environmental costs of present day energy consumption will be felt, not by the generation that benefited from the usage, but by future generations. This is true of $CO_2$ emissions, where there is a predicted time lag of fifty years between rises in atmospheric $CO_2$ and changes in global climate. It is also true of nuclear power: the timetable for decommissioning stations is of the order of a century, while plutonium waste from thermal stations has a radioactive half-life of 25 000 years.

On an intragenerational timescale, the avoidance of fuel poverty is the most obvious equity consideration. Affordable energy services for the least well-off will not be guaranteed by the market alone, anymore than this was achieved by the nationalised ESI. Targeted intervention to improve end-use efficiency by low income groups is the most effective way to alleviate fuel poverty, and the institutional and regulatory framework of the ESI should be designed to facilitate and encourage such initiatives.

A different aspect of equity is that of equality between different technologies: the concept of the 'level playing field'. Chapter 3 described the exclusion of some technologies enforced by the structure of the nationalised ESI. In Chapter 6 it was shown how irrational favouritism towards nuclear power had adversely affected, not just other technologies, but also wider political objectives, such as competition. Prejudice will always colour decision making: the issue is not rationality *per se*, but power. An equitable ESI will be one where the power of vested interest has been dispersed. Dispersal of producer power could lead to more equal consumer/producer relations, and to greater equality between advocates of demand and supply side measures – as well as a more level playing field between different generating technologies.

The new ESI fails to meet this requirement. The generating duopoly, although much less powerful than its predecessor, still commands monopoly power to such an extent as to be described as 'corporatist' by a *Financial Times* Editorial (13 February 1990). The nuclear power lobby, now again firmly ensconced in the public sector, is rapidly reforming itself

178

in order to prepare for the 1994 review. Meanwhile, proponents of alternative generating technologies and energy efficiency are finding the struggle to implement their ideas as difficult as ever.

International equity is also an issue. The present unsustainable patterns of fossil fuel use in the developed world have so adversely affected the atmosphere that it is very likely that the global climate is changing. Repetition of similar development paths by the Third World is, therefore, incompatible with greenhouse damage limitation. International equity demands that not only should the First World do all it can to ameliorate the effects of its energy profligacy on the global commons, but also compensate the developing nations for this damage. An equitable, if utopian, solution is an international carbon permit scheme (Grubb 1990). The proposal is for a global agency to lease carbon permits. Each country would be permitted to emit a per capita quota of $CO_2$. Emissions in excess of this quota would require the emitting nation to purchase the allocation of a less developed country. Ideally the quota would be paid for by $CO_2$ reducing technology transfer, not money.

Whatever the likelihood of implementation of such a scheme, it deals mainly with the greenhouse effect, yet this is only one constraint on the potential energy use by developing countries. Finite resources, of both fossil fuels and uranium, will place ceilings on the capacity of the South to match the energy consumption of the North. Fortunately, meaningful equity relates not to energy consumption, but to the benefit that nations derive from the fuels they use. Increased efficiency and rapid deployment of renewables, North and South, are the necessary precursors of a shift towards greater equality. This implies substantial technology transfer in order to facilitate a different development pattern in the South to the disastrous one followed by the North.

*Efficiency*

Energy policy should include within its objectives both economic and energy efficiency. There is, of course, considerable overlap between these concepts. Wasted energy is wasted money. However, the two are not synonymous. Both the nationalised and the restructured ESI have been subject to a regulatory system, which, while ostensibly designed to promote economic efficiency, has encouraged over-production and wasteful consumption of energy.

The narrow economic goals of productive and allocative efficiencies have been prejudiced by the failure to liberalise the generating industry more radically. Private ownership gives an increased incentive to productive efficiency (including thermal efficiency in conventional plant), but in a firm with substantial market power this spur is weakened (Kay and Thompson 1986). Allocative efficiency is promoted by competition: again, market power diminishes this effect. The break-up of power blocs by liberalisation and decentralisation is a prerequisite of economic efficiency. Such a break-up will tend to result in energy prices being set at a level that reflects the costs of production. Regulation can ensure the incorporation of at least some externalities into this cost structure. End-use efficiency can be encouraged by pricing policies based on true marginal costs – but only to some extent. Market imperfections mean that liberalisation of the supply-side does not bring end-use efficiency automatically through the operation of market forces. Consumer inertia may make the response to higher energy prices inelastic.

Intervention to promote end-use efficiency must therefore be two pronged, acting simultaneously at the supply and at the demand level in order to provide enhanced incentives to efficiency. Demand management is best facilitated by a decentralised approach. Thus, decentralisation promotes efficiency in both its senses.

Thermal efficiency at the point of generation, defined as units of electricity produced from a given quantity of primary fuel, is an aspect of productive efficiency. Adapting generating technology in order to utilise waste heat, via CHP and District Heating schemes, is a different matter. Such schemes can make economic as well as environmental sense, but substantial organisation and investment is necessary in order to reap the benefits. Yet again, a decentralised approach is advantageous. For a large, supply-orientated, generating company, a CHP scheme may appear to be more trouble than it is worth: a REC, a local authority or independent generator, more in touch with the potential consumers of the heat and power, may have a better perception of the need, and a realisation of the scale of any difficulties and how these can be overcome.

*Flexibility*

The last twenty years have been littered with unexpected events demanding an energy policy response. From the Yom Kippur War, to the OPEC dispute of 1985–6, to the Kuwaiti conflagration which overshadowed the final stages of the ESI privatisation, the volatility of oil prices, and the insecurity inherent in dependence on imported fuels, has been amply demonstrated. Warnings from environmentalists about the planetary implications of profligate energy consumption, dismissed as laughable in the early 1970s, are now solemnly intoned by senior politicians. Cassandra-like predictions from the same quarter about the safety and cost of nuclear power, similarly dismissed at first, are far less open to question in the post-Chernobyl, and post-ESI privatisation eras.

It seems certain that such changes will continue, and that some will be sudden. What is uncertain is the precise nature of these shocks. Preparation for response must therefore be based on flexibility, with an eye to self sufficiency and security of supply. Market mechanisms are, in general, more flexible than command structures, provided they are structured so that the correct messages are transmitted through the price structure. Diversity is another obvious prescription, but this must be true diversity, not the narrow fossil/non-fossil dichotomy used by the Government in its futile defence of nuclear power during 1988–9.

An energy policy seeking genuine diversity would promote multiplicity of generators (decentralisation again) and of generating technologies (including renewables and CHP). Flexibility also demands that most power stations should be on a smaller, rather than a larger scale, implying shorter lead times. Because a leaner and less wasteful ESI will be better placed to weather future storms, the need for flexibility reinforces the need for efficient use of energy.

## An idealised structure for the ESI

If the four objectives outlined above, rather than Cecil Parkinson's six principles, had guided the restructuring of the ESI, what would have been the outcome? An electricity industry best able to facilitate these objectives would be:

- decentralised and fragmented
- market-based
- regulated to provide command and market incentives for end-use efficiency and good environmental practice
- regulated to prevent abuse of residual monopoly power
- diverse
- subject to strategic Government intervention in pursuit of long term policy goals

Power blocs on the generating side could have been dispersed by the creation of at least six, and possibly more, competing companies. On the supply and distribution side, natural monopoly limits the potential for competition, but there is no inherent reason why there have to be only twelve distribution companies. Much further breakdown into county or metropolitan sized areas (the precise boundaries based on technical considerations) would have been possible without unduly compromising economies of scale. Such a breakdown would increase the potential for competition at area boundaries and increase the potential for community based demand management and CHP schemes (Armstrong and Cooper 1990). In Sweden, for example, municipalities play an important role in the energy economy running CHP.

Market forces within such a liberalised ESI would give the best guarantee of prices which reflected the true costs of production. Lack of market power would prevent anomalies, such as those found by the Price Waterhouse review of the CEGB's Bulk Supply Tariff, which lead to inefficient over-production of electricity. Over-pricing by generators would be similarly discouraged, although the monopoly activities of transmission and distribution would still need to be price regulated. However, decentralisation should not be taken as far as the dismantling of the National Grid. The operation of the Grid enhances flexibility and efficiency and facilitates decentralisation in generation and supply. The transfer of bulk supplies between regions means there is an overall need for a much smaller capacity margin to cover plant breakdown. With the increased deployment of intermittent renewable sources of power, the ability of the Grid to absorb these will be vital. In addition, a National Grid, acting as a market maker between the generating and supply sides, would have a potentially vital role to play in regulating (via price signals, or command, or most likely both) the market in accordance with the four prime objectives.

In a decentralised ESI the Grid would, therefore, be the most powerful body. The impetus for abuse of this power would not be as great as for the generators or distributors. As a predominantly regulatory and mediatory body, the potential for the Grid company to pursue the policies of aggrandisement for which the nationalised industries have become renowned would be limited, but not altogether absent. It would be essential for a Grid Company in such a powerful position to be made fully accountable to the community at large. This would be best achieved by a return to public ownership and control.

For the smaller bodies in a thoroughly decentralised and properly regulated ESI the issue of ownership would be less important. Competition is a better guarantee of economic efficiency than private ownership (Kay and Thompson 1986) – public ownership can lead to corporatism, not democratic control. Once fragmentation has been achieved the public/private ownership debate becomes unimportant. Having said this, there is no reason why the principle of diversity is not worth considering here. A diversity of styles of ownership would perhaps enhance the vitality and flexibility of the ESI. The potential role of municipally owned distribution companies in facilitating CHP has already been mentioned. Other forms of socialised ownership, such as workers' or consumers' co-operatives are worth experimenting with as alternatives to plcs and management buy-outs. The role of Swedish municipalities as operators of CHP plant has already been noted, whereas in Denmark half the wind power schemes are cooperatively owned. The central state also has a role to play as owner of some power stations, especially demonstration and experimental plant.

## A national energy policy for the UK

The main role of the state, however, should be to ensure that the overall direction of the ESI is compatible with the objectives of sustainability and equity. Given sufficient liberalisation, flexibility and efficiency will virtually take care of themselves. Intervention would however be necessary, via primary legislation and via the Grid Company, to ensure that the industry operated in a way that did not prejudice the security of present and future generations. In particular, the Grid Company should have the responsibility of forecasting future electricity demand plus regulatory powers to induce action (whether demand management or construction of new capacity) to ensure that supply will be adequate. Responsibility for research and development would also fall onto the State, as a diversified ESI will be unlikely to be able to muster sufficient resources. Likewise, equity would demand State intervention.

In this context, the rumoured abolition of the Department of Energy, should the Conservatives win the General Election due in 1991 or 1992, is disquieting. In the nationalised past, the Department has been implicated as being in thrall to various pressure groups acting within the ESI caucus (Sedgemore 1980). Such 'capture' of a Government department by its client group is neither unique nor confined to industries organised on a centralised basis, as the history of UK agriculture shows. The diverse and decentralised farming industry, combined under the banner of the National Union of Farmers, operates as an extremely powerful pressure group within the Ministry of Agriculture, Fisheries and Food, to the exclusion of other lobbies, such as food consumers.

Planning always carries the danger that such corporatism might develop. Corporatism will tend to induce inflexibility, inefficiency, inequity and, therefore, in the energy sector, unsustainable policies. Yet neither would reliance on market forces alone deliver the four objectives. Given that a balance between planning and markets must be struck, precautions to minimise the dangers of incorporation can be taken. The most important of these is a commitment to open Government and freedom of information in order to throw light into the shadier corners of decision making, where caucuses, like spiders, spin their webs.

Sustainability demands a national energy policy, and therefore an authoritative Government Department responsible for formulating and executing this. Although the Grid Company has a potentially important role as an instrument of this policy, it obviously cannot take responsibility for matters beyond the ESI. The track record of the Department might lead those seeking radical changes in energy policy along the lines suggested in this chapter to welcome its abolition – yet the need for a national energy policy means that, while it may be in much need of reform, the Department of Energy is by no means redundant. Indeed, press reports that the UKAEA is seeking 'a central role in directing energy policy' (*The Guardian* 13.2.91) in the wake of the Department of Energy's demise may make the Department's critics, both within and without Government circles, think twice before recommending its abolition.

## The missed opportunities

Set against the four objectives proposed in this chapter, the six principles on which Cecil Parkinson based the White Paper seem hopelessly limited. Yet it could be argued that large parts of even the White Paper agenda turned out to be over-ambitious. If the six principles proved impossible to implement, how can a wider agenda be contemplated?

Substantial liberalisation of the ESI, in line with the six principles, was not inherently impossible to achieve, anymore than substantial changes in accordance with the new agenda outlined above would be. The possible extent of liberalisation of the ESI was limited by the very process of privatisation. The constraints on liberalisation undertaken in preparation for a transfer from public to private ownership were described in Chapter 2. The triangular model of conflict developed there describes the conflict between privatisation, liberalisation and non-market objectives *within the context of the privatisation process*. Divorce liberalisation from privatisation and many of these constraints disappear. Liberalisation of the nationalised ESI would have been possible by sub-dividing corporations on a geographical or on a functional basis. Once the new industry structure was established, transfer of ownership, by flotation or buy-out of individual companies, or to local authority ownership, would have been an option. Even within the privatisation process there was much unrealised potential for liberalisation gains. An obvious scapegoat, for the failure of the Government to implement such a large part of its initial objectives, is the nuclear power programme. Had the eventual solution which was forced upon the Government – that of keeping nuclear in the public sector – been adopted at the outset, the scope for liberalisation would have been much greater.

The fundamental restructuring of the ESI occasioned by electricity privatisation therefore represents two missed opportunities. The first was lost when (as was seen in Chapter 9), in contravention of the growing mass of evidence that sustainability ought to be the cornerstone of energy policy, a narrow, economic view was taken in framing the six principles and the Electricity Bill. The second was the failure fully to destroy the corporatist basis of the ESI by fulfilling even the limited aims of the six principles.

In searching for the blame for these failures, Thatcherite ideology undoubtedly was responsible for the first. There was never the slightest possibility that the 1987 Conservative Government might develop radical policies in line with sustainable development, whatever the rhetoric to the contrary. The reasons for the subsequent failure, successfully to negotiate even the limited course it had chosen, lay in over-ambition, incompetence and an irrational attachment to nuclear power.

## From bad to worse – to better?

It is to be hoped that readers of the previous chapters need no more evidence of the serious deficiencies of the nationalised ESI. Corporatist, monopolistic, unaccountable, arrogant, with a built-in tendency to strive to increase its size, influence and production, there is no doubt that reform and restructuring were long overdue. The question is, has the privatisation process left the ESI in an even worse state?

Despite the limited scope and success of the privatisation objectives, there have been many gains. The full cost of the nuclear power programme has been revealed and the power of the nuclear lobby disrupted, at least temporarily. The generating industry is considerably more liberal than before, and some large customers are able to choose where to buy their electricity. The inflexible CEGB policy of building large plant has been superseded. Renewables now have a small protected market share.

On the minus side, the new institutional arrangements bode well for the restitution of an unaccountable nuclear lobby, which is now preparing for the 1994 review. The generating duopoly commands considerable market power, and the DGES will need much skill and cunning to prevent this from being abused. The benefits of competition have yet to reach the majority of electricity consumers. The switch to gas, for all its environmental advantages, poses many questions of long term fuel security and these questions are posed even more acutely by the potential devastation of the UK coal industry once the generators are free to buy unlimited low-sulphur imported coal in 1993. The likely lack of research and development funding from the privatised ESI for renewables may do these technologies more harm in the long term than the good wrought by the non-fossil fuel obligation. Adequate generating capacity to meet future demand is not assured.

In some respects the nationalised and privatised ESIs are equally inadequate: energy efficiency is the best example. Balancing of the pluses and minuses in these lists of static characteristics would probably leave the privatised industry as marginally better than the nationalised in terms of the objectives set by the new agenda above. But, in one overwhelmingly important respect, the ESI is now in a much worse position to meet the environmental challenge of the last decade of the Twentieth Century. Now that the majority of the industry is in the private sector, the potential for future liberalisation is much diminished.

The best chance to dismantle market power in the ESI has been squandered. As the owner of the nationalised ESI the Government was in a position to choose from a menu of many options. As the Institute for Fiscal Studies has noted, once sold, privatised industries are difficult to liberalise further:

'If . . . the privatisation of large dominant firms is at best pointless and possibly harmful in the absence of effective competition, the result is that no benefits to economic performance are likely to be achieved. Privatisation of this kind would not, of course, be the first ineffectual restructuring of relationships between Government and nationalised industries, which has had a lengthy history. But it is potentially more damaging than the others because privatisation makes it more difficult to introduce competitive incentives in the future. Future liberalisation of airline routes would, for example, devalue shares of the privatised British

Airways. Also fragmentation into smaller operating units is harder to impose on a private firm than a public one.' (Kay and Thompson 1986)

This is not to say that there is no scope for Government intervention to reduce further market power. The Fair Trading Provisions of the Electricity Act prohibit anti-competitive practices and will deter monopolistic abuse to some extent. The break-up of the US giant ATT has shown that compulsory restructuring of private sector companies is possible, if tortuously difficult to achieve. The Director-General has stated:

'It is important to the evolution of a competitive market that all parties to the Pooling and Settlement Agreement trade under it in a way that does not disadvantage others. I believe that the present parties to the agreement recognise this. I shall be monitoring the way in which the Pooling and Settlement Agreement works in practice. I recognise that generators should be free to assess the viability of plant and to decide its availability for generation, but if evidence of monopolistic abuse or anti-competitive behaviour were to emerge, I would need to take appropriate action.' (DGES 1990)

In December 1990 James McKinnon, head of the gas industry regulatory body, OFGAS, hinted strongly that British Gas might be broken into separate regional bodies if competitors continued to be excluded from the gas contract market. Liberalisation of British Gas in this way would almost certainly result in a fall in the value of the company's shares. Whatever the deterrent effect of such a threat the vested interest of BG's institutional investors would make its manifestation politically difficult. The votes of individual shareholders make this even less likely, particularly under a Conservative Government.

More importantly, the scope of competition law and current regulatory practice is limited to amelioration of the adverse effects of market power on economic efficiency, measured in a narrow sense. Competition *per se* is the objective, rather than competition as a means to the wider goals encompassed by the new agenda. As such, fair trading provisions will be grossly inadequate to bring about the radical changes in the ESI structure that are now so badly needed.

## Making the best of a bad job

### Energy efficiency

The question is not, will the prospects for energy efficiency improve, but when will they and in which ways? The present unsatisfactory situation cannot pertain for long. The likelihood of pressure from the EC bringing about the interventions necessary to secure improvements in energy efficiency make this policy area one where optimism is justified, although this is in spite of, rather than because of, the Government's original intentions. Substantial scope exists for marginal adjustments to the regulatory framework and to its interpretation by the Director General which could result in major improvements in the prospects for efficiency. More fundamental changes, especially to the mechanism whereby REC distribution prices are regulated, could give further incentives for improvement.

In addition, the Secretary of State holds substantial powers under the legislation. These were intended for use only during times of national emergency, but could be brought into play on a pretext. The mechanisms exist: there remains the short-term problem of political will. It might have been thought, with the ESI privatisation mostly completed and with a General Election pending, that the 1991 Budget might have boosted the cause of energy efficiency. Indeed, it was rumoured, prior to the Budget speech, that although a carbon tax was out of the question, zero-rating for VAT might be introduced on efficient boilers and home insulation products. This would not have been an expensive concession, and would have given an important boost to the energy efficiency industry at a time when, as well as its traditional problems, it was suffering with the rest of the economy as a result of the recession. In the event the only Budget sop to energy efficiency was an above-inflation rise in petrol duty. In deciding against a VAT concession, lost revenue probably weighed less with the Treasury than administrative simplicity. The post-Thatcher philosophy driving fiscal policy, it would seem, is still very far from the ideas advocated in the Pearce Report.

*Renewable energy*

Progress in line with the the objectives of the new agenda requires a shift towards renewable energy technology. In the promotion of renewables both the public and the private sector have a role – the Government at the very least assessing rival proposals, regulating the development process and intervening more directly by setting targets and goals. There is also clearly a role for the state in supporting research and development. The aim of such Government intervention should be to facilitate the commercial deployment of renewables by the private sector: all of this is happening, to a limited extent, at present. The contested issue is how much further public sector involvement should extend.

The capital structure of large, long term projects such as the proposed Severn barrage destines them, like nuclear power, to long term public sector support. But this is not the case for most renewables. Essentially we are talking about short- to medium-term subsidies, to carry emergent technologies through the difficult transition (to which the private sector is averse) from research through to commercial scale deployment. Both the USA and Denmark have operated subsidy schemes with wind power.

In the USA relatively generous R&D budgets for renewables in the 1970s (e.g. under President Carter) were followed in the early Eighties by tax concession schemes which led to the so-called Californian wind rush, with

16 000 or so privately owned wind turbines (1.5 GW total capacity) being installed in a few years, mainly wind farms in California. However this boom was rather chaotic – the machines were often poorly designed and sited, and installed just to exploit the tax concession. When this was withdrawn in 1985 the industry contracted but now is, arguably, leaner, fitter and more mature – having benefited from the 'experimental' period. Significantly, some 622 MW of capacity has been installed since 1985. The front-runners, however, are no longer US companies – Denmark, the UK, and more recently Japan have made major inroads into the US market.

In Holland and Denmark a more careful, targeted approach was adopted. Reasonably generous capital grants for private developers (up to 40 per cent in Holland) were conditional on performance and environmental criteria, including careful attention to location. Another objective was the consolidation of the industrial infrastructure. In 1989 the Danish Government decided that its wind subsidy programme, which had cost a total of $40 million, had achieved its purpose. 2500 turbines had been installed (around 300 MW) including several wind farms and, although not without its problems, the Danish wind industry was well on the way to being viable, with a national wind power target of 1 GW installed by around the year 2000, supplying ten per cent of the country's electricity.

These examples contrast strongly with the UK approach. The NFFO/levy scheme represents at least a start, but so far it seems to have been too penny pinching and too short term, with renewables expected to stand on their own feet rather too quickly. Many are likely to become fully competitive, but most need just a few more years of support – less for some options (like wind), and more for others (like wave and geothermal). Of course there are exceptions, such as large scale tidal barrages, but most renewables are smaller scale, more modular and flexible, with incremental improvements possible as operating experience is gained and technology advances. What seems to be needed is relatively small amounts of pump-priming money, tens of millions rather than billions, and in some cases much less. Around £10 million p.a., for example, could compensate for the shortfall due to the eight year limitation on the levy, depending on the exact number of projects, and could tease out capital from the private sector for perhaps 1 GW worth of renewables. This is the sort of approach that would be likely to appeal to an incoming Labour Government, without the cash to fund major new projects itself, but keen to see renewables developed.

There are several specific areas where public funding would lubricate the transition to market. While much of the basic research has now been completed, there is clearly still a need for more (for example, in photovoltaics, geothermal and wave power) as well as for more development work (e.g. to increase energy conversion efficiencies and technical reliability, and to reduce unit costs). The layout of wind farms can be improved to reduce array interaction losses, and blade design might be improved by the use of new materials. A recent report for the US Department of Energy on the potential of renewable energy (US Department of Energy 1990) estimated that, while wind turbines on good sites can currently generate at around 7c/kWh, this could drop to around 4c/kWh within around five years if suitable funding was provided, making wind power clearly competitive with gas. Given developments like this, the USA might expect the renewables to supply around 28 per cent of total energy requirements by 2030. To achieve this end, the US report calls for a major expansion of renewable R & D to two to three times current levels, involving the allocation of around $3 billion over the next two decades, coupling this 'technology push' approach with a 'market pull' incentives approach, based on short term grants and subsidies. In particular it calls for low interest loans, or loan guarantees, to reduce the high risks investors perceive to be involved with the new technologies, possibly along with tax credits during the early, high risk years.

Assuming such a policy shift in the UK still begs the question of which of the renewables should be emphasised. Currently market criteria dominate, with wind power consequently being seen as one of the front runners along with passive solar design, micro-hydroelectric turbines and some biofuels. These may be the best bets, but current unit cost estimates may not be the best guide to long term costs and benefits. There are other strategic and environmental factors to consider, not least the scale of the resource and the associated environmental impact. For example, on land wind could perhaps ultimately supply up to 20 per cent or more of our electricity, but finding suitable and acceptable sites may limit it to, say, ten per cent. However, even though the associated unit cost may be higher, the off-shore wind resource is much larger and is much less environmentally constrained. The same is true of deep sea wave power.

Strategic concerns and trade-offs like this imply the need for careful assessment of priorities within an overall context of a fully developed national energy policy, this in turn reflecting wider global environmental and resource constraints. Unfortunately, this is just what is missing at present in the UK. Energy choices have been left to the market to decide, with minimum state intervention apart from a few *ad hoc* schemes. The message of this book is that this will not be sufficient for the future. There is a need for more comprehensive strategic assessment, overseen perhaps as Labour has recently suggested, by a new Renewable Energy Development Agency (Labour Party 1990). Along with serious, but not necessarily vast, financial commitment both to developing the renewable technologies and stimulating markets for their energy, this could ensure that we can move towards the full scale deployment of an economically sustainable and commercially viable set of technologies.

During the sixteen years between the first oil crisis and the completion of the privatisation of the ESI the lion's share of research funding has gone to nuclear power – an option which seems now to have finally failed the market test, and which still has many environmental problems unresolved, not least the problem of long term waste storage. Perhaps it is now time to give the alternatives an opportunity to show what they can do. Privatisation alone will not ensure this will happen – there also is a need for a policy switch, matched by a limited but serious public financial commitment.

## Nuclear power

John Collier, Chairman of Nuclear Electric, said in February 1990: 'I am full of confidence about the future of the nuclear energy industry here in the UK and worldwide . . .' (Collier 1990). How realistic is this confidence? A successful nuclear programme depends on a strong nuclear lobby, supported by Government and unimpeded by outside influences. Privatisation profoundly weakened, but did not destroy, both Government support for further development and the nuclear caucus. This is now regrouping.

Current Department of Energy talk is of a future for '*economic* nuclear power', within the context of the new accounting methodology (which was described in Chapter 9). The qualification is significant. Should the construction of Sizewell 'B' suffer delays and further cost escalations, the industry may have had its last chance as far as the Conservatives are concerned. Even if it does not, the economics of Sizewell 'B' as a one-off station are poor (Energy Committee 1989c) and the non-fossil fuel obligation may be proscribed by the EC after 1998. However, should evidence of global warming continue to mount, so will pressure for political action to curb carbon dioxide emissions.

These considerations will also apply should a Labour Government be returned in a 1991 or 1992 General Election. Although there is a policy stance for diminished dependence on nuclear power, pressure from the ESI unions remains intense on the Labour leadership to reverse this. The greenhouse effect will be invoked by the nuclear lobby. The depth of Labour's anti-nuclear commitment will be quickly demonstrated, as both Sizewell 'B' and the THORP reprocessing plant at Sellafield are due for commissioning early in the next Parliament.

Should a Government of any political hue decide to revive the UK nuclear programme, whether in 1994 or in the future, it will not succeed unless it has learnt the lessons of the past. If the programme is to be successfully implemented, corporatist institutions must be allowed to work unhindered. There will be a short term political price to pay but, if public concern about climate change is sufficient and belief is widespread that nuclear is the answer, authoritarian solutions may be deemed acceptable. The implications for liberalisation in the rest of the ESI of such a development are not good. A strong, nationalised, growing nuclear power industry, in quasi-competition with the generating duopoly could squeeze out independent new entrants by mopping up projected increases in demand. However, the botched privatisation of nuclear power dealt the industry a severe blow, from which it may not easily recover. The PWR programme of four stations would merely have replaced retiring Magnox capacity, thereby keeping nuclear generation at its 1988 level by the year 2000. With the abandonment of three of these stations, nuclear's share is in decline, despite the planned life extension of Magnoxes. Now that consent has been granted for Hinkley 'C', construction of this station would give the fastest restart to the nuclear programme subsequent to a 1994 review. A start in the second half of that year would, on CEGB estimates, give a commissioning date of 2000 at the earliest.

The further stations that would be necessary to have an impact on overall UK $CO_2$ emissions would not necessarily be based on what is now an elderly Sizewell 'B' design. Planning and licensing would therefore take much longer, although it is unlikely that a new nuclear programme will be subjected to the station-by-station scrutiny by Public Inquiry that proved so time consuming for the PWR programme. It has already emerged that the Inquiry into the deep underground repository planned by NIREX will not consider the full safety case. The reason was given by Dr Ron Flowers, a director of UK NIREX: 'it is not a planning matter.' (*The Independent* 21 January 1991). Should the remit of nuclear power station inquiry procedures be severely curtailed, it will raise important issues of legitimation (Roberts 1991). As Thomas (1988a) has observed in respect of the French programme, should a serious accident ever occur in an imposed nuclear programme, the long term political price would be great.

## 'A market is like a tool . . .'

The quotation which opened this book could as easily be used to close it. The enthusiasm for markets, which so radically shaped the 1980s, must now be moderated by a growing realisation that, after all, a balance must be struck between intervention and liberalisation – between the rights of individuals to personal freedom and their obligations to a community of present and future generations. The choice is not between Stalin and Adam Smith: many modes of operation lie between these two extremes.

Since 1979 the predominant UK Government ideology has preferred individual to collective solutions. Thatcherism developed as a response to the inherited problems of the 1970s, the problems of corporatism and overload. The arrival of the global environment onto the political agenda has made her ideology as outdated as that of Morrison. For the 1990s, the challenge is to find new political and institutional forms which can harness the actions of individuals and sovereign states to collective purposes.

As the resource and environmental problems now on the horizon are manifested in the coming years, a retreat from the *laissez-faire* philosophy that guided energy policy in the Eighties is inevitable. The Lawson doctrine, based on a narrow economic view of efficiency and having no regard for sustainability or equity, is woefully inadequate to meet the coming challenge. An apology is anyway due to Mr Lawson at this point. Throughout this book we have used his name as a shorthand for the advocacy of market forces alone as energy policy. Yet, when formulating his 'doctrine', he specifically excluded electricity from this analysis, because of its special characteristics (Lawson 1982). It is unfortunate that his successors as Secretary of State for Energy have been less cautious.

As Adam Smith (quoted by the Watt Committee [1990]) pointed out:

'The sovereign (Government) has the duty of erecting and maintaining certain public works which it can never be for the interest of any small number of individuals to erect and maintain; because the profit could never repay the expense to any small number of individuals though it may frequently do much more than repay it to a great society (1776).'

The lessons of the ESI have more general application beyond the energy sector, and if sustainability is to be achieved there is no time to be lost in learning them.

# References

ACORD. 1981. *Status of renewable energy sources*. London: Chairman of Programme Committee.

Armstrong, N. and Cooper, M. 1990. *Energy for the 1990s: A new policy framework*. Loughborough: Local Economic Policy Review.

Armstrong P., Glyn, A. and Harrison, John 1984. *Capitalism since World War II*. London: Fontana.

Association for the Conservation of Energy. 1988. *Regulating for efficiency*. London: ACE.

Barnes, M. 1990. *The Hinkley Point Public Inquiries*. Vol. 1–9 London: HMSO.

Baumgartner, T. and Midturn, A. 1987. *The politics of energy forecasting*. Oxford: Clarendon Press.

BBC. 1989. *Analysis*. Broadcast Radio 4 10 February 1989.

Benn, T. 1979. *Arguments for socialism*. London: Jonathan Cape.

Birch, A. 1984. 'Overload, ungovernability and delegitimation: the theories and the British case' *British Journal of Political Science*, 14, pp. 135–60.

Boardman, B. 1988. *Proof of evidence to Hinkley Point 'C' public inquiry*. BEC 3. Cannington: Hinkley 'C' Secretariat.

—— 1990. *Fuel poverty and the greenhouse effect*. London: National Right to Fuel Campaign, FOE, NEA, Heatwise Glasgow.

Bolin, B., Doos, B., Jager, J. and Warrick, R. 1986. *The greenhouse effect, climatic change and ecosystems*. Chichester: Wiley.

Bonner, F. E. 1989. 'The electricity supply industry'. *Energy Policy* 17, pp. 15–21.

Bradshaw, J. and Hardman, G. 1988. *Expenditure on fuels 1985*. Gas Consumer Council.

Braun, E. 1990. 'Policy Issues in the development of communications'. *Technology Assessment and Strategic Management* 2, pp. 265–273.

British Nuclear Fuels plc. 1988. *Nuclear Energy: Don't be left in the dark*. Warrington: BNF plc Information Services.

British Wind Energy Association. 1987. *Wind power for the UK*. London: BWEA.

Brittan, S. 1984. 'The politics and economics of privatisation'. *Political Quarterly* 55, pp. 109–128.

—— 1986. 'Privatisation: A comment on Kay and Thompson'. *The Economic Journal* 96, pp. 33–38.

Budge,I.,McKay,D.,Rhodes,R.,Robertson,D.,Sanders,D.,Slater,M.,Wilson,G.and Marsh, D. 1988. *The changing British political system: into the nineties*. London: Longman.

193

Burn, D. 1978. *Nuclear power and the energy crisis*. London: Macmillan.

Central Electricity Generating Board. 1988a. *Proof of evidence to Hinkley Point 'C' public inquiry*. CEGB 4. Cannington: Hinkley 'C' Secretariat.

—— 1988b. *Proof of evidence to Hinkley Point 'C' public inquiry*. CEGB 3. Cannington: Hinkley 'C' Secretariat.

—— 1988c. *Proof of evidence to Hinkley Point 'C' public inquiry*. CEGB 7. Cannington: Hinkley 'C' Secretariat.

—— 1989. *Annual Report and Accounts 1988/89*. London: CEGB.

Christensen, B.A. and Jensen Butler, C. 1982. 'Energy and urban structure – heat planning in Denmark'. *Progress in Planning* 8, p. 69.

Clarke, F. 1984. 'Energy'. in *UK Science Policy*. Ed. Goldsmith, M. London: Longman.

Collier, J. 1990. 'Anniversary Message'. *Atom* 400, p.4.

Collingridge, D. 1984. 'Lessons of nuclear power: US and UK history'. *Energy Policy* 12, pp. 46–67.

COM (89) 369. Final *Communication from the Commission to the Council on 'Energy and the Environment'*. Commission of the European Communities. 27.3.90.

COM (90) 365. Final *Proposal for a Council decision concerning the promotion of energy efficiency in the Community*. Commission of the European Communities. 13.11.90.

Commission of the EC. 1988. *The Internal Energy Market*. Energy in Europe. Special issue.

Comptroller and Auditor General. 1989. *National Energy Efficiency*. National Audit Office London: HMSO.

Cook, P. and Surrey, A. 1977. *Energy policy*. London: Martin Robertson.

Conservative Party. 1987. *Manifesto*. London: Conservative Party.

Consortium of Opposed Local Authorities (COLA). 1988. *Proof of evidence to Hinkley Point 'C' public inquiry*. COLA 16. Cannington: Hinkley 'C' Secretariat.

Cotgrove, S. 1979. 'Risk, value conflict and political legitimacy' . *Symposium on the acceptability of risk: UMIST 17/18 December*. Manchester: MUP.

Cotgrove, S. and Duff, A. 1981. 'Environmentalism, values and social change'. *British Journal of Sociology* 32, pp. 92–110.

Cotgrove, S. 1982. *Catastrophe or cornucopia?* Chichester: John Wiley and Sons.

Curwen, P. 1986. *Public Enterprise*. Brighton: Harvester Press.

Dawson, J. 1980. *Atom*. December.

Department of Energy. 1977. *Coal for the future*. London: HMSO.

—— 1983. *Investment in energy use as an alternative to investment in energy supply*. London: Department of Energy.

—— 1988a. *Privatising Electricity*. Cm 322. London: HMSO.

—— 1988b. *Renewable energy in the UK: the way forward*. Energy Paper No 55. London: Department of Energy.

—— 1990a. *Memorandum* to Energy Committee. 1990b.

—— 1990b. *Letter from the Secretary of State dated 6 September re consent for Hinkley Point 'C'*. London: Department of Energy.

Department of Environment 1990. *This Common Inheritance: Britain's Environmental Strategy*. Cm 1200. London: HMSO.

Director General of Electricity Supply. 1990. *Report to the Secretary of State for Energy and Secretary of State for Scotland*. HC 367 (89/90). London: HMSO.

Donaldson, D.M. and Betteridge, G.E. 1990. 'Carbon dioxide emissions from nuclear power stations – a critical analysis of FOE 9'. *Atom* 400, pp. 18–22.

Earth Resources Research. 1983. *Energy Efficient Futures*. London: ERR.

East Midlands Electricity. 1990. *Energy efficiency for the neighbourhood*. Press release 2.10.90.

Eckstein, H. 1958. *The English Health Service*. Cambridge Mass.: Harvard University Press.

Electricity Consumers' Council. 1982. *Memorandum in response to the Department of Trade's consultative document 'Consumers' interests and the Nationalised Industries'*. London: ECC.

Elliott, D. 1987. *Ruling out the waves*. Milton Keynes: NATTA.

—— 1988a. *Nuclear power and the UK Trade Union and Labour movement: The erosion of opposition?*. Milton Keynes: Open University Technology Policy Group.

—— 1988b. *Renewable energy: a review of the government's strategy*. NATTA Discussion Paper 8. Milton Keynes: NATTA.

—— 1989. *Privatisation, Nuclear Power and the Trade Union and Labour Movement*. Milton Keynes: Open University Technology Policy Group.

Energy Committee. 1985. *The Energy Efficiency Office*. London: HMSO.

—— 1988a. Third Report: *The Structure, Regulation and Economic Consequences of Electricity Supply in the Private Sector*. HC 307 (87–88), Vol I, II and III. London: HMSO.

—— 1988b. Third Special Report: *Government Observations on the Third Report from the Committee (Session 87-88) on The Structure, Regulation and Economic Consequences of Electricity Supply in the Private Sector*. HC 701 (87–88). London: HMSO.

—— 1989a. *Energy Policy Implications of the Greenhouse Effect*. HC 192 (88–89). London: HMSO.

—— 1989b. Fifth Report: *Electricity Bill: Lords Amendment on Efficient Use of Electricity*. HC 478 (88–89). London: HMSO.

—— 1989c. Fourth Special Report: *Government Observations on the Sixth Report from the Committee (Session 1988-89) on the Energy Policy Implications of the Greenhouse Effect*. HC 611 (88–89). London: HMSO.

—— 1990a. Seventh Report: *The Department of Energy's spending plans 1990-91*. HC 462 (89–90). London: HMSO.

—— 1990b. Third Report: *The Flue Gas Desulphurisation Programme*. HC 371 (89–90). London: HMSO.

—— 1990c. Fourth Report: *The Cost of Nuclear Power*. HC 205 (89–90). Vol I and II. London: HMSO.

—— 1990d. Third Special Report: *Government observations on the fourth report from the Committee (Session 1989-90) on the cost of nuclear power*. HC 92 (90–91). London: HMSO.

Energy Technology Support Unit. 1979. *Energy technologies for the UK*. Energy Paper 39. London: HMSO.

—— 1982a. *Strategic review of renewable energy technologies* Report no. 13. London: HMSO.

—— 1982b. *Contribution of renewable energy technologies to future energy requirements*. Report no. 14. London: HMSO.

—— 1985. *Prospects for the exploitation of renewable energy technologies in the UK*. Report no. 30. London: HMSO.

England, G. 1978. 'Renewable sources of energy – the prospects for electricity'. *Atom*. October.

Fagan, M. 1990. 'Electricity sales system queried'. *The Independent* 5 September 1990.

195

Family Expenditure Survey 1989. 1990. London: HMSO.
Fine, B. 1989. 'Privatisation of the ESI: broadening the debate'. *Energy Policy* **17**, pp. 202–207.
Friedman, M. 1962. *Capitalism and Freedom*. Chicago: University of Chicago Press.
Friends of the Earth. 1986. *Critical decision*. London: FoE.
—— 1989. *Proof of evidence to Hinkley Point 'C' public inquiry*. **FOE 9**. Cannington: Hinkley 'C' Secretariat.
—— 1990. *Cutting your electricity use: A step-by-step guide*. London: Friends of the Earth.
Gamble, A. *The Free Economy and the Strong State*. London: Macmillan Education, pp. 126.
Greenpeace. 1989. *The Powerline*. London: Greenpeace.
Griffiths, I. 1991. 'Tackle the divide-and-rule bully', *The Independent*, 16 January 1991.
Grubb, M. 1990. *The greenhouse effect: negotiating targets*. London: Royal Institute for International Affairs.
Habermas, J. 1976. *Legitimation Crisis*. London: Heinemann Education.
Ham, C. and Hill, M. 1984. *The policy process in the modern capitalist state*. London: Wheatsheaf Books.
Hammond, E., Helm, D. and Thompson, D. 1986. In *Privatisation and regulation*. Eds Kay, J., Mayer, C. and Thompson, D. Oxford: Clarendon Press.
—— 1989. 'Competition in Electricity Supply: Has the Energy Act failed?' in *The market for energy* ed. Helm. D., Kay, J. and Thompson, D. Oxford: Clarendon Press pp. 157–177.
Hansard. 1984. *Official Report HC 17 December*. Col. 10. London: HMSO.
—— 1987. *Official Report HC 17 December*. Col. 639–640. London: HMSO.
—— 1988a. *Official Report HC 13 December*. Col. 799. London: HMSO.
—— 1988b. Official Report HC 13 December. Col. 820. London: HMSO.
—— 1989a. *Official Report Standing Committee E 19 January*. Col 240. London: HMSO.
—— 1989b. *Official Report Standing Committee E 12 January*. Col 120. London: HMSO.
—— 1989c. *Official Report Standing Committee E 17 January*. Col 172. London: HMSO.
—— 1989d. *Official Report Standing Committee E 9 February*. Col 906–7. London: HMSO.
—— 1989e. *Official Report HC 9 November*. Col 1175–83. London: HMSO.
—— 1989f. *Official Report HC 24 July*. Col 744–7. London: HMSO.
—— 1989g. *Official Report HC 24 July*. Col 769. London: HMSO.
Heald, D. and Steel, D. 1986. 'Privatising public enterprise: An analysis of the government's case' in *Privatisation and regulation*. Eds Kay, J., Mayer, C. and Thompson, D. Oxford: Clarendon Press. pp. 58–77.
Helm, D. 1988. 'Memorandum 44' to Energy Committee (1988a).
HM Treasury. 1961. *The financial and economic obligations of the nationalised industries*. Cmnd 1337. London: HMSO.
—— 1967. *Nationalised industries: A review of economic and financial objectives*. Cmnd 3437. London: HMSO.
—— 1978. *The nationalised industries*. Cmnd 7131. London: HMSO.
Herbert Committee. 1956. *Report of the Committee of Enquiry into the Electricity Supply Industry*. Cmnd. 9672. London: HMSO.
Hinkley 'C' Public Inquiry. 1988/9. *Transcript*. Cannington: Hinkley 'C' Inquiry

196

Secretariat.

Holland, S. 1987. *The Market Economy*. London: Weidenfeld and Nicolson.

Huhne, C. 1990. *Real World Economics*. London: Macmillan.

Ince, M. 1988. 'Industrial effects of UK electricity privatisation'. *Energy Policy* **16**, pp. 409–14.

Industry Department for Scotland. 1988. *Privatisation of the Scottish Electricity Industry*. Cm 327. (87–88). London: HMSO.

Jackson, T. and Roberts, S. 1989. *Getting out of the Greenhouse*. London: Friends of the Earth.

Jacobs, M. 1990. 'Costing the earth'. *New Ground*, Spring. p. 21.

Jessop, B. 1979. 'Corporatism, Parliamentarism and Social Democracy' in *Trends toward corporatist intermediation*. eds Schmitter, P. and Lehmbruch, G. London: Sage. pp. 185–212.

Jones, C. 1989. 'Europe's energy policy after 1992'. *Energy in Europe* **14**, December 1989.

Jordan, A.G. and Richardson, J.J. 1987. *Government and Pressure Groups in Britain*. Oxford: Clarendon Press.

Kay, J.A. and Thompson, D.J. 1986. 'Privatisation: a policy in search of a rationale'. *The Economic Journal* **96**, pp. 18–32.

Keepin, B. and Kats, G. 1988. 'Greenhouse warming: Comparative analysis of nuclear and efficiency abatement strategies'. *Energy Policy* **16**, pp. 538–561.

Kellner, P. 1989. 'Labour has a power of choice'. *The Independent*, 1 May 1989.

Kleinwort Benson. 1990a. *The Regional Electricity Companies Share Offers: Mini Prospectus*. London: Kleinwort Benson.

—— 1990b. *The Regional Electricity Companies Share Offers: Main Prospectus*. London: Kleinwort Benson.

—— 1991. *The Generating Companies Share Offers: Main Prospectus*. London: Kleinwort Benson.

Labour Party. 1990. *An earthly chance*. London: The Labour Party.

Lawson, N. 1982. 'Energy Policy'. In *The market for energy*. 1989. Eds Helm, D., Kay, J. and Thompson, D. Oxford: Clarendon Press. pp. 23–9.

Layfield, F. 1987. *Sizewell 'B' Public Inquiry*. London: HMSO.

Leach, G., Lewis, C., van Buren, A. and Foley, G. 1979. *A low energy strategy for the UK*. London: IIED.

Lindblom, C. 1977. *Politics and Markets*. New York: Basic Books.

Lyons, J. 1989. 'Privatising electricity supply cannot be justified'. *Energy Policy* **17**, pp. 149–154.

Marsh, D. 1983. 'Interest groups in Britain: Their Access and Power' in *Pressure Politics*. Ed. D. Marsh. London: Junction Books. pp 1–19.

Marshall, W. 1979. *Combined heat and electrical power generation in the UK*. Energy paper 35. London: HMSO.

—— 1990. 'The future for nuclear power'. *Atom* **400**, pp. 5–13.

Martin, D. 1991. 'Independents struggle for power'. *Electrical Review* 22 February, p. 22.

McGowan, F. 1988. 'Public ownership and the performance of the UK ESI'. *Energy Policy* **16**, pp. 221–5.

—— 1990. 'European energy policy: 1992 vs 1995'. *ENER bulletin European Network Energy Economics Research*. March 1990.

Middlemas, K. 1979. *Politics in Industrial Society*. London: Andre Deutsch.

—— 1983. 'The Supremacy of Party'. *New Statesman* 10 June, pp. 8–10.

Miller, D. 1989. 'Why markets?' in *Market Socialism*. Ed. Le Grand, J. and Estrin, S.

Oxford: Clarendon Press. pp. 25–49.

Monopolies and Mergers Commission. 1981. *Central Electricity Generating Board.* HC 315 80–81. London: HMSO.

Moore, J. 1986. 'The success of privatisation' in *Privatisation and regulation.* Eds Kay, J., Mayer, C. and Thompson, D. Oxford: Clarendon Press. pp. 94–7.

Mortimer, N. 1990. *The controversial impact of nuclear power on global warming.* Milton Keynes: NATTA.

—— 1991. 'Nuclear power and global warming'. *Energy Policy* **19**, pp. 76–78.

Mulgen, G. 1988. 'The power of the weak'. *Marxism Today.* December, pp. 24–31.

Musgrove, P. 1990. 'Wind energy: a reality after privatisation'. *Parliamentary Alternative Energy Group seminar.* February.

National Consumer Council. 1989. *In the absence of competition.* London: HMSO.

National Economic Development Office. (NEDO). 1976. *A study of UK nationalised industries.* London: NEDO.

NORWEB/ETSU. 1989. *The prospects for renewable energy in the NORWEB area.*

OFGAS. 1990. *Least cost planning in the gas industry.* Office of Gas Regulation.

OJ 89 No C158/514. *Resolution on the Internal Energy Market.* Official Journal of the European Communities 26.5.89.

OJ 90 No C75/23. *Opinion on the proposal for a Council Directive on the transit of electricity through transmission grids.* Official Journal of the European Communities 26.3.90.

OJ No C241. *Council Resolution on Community Energy Policy.* Official Journal of the European Communities 25.9.86.

OJ 89 No L157. *Council Decision 5/6/89 on a Community action programme for improving the efficiency of electricity use.* Official Journal of the European Communities 9.6.89.

O'Riordan, T. 1981. *Environmentalism.* London: Pion.

O'Riordan, T., Kemp, R. and Purdue, M. 1988. *Sizewell B: An anatomy of the Inquiry.* London: Macmillan.

Owens, S., Anderson, V. and Brunskill, I. 1990. *Green taxes – A budget memorandum.* Green Paper No.2. London: IPPC.

Pahl, R.E. and Winkler, J.T. 1974. 'The coming corporatism'. *New Society,* 10 October, pp. 6–10.

Panitch, L. 1980. 'Recent theorizations of corporatism: reflections on a growth industry'. *British Journal of Sociology* **31**, pp. 159–187.

Passant, F.H. 1990. 'Decommissioning – you can take it or leave it'. *British Nuclear Forum Conference 25–7 June.*

Pearce, D., Markandya, A. and Barbier, E. 1989. *Blueprint for a green economy.* London: Earthscan.

Prior, M. 1989. 'Power privatisation and the UK coal industry'. *Energy Policy* **17**, pp 208–14.

Prior, M. and McCloskey, G. 1988. *Coal on the market: can British Coal survive privatisation?* London: Financial Times Business Information.

Roberts, J. 1991. 'Clarity, ambivalence or confusion? An assessment of pressure group motives at the Hinkley 'C' Public Inquiry'. *Energy and Environment.* (In press.)

Robinson, C. and Sykes, A. 1988. 'Memorandum 58' to Energy Committee (1988a).

Robinson, C. 1989. 'The economics of coal' in *The market for energy.* Eds. Helm, D., Kay, J. and Thompson, D. Oxford: Clarendon Press. pp. 313–46.

Rodriguez, F. 1987. 'UK government controls and the ESI since 1980'. *Energy Policy* **15**, pp 22–6.

Royal Commission on Environmental Pollution. 1976. 6th Report: *Nuclear Power and the Environment*. Cmnd. 6618. London: HMSO.

Rudig, W. 1983. 'Capitalism and Nuclear Power: A Reassessment'. *Capital and Class*, Summer, pp. 117–156.

Sayer, A. 1984. *Method in social science*. London: Hutchinson.

Schmitter, P. 1979. 'Still the Century of corporatism?' in *Trends toward corporatist intermediation*. Eds Schmitter, P. and Lehmbruch, G. London: Sage. pp. 7–52.

Sedgemore, B. 1980. *The secret constitution*. London: Hodder and Stoughton.

Select Committee on the European Communities. 1988. Sixteenth Report: *Alternative energy sources*. HL 88 (87–88). London: HMSO.

Select Committee on the Nationalised Industries. 1963. *The Electricity Supply Industry*. HC 236 (1962–3). London: HMSO.

Skea, J. 1988. *Electricity for Life*. London: Friends of the Earth/CPRE.

—— 1990. Memorandum submitted to Energy Committee. (1990a).

Sutherland. 1990. *Sutherland's Comparative domestic heating cost tables – UK September 1990*. Sutherland Associates.

Thomas, D. and Sychrava, J. 1990. 'Thatcherite sell–off poised for market' *Financial Times*, 22 November.

Thomas, S. 1988a. 'The development and appraisal of nuclear power Part 1. Regulatory and institutional aspects'. *Technovation 7*, pp. 281–304.

—— 1988b. *The realities of nuclear power*. Cambridge: CUP.

—— 1988c. 'The development and appraisal of nuclear power Part 2. The role of technical change' *Technovation 7*, pp.305–339.

Thompson, G. 1986. *The Conservatives' economic policy*. London: Croom Helm.

Toke, D. 1989. *Critique of 'Getting out of the Greenhouse'*. London: SERA.

—— 1990. *Green energy*. London: Green Print.

United States Department of Energy. 1985. *State of the art report on the carbon dioxide research programme*. Washington DC: Department of Energy.

—— 1990. *Potential for renewable energy*. Interlab Report. Washington DC: Department of Energy.

Veljanovski, C. 1987. *Selling the State*. London: Weidenfeld and Nicolson.

Watt Committee on Energy. 1990. *Renewable energy sources*. Ed. M. Laughton. Report No. 22: Elsevier Applied Science.

Ward, H. 1983. 'The anti-nuclear movement: A unequal struggle?' in Marsh, D. *Pressure Politics*. London: Junction Books. pp. 182–210.

Williams, R. 1980. *The Nuclear Power Decisions: British Policies 1953–78*. London: Croom Helm.

Yarrow, G. 1986. 'Regulation and competition in the electricity supply industry' in *Privatisation and regulation*. Eds Kay, J., Mayer, C. and Thompson, D. Oxford: Clarendon Press. pp. 189–209.

# Index

*Introductory Note*: No abbreviations or acronyms have been used in the index, please refer to the separate listing